THE
MASSACRE
ON THE
MARNE

THE
MASSACRE
ON THE
MARNE

*The Life and Death of the
2/5th Battalion West Yorkshire Regiment
in the Great War*

Fraser Skirrow

Pen & Sword
MILITARY

First published in Great Britain in 2007 by
Pen & Sword Military
an imprint of
Pen & Sword Books Ltd
47 Church Street
Barnsley
South Yorkshire
S70 2AS

ISBN 1 84415 496 3

A CIP catalogue record for this book is
available from the British Library

Typeset in Plantin by
Phoenix Typesetting, Auldgirth, Dumfriesshire

Printed and bound in England by
CPI UK

Pen & Sword Books Ltd incorporates the Imprints of Pen & Sword Aviation,
Pen & Sword Maritime, Pen & Sword Military, Wharncliffe Local History,
Pen & Sword Select, Pen & Sword Military Classics and Leo Cooper.

For a complete list of Pen & Sword titles please contact
PEN & SWORD BOOKS LIMITED
47 Church Street, Barnsley, South Yorkshire, S70 2AS, England
E-mail: enquiries@pen-and-sword.co.uk
Website: www.pen-and-sword.co.uk

Contents

Preface

In the 1970s I accompanied my parents on their 'ancestor hunting' trips to the West Riding. In the churchyard at Addingham is the tomb of a branch of my family. Added to the inscriptions is a memorial to Captain Geoffrey Skirrow, a Territorial officer killed near Bapaume in 1918. Many years later, when I had also been a Territorial officer, I decided to find out more about this young man. The researcher helping me at the National Archives, Roger Nixon, told me that I was the second person to ask him to look at these records and so I met Susan Ward, Geoffrey Skirrow's niece. Susan was trying to find out how her uncle had won the Croix de Guerre. The search for that decoration and the circumstances of its award grew into the search for the men of the Battalion and then their whole history. It went on for five years, took me to all of the Battalion's battle grounds and culminated in this book.

Fraser Skirrow

Acknowledgements

Even a small book takes a lot of people to make it happen. My thanks
go to Major N Allbuery MBE and Mrs Pat Boyd at the Prince of Wales's
Own Regiment of Yorkshire Museum for access to the Regimental
Archives, and for their help and tolerance during my researches. My
thanks to the relations of the Battalion's officers, to Lucy Harrison for
material on Hedley Heaton and Arthur Smith, to Rodney and Audrey
Bottomley and Trevor Johnson for information and photographs of
Colonel Bottomley, to Carol Wright and Audrey Mylne, the grand
daughters of Colonel Josselyn, to Colonel John Waddy for material
about his father Colonel R H Waddy and to Michael Wilson for per-
mission to use quotations and photographs from *Peter, A Life
Remembered*. Robert Carrington, Pat and Tony Bedingham, Sandra
Ascough, David Lockwood and Brian and Sue Mullarvey all provided
material from their archives for which I am very grateful. Richard
Davies of the Liddle Collection has been a great help and guide through
that magnificent archive and thanks to Mrs Margaret Power of
Harrogate Library for her help and enthusiasm. Tony Cheal's website
has been a superb source of correspondence and background on the
Harrogate men and I am very grateful to him. The professional
researcher Roger Nixon undertook a huge amount of effort at the
National Archives as did Brian Jones in Leeds and Bradford – my thanks
to them both.

Photographs have been hard to come by and I am grateful to Don
Jackson for unpublished photographs of the Battalion in the UK and for
his invaluable assistance in the compilation of the honours and awards
list, to Harriet Bennett for photos of Geoffrey Skirrow and to Tracy
Leung and Paul Cooper for guiding me to Ackrill's Annuals. Thanks
also to Malcolm Neesam for photographs from Ackrill's and to Colonel
Charles Crossland, formerly adjutant of the 5th Battalion, for

photographs from the later days of the Battalion. Analysis of casualties has been based on the Naval and Military press CD *Soldiers Died in the Great War*.

My thanks to Dr Mark Beggs and Adam Cowley for accompanying me across many battlefields, tolerating my enthusiasms and assisting with the editing. Lieutenant Colonel Collins (Royal Signals) has been an invaluable help throughout the creation of this book both on military matters and on style. Thanks also to Mrs Vanessa Skirrow Gray for a huge amount of research on the background of the officers and men and to Jonathan Falconer for his encouragement and advice. I would also like to express my gratitude to Susan Econicoff and Rupert Harding of Pen & Sword without whom this project could never have taken place.

Lastly to my wife Lisa, who was not aware when marrying me that she was also hitched to this book.

Copyright – while every attempt has been made to find copyright owners, the passage of time has worked against me. Should any copyright holder come forward after publication I would be delighted to make the proper acknowledgements. In particular, efforts to find the descendants of Captain Green, whose letters made this work possible, have failed and I would be very keen to hear from them.

A note on sources – much of the original material comes from soldiers' letters, many written in the trenches. As little change as possible has been made to their spelling and grammar so there are some inconsistencies in the text e.g. Arthur Green habitually nicknames the Germans 'Bosche' where the correct spelling is 'Boche'. His usage remains unaltered.

Time Line and Locations

Date	Location	Notes
1914		
28 September	Strensall Camp York	Formation of 5th (Reserve) Battalion
24 November	Harrogate	Billeted in hotels and schools
1915		
5 March	Matlock	Billeted in Matlock Bath Hotel
9 April	Doncaster Race Course	Under canvas
17 May	Thoresby Park,	Under canvas
11 October	York	Fulford barracks
28 November	Newcastle upon Tyne	Billets
1916		
13 January	Salisbury Plan	No 1 Camp Canada Lines, Larkhill
8 June	Somerleyton,	Coastal Defence near Lowestoft
1 November	Bedford	Billeted in Queen's Park
1917		
5 January	Southampton	Embarkation
6 January	Le Havre	Re organizing
8 January	Fortel	Training
23 January	Couin	Trench familiarization
31 January	Mailley Wood	Working Parties at Beaumont Hamel
14 February	Ten Tree Alley	Front Line
18 February	Y Ravine, Beaumont Hamel	In support

21 February	Bolton Camp, Mailley Wood & Forceville	Rest & Working Parties
26 February	Gudgeon Trench	Pursuit to Hindenburg Line
2 March	Miraumont	In Support
5 March	Miraumont	Front Line
7 March	Mailley Wood	In Reserve – No 4 Camp
16 March	Station Road Beaumont Hamel	Working Parties
24 March	Bihucourt	Working Parties
27 March	Camp G10a Central	Working Parties
3 April	Ervillers	Moving Up
4 April	Bullecourt Sector U	Front Line
13 April	Sapignies & Behagnies	Training
2 May	Bullecourt	Moving up for attack on Bullecourt
3 May	Bullecourt	Attack on Bullecourt
4 May	Ecoust	Reorganization
5 May	Ervillers	Reorganization
14 May	Courcelles	Training
20 May	Ervillers	Training
29 May	Gomiecourt	Rest and working parties
25 June	Vaux - Vraucourt	Front Line
1 July	Near Lagnicourt	Front Line
5 July	Near Lagnicourt	Support
14 July	Favreuil	A Camp
22 July	Noreuil	Front Line
4 August	Favreuil	A Camp
9 August	Ecoust - Longatte	In Support
15 August	Bullecourt	Front Line
21 August	A Camp Favreuil	Camp – rest and working parties
28 August	Bullecourt	Front Line
14 September	Favreuil	A Camp
21 September	Ecoust - Vraucourt	Support
30 September	Bullecourt	Front Line
12 October	Barastre Camp	Training and Rest
30 October	Barly	Training for Cambrai Offensive
8 November	Semincourt	Training for Cambrai Offensive
13 November	Gommiecourt Camp	Staging camp
14 November	Lechelles	Staging camp
16 November	Ruyaulcourt	Staging camp
18 November	Havrincourt Wood	Forming up for Attack

20 November	Havrincourt	Attack and capture of Havrincourt
21 November	Graincourt	Front Line
22 November	Bourlon Wood	Front Line
23 November	Lechelles	Reorganization
25 November	Bourlon Wood	Attack north of Bourlon – Bapaume Road
29 November	Beaumetz	Reorganization
30 November	Hermies	Reorganization
1 December	Near Havrincourt	Hindenburg Line
4 December	Fremicourt/ Arras	Entrained for Arras
5 December	Arras	Levis Barracks
6 December	Camblain L'abbe	Training and cleaning up
15 December	Annezin	Rest
19 December	La Thieuloye	Training

1918

1 January	Roclincourt	Working Parties and training
17 January	Oppy	Front Line
21 January	Roclincourt	Diary Missing
25 January	Oppy	Support
25 January	Oppy	Front Line
3 February	Roclincourt	Camp
7 February	Oppy S	Front Line
11 February	La Thieuloye	Training and Drill
12 March	North West of Oppy	Front Line
16 March	West of Bailleul	Reserve
18 March	Roclincourt	Reserve - Stewarts Camp
20 March	Willerval	Reserve
23 March	Ecurie Wood Camp	On the move
24 March	Agny	On the move
25 March	Bucquoy	Front Line
31 March	Biez Wood	Support
1 April	Coigneux	Cleaning up
3 April	Marieux	Rest
7 April	Fonquevillers - Essart	Front Line
12 April	Essart 'Purple Line'	Reserve
21 April	Essart	Front Line
24 April	Essart	Support
25 April	Louvencourt	Rest, Training and working Parties
18 May	Biez Wood	Front Line
26 May	Souastre	Training
30 May	East of Fonquevillers	Front Line
3 June	Bucquoy	Front Line

8 June	Bucquoy	Support
14 June	Bucquoy	Front Line
19 June	Souastre	Training
25 June	Authieule	Division in Rest and Training
15 July	On the Move	
19 July	St Imoges	Moving up to attack
20 July	Pourcy	Front Line – attack on Marfaux
27 July	Chaumuzy	Support and attack on Bligny
31 July	St Imoges	Reorganization
1 August	On the Move	
5 August	Vauchelles	Cleaning up and reorganization
9 August	Vauchelles	Ordered to Disband
18 August	Vauchelles	Battalion formally ceased to function

Chapter 1

The Territorial Force
at the start of the Great War

In April 1919, Winston Churchill, then Secretary of State for War, reviewed the contribution to victory made by the Territorials. The Territorial Force had provided 1,045,000 men to the war, of whom nearly 600,000 had become casualties. Amongst these 105,000 men had been killed, along with 6,500 of their officers. Together the officers and men won seventy-one Victoria Crosses. He also related how this contribution was made by an organization that, prior to the war, was reliant on second rate weapons and consistently poor in resources.

The Territorials form an obscure element in the history of the Great War. This book records the history of the officers and men of the 2/5th West Yorkshire Regiment, a second line Territorial battalion. It follows them through the experience of turning a peacetime, part time organization into a fighting unit, through the tests that they underwent in France in 1917 and 1918, through to its disbandment and descent into obscurity. It is a patchy story, with many documents lost and all the participants dead but it serves to record the contribution of one small part of the Territorial Force to the overall victory.

The Regulars defend the Empire; the Territorials defend the mainland

Volunteer Reserves have existed in England for hundreds of years, waxing and waning depending on the level of threat perceived by the nation in general.

In 1794, as a response to the threat of French invasion, the Militia units were regulated nationally for the first time. They were largely infantry and filled a part time, home defence role. A further invasion threat in the 1850s again produced a flourishing of volunteer forces. These were then adopted as a formal auxiliary to the professionals. By Victorian times the Volunteer Movement was fashionable and groups of gentleman banded together, providing their own weapons and electing their own officers in a rather unofficial way. A slow process of assimilation brought these units under control; in the Cardwell reforms of 1881 the Regulars reorganized on a county basis, which brought them into alignment with the Militia and allowed direct links between the Regular forces and the reserves. However, in reality the efforts of these amateurs did not provide an effective military force for the nation to fall back on in time of war.

In 1904, a royal commission reported that the Militia and Volunteer units were entirely unable to defend the country against a European army. As a response, in 1907, the Haldane Act came into force to:

> Provide for the reorganization of His Majesty's military forces, and for that purpose to authorize the establishment of County Associations and the raising and maintaining of a Territorial Force. [1]

These County Associations were responsible for raising, paying, equipping and housing the forces in their area. This act brought together the Volunteer forces and the Yeomanry into the Territorial Force (TF) and formally linked them to the Regulars. The common format for a regiment was to have Regular first and second battalions, a special reserve made out of the old militia and comprising time expired soldiers who still had an obligation to serve in some circumstances and then a fourth, fifth or more battalions of Territorials. Across the country were fourteen Territorial Divisions, each designed to resemble a Regular division in scale and equipment. For West Yorkshire the TF was to be 18,000 men.

Service in the TF
The purpose of the Regular Army, it was felt, was to police the Empire. The Militia, as the Special Reserve was still generally referred to, was an emergency body of replacements and the Territorial Force was concerned with home defence. Men enlisted in the TF could not be sent abroad without their consent. Section XIII of the Haldane Act reads:

> Any part of the Territorial Force shall be liable to serve in any part of the United Kingdom but no part of the Territorial Force shall be carried or ordered to go out of the United Kingdom.[2]

5th Battalion TF marching past at Ramsey Camp 1910.
Prince of Wales's Own Regiment of Yorkshire Museum

The units of the TF were locally based, drill halls were part of local society, men often trained with their work mates, the officers were often local gentry or business men. The gibe of the TF being the 'Town Clerk's Army' was painful to them in that it was not entirely unjustified. Some regiments had a great social cachet, London TF battalions were particularly well staffed and equipped – their officers had introduced the Maxim machine gun at their own expense. The officers and men of the northern TF were largely drawn from the business and skilled working classes – the 6th Battalion West Yorkshire Regiment had a company raised from old boys of Bradford Grammar School. Their battalion historian states that most men enlisted not for militaristic reasons but:

> as a relief from the monotony of civil life, as an outlet for high spirits and as a means of spending a healthy holiday with good comrades.[3]

Keeping units up to strength was a challenge. There was considerable turnover in the battalions – annual wastage ran at 12 per cent per annum rather than the Regular Army's 6 per cent. Overall the Territorial force peaked at 270,000 in 1909 and was down to 245,000 in 1914[4]. Young men would join up, spend a year or two attending regularly and then move off to spend their leisure time elsewhere, many did not re enlist at

5th Battalion assembling prior to a parade at Ramsey Camp 1910.
Prince of Wales's Own Regiment of Yorkshire Museum

the end of their four year term of service and sometimes up to a third of a battalion was eligible for discharge in a single year. There was also passive resistance among employers (some indeed advertised 'No Territorials need apply') and a general tone of pacifism in the press in the early years of the century that was discouraging. In each Territorial battalion numbers were almost never up to full complement. Even though for annual camps many battalions had attendances of over 80 per cent, many ran their usual training on less than 60 per cent of their complement. While the turnover limited the level of expertise that each battalion might achieve, it did provide a large number of local men with some military experience and a link into a specific place in the military organization.

In 1914 the West Riding Territorials ought to have had 574 officers and 17,680 men as well as all the equipment and support needed for operating as a full part of the Army – a brigade of cavalry, four brigades of Field Artillery, Horse Artillery, Engineers, Medical Corps, field hospitals, transport and twelve full battalions of infantry. The truth was slightly different. To begin with, they were 58 officers and 3,082 men below complement. They were armed, but with the obsolete Long Lee Enfield rifle. Despite the name – Lee Enfield being associated with some very fine weaponry – this was not the best of the breed. It was based on a design of 1881 for a black powder weapon and did not work well with modern ammunition. They were in the process of being reworked at the arsenal when war broke out and some units actually took them to France where they were a serious problem. The artillery was also obsolete – 15-pounders with little ammunition and four guns to a battery rather

Tented accommodation at Ramsey. The 2/5th would live in similar camps
for much of 1915.
Prince of Wales's Own Regiment of Yorkshire Museum

The camp cookhouse and staff.
Prince of Wales's Own Regiment of Yorkshire Museum

than the Regular's six. There was a general perception that standards of artillery were not good but it is unclear how much worse they were than the Regulars whose ability, at the time, to hit anything not clearly visible from their gun was pretty patchy as well. Their internal organization was obsolete, the TF units had retained the eight company structure which was convenient for spreading companies across drill halls but did not match the Regulars. The Regulars had adopted a four Company structure in 1913. As with the Regulars, each battalion had two Maxim guns.

The training was of a reasonable standard. The University Officer Training Corps of the time were turning out men with Certificates of Military Training (A or B). These provided a good basic understanding of the military and in 1914 there were 25,000 men so qualified. Many of the TF officers had attended courses run by the Regular army in order to achieve their rank, and as it was their hobby rather than their profession many were assiduous readers of military material. The TF Handbook of 1910 sets out the courses available to officers; before passing for captain all were to have attended the musketry course and further compulsory courses covered signalling, advanced musketry and the use of machine guns. The most intense training took place at camps where each battalion would work on company and battalion level tactics so at least the men knew each other and their officers and had a basic grounding in what to do.

In using their equipment there was also a reasonable standard. The Musketry Regulations of 1909 lay down the marksmanship tests for both Regular and Reserve soldiers and they are not dissimilar[5]. The proliferation of equipment – light machine guns, trench mortars, hand grenades, flamethrowers, Bangalore Torpedoes, gas – had not occurred in 1914 and a body of men capable of marching, digging and shooting in an organized way was about as good as a reserve unit was likely to achieve. However, it was a long way from what Haldane had conceived and its members had hoped. In February 1913 an open letter from Lord Scarborough and other supporters of the TF to the National Defence Association stated:

> If such a situation as existed in the autumn of 1911 recurred, [a perceived invasion threat] the present training, equipment and numbers of the Territorial Force are inadequate for the task that would only too probably be laid upon it.[6]

The Territorial style
Running a military unit where the men can decide whether or not to take part on a week by week basis necessitates a different style of

leadership from that of Regular units. The historian of the 6th West Yorks states:

> [The men] obeyed orders simply because of a mutual confidence and respect between officers and men similar to that in a workshop, or any small society.[7]

The histories of Territorial battalions stress the easy yet respectful relationship between officers and men, who often knew each other in the workplace, and a discipline based on peer group pressure, tact and the personal style of the officers rather than on formal military law. This is an important factor in the history of the TF, this different style was not easily comprehensible to Regular officers and they had serious, and often well justified, reservations about the usefulness of the Territorials. The precedents were bad - the old Militia had been a laughing stock and the Yeomanry who had gone to the South African war had generally performed badly. Views were expressed in army reports that even after four months' intensive training, TF infantry would still be only 50 per cent as effective as Regulars. At best, few professions liked part timers.

> Relations between Regular and Territorial officers were not always marked by outstanding cordiality. The Regular mitigated his enthusiasm for amateur soldiers largely for one often

The officers at rest. Left to right Lt Dale (later 2i/c of 2/5th), Capt Platnauer (later a company commander in 2/5th), Lt Scott, Lt D Mackay.
Prince of Wales's Own Regiment of Yorkshire Museum

mentioned reason; no matter how indifferently they might have performed a given piece of work they expected a praise verging on the extravagant. The Territorial not uncommonly held to the view that Regular officers were better pleased with themselves than their experience and ability warranted and their condescension was misplaced.[8]

Much of the confusion for the TF in the early years of the war, about its role, plans for deployment and even its use in battle stem from this fundamental difference in the way TF and Regular officers saw themselves and each other. This started at the top with Kitchener himself.

Kitchener and the TF

The driving force behind the Empire's response to the German invasion of France and Belgium was Lord Kitchener. He was not the product of the peacetime Regular Army, but had huge experience in raising and training armies in India and Africa. He had seen the modernization of the German and Japanese Armies (he had met the Kaiser) and had a clear vision of what a modern European war was likely to entail. Once the BEF was on its to way to France there was little left to support it, the bulk of the remaining Regulars then being in India. The limitations of the Regular Army in 1914 have been well examined and it was accused of being a colonial police force ill prepared by almost a century of non intervention on the Continent to take on modern armies. Kitchener's belief was that this would be a war for years, requiring up to seventy Divisions of 25,000 men and that it would not be at its peak until 1917. Long before the casualties among the BEF became significant Kitchener was wondering where he was going to get the forces to win the war. His personal view of his masters being:

> At least no one can say that my colleagues in the cabinet are not courageous, they have no army and they declared war against the mightiest military nation on earth.[9]

In August, the mobilization machine was working. Reservists were called up by letter and telegram, equipped and sent out to the regular battalions but they were not by any means enough. These men may not have been active for over five years and a sudden return to soldiering would have been a shock; returning reservists were often unfit, they were issued with new boots which blistered them making it hard not to fall out on the march and many were unfamiliar with the modern rifle. Kitchener's immediate need for men had to be met. Turning to the TF,

Kitchener required from the battalions which of them would wholly volunteer for service abroad, partially volunteer and if so in what numbers or would want to form part of the Home Defence and not leave the country.

The answer came fast but Kitchener was not pleased with it. Only 20 out of 194 units agreed to go completely – that is to say 75 per cent of the current men ready to go and a source for the further 25 per cent. This is a misleading picture – within a further two weeks sixty-nine battalions had organized themselves to volunteer with many more coming in afterwards. It seems to have been impossible for some units to be sure of this level of commitment in the timescale allowed to answer. In the TF Handbook 1910 it is clearly set out:

> Individual members of the [Territorial] Force may also engage to serve abroad if called up . . . . Each man must sign a special agreement before his CO. The liability to serve is with the unit to which the officer or soldier belongs, or a portion of it, they cannot be drafted to other units.
>
> Territorial units as such may accept liability for Foreign Service and where 90 percent of the strength of a unit has accepted this liability the words Imperial Service will appear under its title in the army list.

Some units made up the numbers by putting together men from different battalions who were willing to go overseas. Again this took time as one of the conditions of service for the TF was that soldiers would not be transferred between units without their consent. Everything to do with changing the role of the TF was held back by the local and personal nature of its organization, the need for consultation with individual soldiers, the role of the officers in persuading the men and the conversations in platoons and isolated drill halls to reach a local consensus on what to do. The County Associations which were a great asset in the raising and equipping of local forces were a great frustration in attempting centralized control; in effect every county had its own 'War Office'. These Associations also had new considerations and had to work out how the men would be paid overseas allowances and dependants would be looked after; problems that married soldiers with civilian employers would need to see solved before signing up. It was a considerable organizational task to convert units from Home Defence to Imperial Service.

Kitchener had a low view of 'irregular' troops and had no experience of the TF. He also had no time. By 7 August he decided that a New

Army would be needed that was formally part of the Regular Army and he set about raising it. He wrote to the Lord Lieutenants of Counties and the Chairmen of the Territorial Force County Associations:

> In the present grave emergency the War Office looks with the utmost confidence to you for a continuance of the invaluable help which you have given in the past . . . I therefore desire to invite your co operation in the work of raising the additional number of regular troops required at once for the army. It is intended to enlist as soon as possible 100,000 men and I would ask you to use your great influence and that of the Territorial Association to secure these necessary recruits as soon as possible.

He goes on to create some problems for the TF:

> Members of the Territorial Force may be enlisted, provided they fulfil the prescribed conditions . . . . Territorial Force units that are at full strength will not recruit additional men until the 100,000 men are provided . . . . It is not the ordinary appeal from the Army for recruits but the formation of a second Army.[10]

Thus, the TF was drained of its troops, could not recruit until the needs of the Regulars were met and now represented a third army behind the New Army – despite the fact that the New Army could not be ready for one to two years and observers saw the TF battalions as requiring only six months before they were battle ready.

Kitchener decided to use those battalions that had volunteered en masse in Europe to reinforce Regular divisions. The London Scottish were the first into a major action in October 1914 at Messines, and did very well. Kitchener's second idea was to use them to relieve Regular battalions in India and on 22 September the Government of India agreed to swap thirty-two Regular battalions and twenty Indian army ones for forty-three Territorial units – three entire TF divisions. However a combination of the successes of the TF battalions in battle and the mounting casualties in the Regulars meant that the deployment of Territorial Divisions into France and Belgium was necessary. The impact of this decision in the West Riding was that the newly renamed 49th West Riding Division would go to France in April 1915.

The 5th Battalion (TF) West Yorkshire Regiment on the eve of war

There is a long history of volunteer soldiering in West Yorkshire. The history of the 5th Battalion goes back, through the 1st Volunteer Battalion of the Regiment, to the West Riding of Yorkshire Rifle Volunteers which was raised in 1859. In 1880 the depot of the 14th Regiment – the Prince of Wales's Own Regiment – was relocated to York from Bradford and became officially the West Yorkshire Regiment. At the same time the number of battalions expanded from two to seven. Of these two were Militia and three were Volunteer Battalions. The 1st Volunteer Battalion (VB) brought together the York Rifle Volunteers and the Claro Rifle Volunteers who had their homes in Harrogate, Ripon and Knaresborough. When the Volunteer Battalions were then merged into the TF the 1st VB became the 5th Battalion headquartered in York. The 2nd VB became the 6th Battalion in Bradford and the 3rd VB became the 7th and 8th Battalions retaining the title 'Leeds Rifles'. All formed part of the 1st West Riding Infantry Brigade in the West Riding Division.

The organization of the 5th Battalion in 1914 was based on company drill halls spread across the County. It had the pre-war eight

5th Battalion on a training march near Strensall 1914.
Prince of Wales's Own Regiment of Yorkshire Museum.

company organization. HQ at York was at 28A Colliergate. The others were spread across the country:

> 'A' Company at York with a drill station at Tadcaster
> 'B' and 'C' Companies at York
> 'D' Company at Selby
> 'E' Company at Harrogate
> 'F' Company at Harrogate with a drill station at Wetherby
> 'G' Company at Knaresborough with drill stations at Borobridge & Starbeck
> 'H' Company at Ripon with a drill station at Pateley Bridge[11]

All of these companies would be brought together for annual camp but largely trained separately under their local officers.

The 5th Battalion goes to war

The establishment of the 5th Battalion on 20 September 1914 was 1,020. Its actual strength on the books was 1,018 of which 834 men were available for Imperial Service, so it was in reasonably good shape for war.

The Commanding Officer was Lieutenant Colonel C E Wood supported by Majors Oddie and Cattley. Both Colonel Wood and Major Cattley had served as company commanders and were Mentioned in Dispatches in the South African war for which the Battalion had provided 9 officers and 210 men. There were seven captains on the list – Thompson, McConnell, Cross, Dale, Mackay, Scott and Lansdale, nine lieutenants, seven second lieutenants and a regular adjutant, Captain Wilkinson, West Yorks Regiment.

The Battalion was at annual camp on Scarborough Race Course when war broke out. Private A G Wilson, later Second Lieutenant Wilson of the 2/5th, was on camp with the Battalion and recalled the atmosphere as they prepared for camp.

> The mid-summer days of 1914 seemed to rush by and a pervading atmosphere of anxiety overshadowed the whole of Europe. There was much excitement at the local Territorial Headquarters in Knaresborough in the final week of July as the troops kitted up in readiness for the move to join up with the battalion in York.
> There was much extra equipment as all the troops were fitted with 'walking out' uniforms, glowing scarlet tunics, smart caps with a silver badge, 'The White Horse of Hanover', the West

Yorks Regimental badge. On arrival at Scarborough, the Regimental band was soon stationed at the head of the Regiment and the 8 companies A to H lined up outside the station. The holiday season was in full swing and Scarborough was packed with visitors so excited crowds watched the Regiment walk off with rifles at the slope. The band led the long military procession with the Colonel and Adjutant mounted on their horses. Each of the eight companies had a strength of about 120 and as the weather was gloriously fine the citizens and visitors to Scarborough enjoyed the picture of the Regiment on the march.

This rather splendid military idyll was interrupted on 4 August; now promoted lance corporal, Wilson was present as the news of war reached the Battalion:

In the afternoon of my day on duty as Battalion Orderly Corporal, 4th August 1914, almost the whole of the Regiment was free to wander off into Scarborough and enjoy the manifold entertainments. I was reclining near Battalion Headquarters when I heard the thud of a motor bike and as it approached I could see the dispatch rider was from the Corps of Signals. After dismounting, he carried a dispatch case into the orderly room. Within the space of a few minutes there was sudden burst of excitement and a tense atmosphere prevailed. The voice of the RSM boomed out 'Bugler, sound Orderly Sergeants at the double.' From the prevailing peace of a quiet, hot sunny afternoon the whole scene was transformed into hectic activity. It was clear the despatch contained orders of vital importance as the Adjutant gave orders for immediate striking of camp and plans were put out to collect the hundreds of troops enjoying their relaxation in the widespread coastal resort of Scarborough.[12]

The Battalion reassembled at speed and their scarlet walking out uniforms were quickly replaced by khaki, never to be returned. By 9:00 p.m. they were marching out of the racecourse and heading to entrain for York. Corporal Wilson was carrying the secret despatch and thus marched behind the adjutant with an escort of four men with fixed bayonets, causing one of the young ladies in the cheering crowd to exclaim 'oh look, that young lad's off to prison'.

They were ordered to a concentration of the Brigade at Selby by 10

A G Wilson in 1914; he escorted the mobilization orders through Scarborough. *Peter, A Life Remembered. Michael Wilson*

August. The first set of duties was to guard the railways. The excitement of the men was very great and invasion was expected at any moment resulting in the 5th Battalion's first engagement of the enemy. A sentry opened fire one night on a man who did not answer his challenge. Dawn revealed the intruder to be a figure on an advertising hoarding by the railway; however the marksmanship was good, the painted image had been shot through the thigh. This belief in an immediate invasion threat was not unfounded; the Battalion heard the bombardment of Scarborough on 16 December 1914 and was formed up at the railway station to respond should it have been a landing.

The pre-war instructions for the mobilization of the Battalion would naturally have led the officers to believe that theirs would be a home defence role. It became very clear within a matter of days that the war was going to be a very different one from that expected and that the assumed home defence role for the TF was not a given. In the early days of August when the recruiting call was going out for the new army and recruits were flooding in, the 5th Battalion had few of the organizational issues of other TF units in that it was already embodied. TF soldiers who had been unable to come to camp for work reasons or who were 'time expired' rejoined quickly in the emergency, believing that their state of training would ensure an early move to France. As such, the response of the 5th Battalion to Kitchener's call to the TF was whole-hearted. The report of the West Riding County Association (given by Lord Scarborough who had helped to pen the open letter about the poor state of the TF) reported that every unit in the West Riding Brigade had, by 9 September 1914 reported above 60 per cent volunteered for overseas service and been accepted. The report went on to state that the establishment of Officers was 580 and other ranks 17,780, the current enlisted strength was 608 officers ands 20,211 men[13], demonstrating how many former Territorials had returned to their units despite being time expired.

Among the officers of the 5th, signing up to go was almost universal. The exception, a young Second Lieutenant Arthur Green from Leeds, wrote home from Strensall camp in early September with a grievance. He needed his father's approval to allow him to go overseas.

> During the day everyone has been signing up their papers for Foreign Service. The bulk of the men are keen and as far as I can see I appear to be the only officer not to have signed . . . . I should love to have a trip abroad with these chaps; we could not be ready for service in under 3 or 4 months, the only chance we have is to be sent to relieve some garrison at Gibraltar or Malta or some such place and there is no distinction between Colonial and Foreign service. If you don't want me to go out then I've nothing more to say.[14]

He did have more to say and his frustrations continued into October. Already he felt disadvantaged within the TF by not having made himself available for Imperial Service. He wrote to his father again using a different set of arguments:

> to ask if you were willing for me to sign the Imperial Service Form which will render me liable for service anywhere. I can't

see any possibility of being sent out to France, with things as black as they are now, a Zeppelin invasion any time or an army invasion will require the Territorials to stay at home. Then, owing to not having volunteered I have been sent to the reserve battalion where we are drilling the rawest recruits and we have not even touched a rifle yet and who can not possibly be ready for use before February or March so I can't see any possibility of going abroad, either to the colonies or to France.

But still, at the same time, I feel that if the call did come later on in the war – I should not be quite playing the game if I smugly hid behind the excuse of 'home service' and refuse to go away with the officers I have grown up with, and with the men whom I am doing my best to prepare for the worst.[15]

His father clearly preferred him out of harm's way and much to his fury Second Lieutenant Green was unable to accompany the Battalion when, after a hard period of training and a brief period of duty on the Lincolnshire coastline, the original TF 5th Battalion went to war. In October 1914, many of the officers did believe that the 5th was destined for India; having mostly volunteered for overseas service it was clear that they would be going somewhere. This left a question of who would fulfil the home defence role and where the recruits for the TF units in France and India would come from. What was not stated at the time was the hovering question that, if casualties continued at the present rate, the TF in France might be used up before the New Army could be put into action. Kitchener was forced to turn back to the County Associations again to resolve this and to form the Second Line TF units – among which would number the 2/5th.

Chapter 2
The Raising of the 2/5th

The 5th (Reserve) West Yorks

Once the First Line TF units were definitely to go to France the
authorities had to answer how the vacant home defence role was to be
filled, and how recruits and replacements were to be provided to them.
The solution was patterned on the Regular Army peacetime organization, where the First Battalion might be in India and the Second
would be in the depot recruiting and training. The *Yorkshire Herald*
announced:

> County Associations have now been authorized to form a home
> service unit for each Territorial unit which has been accepted
> for Imperial Service . . . . According to an Army Order just
> issued the new Home Service units take the place of Imperial
> Service units when sent abroad and act as a feeder to replace
> wastage. The new corps consists of all men not able to go
> abroad and recruits enlisted for both home and Imperial
> service. [1]

The role of the Second Line would be a 'home battalion' for re-supply
and training, a force to fill the home defence role left empty by the
deployment of the First Line TF units to France or India and a place to
put half trained men and returning reservists before a speedy deployment to the Front. However, mindful of the difficulties in sorting out
the original TF for overseas service, recruits to the reserve units would
be required to sign the Imperial Service Form. The West Riding
Territorial Association was now responsible for finding a complete
replacement for its original division – another 18,000 men fully trained
and equipped and willing to serve overseas.

The founding officers

The dividing line between the officers of the 5th and 5th (Reserve) Battalions did not become clear for some time. The Army Lists do not separate them consistently until early 1915 nor did units at home keep particularly detailed war diaries. However letters identify some of the founders and this helps to construct a picture of the skills and experience leading the Battalion in 1914 and early 1915.

The *Yorkshire Herald* announced the appointment of Lieutenant Colonel Richard Arthur Augustus Bottomley, as Commanding Officer of the 5th (Reserve) on 29 September 1914. He was 43 years old and an experienced Territorial officer. He came from a wealthy family of mill owners and had attended Giggleswick School before going up to Clare College Cambridge in 1889, where he rowed for the College. Commissioned as a second lieutenant in August 1889 he was a captain by February 1895, a major in December 1898 and rose to be colonel of the 2nd (Volunteer) Battalion of the West Yorks at Bradford by May 1906 and held this command into 1908. This Battalion would become the 6th West Yorks and was stationed at Belle Vue Barracks in

The officers of the 5th Reserve at Harrogate in early 1915.
Back Row. Left to Right, unknown, 2/Lt N Allen, 2/Lt G Skirrow, unknown,
Lt AWL Smith, Lt H Heaton, Lt AE Green, 2/Lt P Clubb.
Front Row. Left to Right, Lt F Knowles, Lt J L Thompson,
Capt C Bulmer, unknown, Capt E Cross and Scottie,
Lt Colonel RAA Bottomley, unknown, Capt HM Platnauer, unknown
Ackrill's Harrogate War Souvenir, 1915

Woodleigh Hall, Col Bottomley's family home. *Lucy Harrison*

Bradford. Among his officers was John Hastings who commanded the 6th after Colonel Bottomley and then the 2/6th Battalion from its formation. Colonel Bottomley describes his occupation as 'Retired Lt. Colonel' and he was a gentleman farmer.

His second in command was Major Alwyn Percy Dale; born in 1882 he was a prosperous York solicitor and the son of one of the city's aldermen. Another pre-war territorial, this time with the 5th Battalion he had been a company commander in the 1st VB West Yorks. Major Dale was popular and photographs show him as a rather jolly pipe-smoking man with a rotund figure. Reports describe him as a conscientious and painstaking officer.

The other senior officers associated with the Battalion at the start were Captain Platnauer, Major McConnell and Captain Bower. Of these, only the records for Captain Bower have survived. He was born in 1854 and was a Justice of the Peace in Ripon. He had served with the Inns of Court Volunteers and had been with the 1st VB West Yorks in the 1890s. He was retired in 1914 but came to the Depot of the 5th West Yorks on the outbreak of war to serve in whatever capacity he could.

The adjutant at the formation of the Battalion was Captain Cross who transferred from the 1/5th. He was also a long term TF officer, he was appointed second lieutenant in the 1 VB West Yorks Regiment in April 1900 and went to the 5th Battalion in April 1908. In civilian life he was also a lawyer. He had administrative responsibility for the Battalion through this very difficult time and faced much unpopularity among the junior officers. In early 1916, at the age of 44, Captain Cross failed the medical examination for going overseas as he had chronic bronchitis. He continued to make a contribution and from 10 April 1916 he was the military representative on the Northumberland County Appeal Tribunal. He remained a supernumerary member of the Regiment.

Captain Robert Green, brick and tile manufacturer, was born in 1872 and went to France as the junior major in the Battalion though his role is uncertain. Prior to the war he had seven years and ten months Volunteer service. In May 1918 he was recommended for a medical board as his chronic rheumatism at age 46 made him unfit to carry out duties of a company officer. He was serving with the 2nd West Yorks at the time.

Captain Frank Knowles was born in 1887 and had been a lieutenant in the 5th before the war and transferred as part of the original nucleus of officers. He was a successful York solicitor with his own practice in Ousegate. He was an only child and his father had died. He was 28 years old when war broke out and was described as being of a genial and boyish disposition.

Captain Watson was born in 1864 and so qualified as one of the oldest members of the Battalion. He had previously been in the 1st (VB) but had left in 1903 as his business was in trouble. He came forward in September 1914, leaving his directorship of a brewery in Skipton. He too had health problems and a report on him in May 1916 notes that he was 51 years old and had chronic bronchitis. He did not get to France with the Battalion and ended the war running 351 Works Company in Scarborough. He corresponded with members of the Battalion throughout the war and visited wounded officers whenever he could. His letters are earthy, good humoured and unfailingly encouraging.

Captain Claude Bulmer was one of the earliest company commanders, most likely of 'C' Company. He was from Sharow near Ripon and was 28 year old at the outbreak of war. He was also a long serving TF officer having been in continuous service since 1905. His occupation is not recorded. He is referred to in letters as 'Bully'.

Captain Joseph Lowes Thompson was 28 years old when he came forward to regain his commission on 29 September 1914. He was late of Shrewsbury School Cadet force and 7th Durham Light Infantry where he was a lieutenant. In civilian life he was a gentleman farmer and was a rotund man with an enjoyment of good living. He was also the proud owner of a 2¼ horse power Triumph motorcycle, licensed to him on 7 October 1914 when living at the officers' mess in 37 St Mary Bootham. This served as the subalterns' personal transport train while in England.

Captain W A Pearson was unusual in that he had some combat experience, having been one of the officers of the 5th Battalion who had served in South Africa. He was frequently selected for detached service and led companies on coastal defence and training assignments throughout 1915. However he was posted to the Command Depot in Buttevant in Ireland in February 1916 having been passed medically unfit for general service.

This early group also had some junior officers. First among these and for a time the senior subaltern was Second Lieutenant Arthur Estough Green. Arthur Green is the accidental historian of the Battalion. Between 1913 and 1919 he wrote at least weekly to his parents who preserved his letters. He was the only son of a government official, attended King's School Pontefract and then Leeds University. He got his BSc in Civil Engineering shortly before the war broke out and joined the 5th Battalion on 29 August 1914 before the split into First and Second Lines. While billeted at York he found himself sharing with the colonel's nephew, Second Lieutenant A W L Smith.

Arthur Wilfred Lucius Smith, second son of the Bishop of Knaresborough was originally recommended to 2/7th West Yorks. Born in February 1894 he had attended Marlborough College where he was a cadet second lieutenant in the OTC. He was interviewed for a commission on 10 September 1914 and was the colonel's nephew. His father, Bishop Lucius Smith, married Lucy Bottomley in 1884. When an undergraduate at Oxford, Lucius, then studying for the Church, stayed with the Bottomley family in the holidays and the families had been closely linked for generations. Colonel Richard Bottomley was Lucy's younger brother. A W L Smith was referred to by the family as Wilfred and in the officers' correspondence, inevitably, as 'Lucy'.

Captain Cross's place as adjutant would later be taken by Hedley Heaton. For much of the war, Captain Hedley Heaton would write the war diaries as the official chronicler of the 2/5th. He was the son of a school master and was 31 years old when the war broke out. By trade he was a bank clerk, but when he was at Grammar School at Ripon he had been a captain in the Cadets. He came forward to be interviewed for a commission on 29 September 1914. In 1916 he married the sister of one of the other officers (A W L Smith) and became the son-in-law of the Bishop of Knaresborough and a relation by marriage of Colonel Bottomley. He was a short, fit, dapper man and a keen hockey player.

Bernard Ernest Ablitt was interviewed for his commission on 26 September 1914 and was with the Battalion by October. He was a bank clerk at the time but had been in the OTC at All Hallows School Honiton where he had been a lance sergeant. He was enlisted into the 2/5th during its time as a feeder for the 1/5th, and went to France with them.

James Henry Armistead was born in January 1892, at Bingley in Yorkshire. He attended Lancing College and Christ Church, Oxford. He then went to London, studying for the Bar at Inner Temple. At Lancing he was in the OTC from 1909 to 1910 and then again at Oxford 1913 to 1914 as a private. He came forward to be interviewed for his commission on 12 September 1914 and was also serving by October. In the 2/5th he was a full lieutenant but he reverted to second lieutenant on joining 1/5th in October 1915. He was wounded in July 1916 when shrapnel burst through his helmet and a section of his skull was blown off.

Second Lieutenant Benjamin Dodsworth was also serving by October 1914; he was born in 1882 and was also a solicitor in York. Educated at Repton and Oriel College, Oxford, he had previously been commissioned into the 1st VB but had left because of pressure of work. He came forward on 12 September 1914 and was swiftly re-commissioned. In January 1915 a medical examination found he had a chronic heart complaint brought on by a bout of flu and he left the Battalion.

As the Battalion started to grow in early 1915, more officers arrived.

Second Lieutenant Geoffrey Skirrow was born into a well-to-do Leeds family in 1896. His father, John William Skirrow, was originally a coal merchant but later prospered and described himself as a stock-broker. He went to Harrow School, where he was in the School Officer Training Corps for four years, and then went up to Clare College, Cambridge, in 1914 to study law. Here he joined the OTC. In January 1915 he cut short his studies and applied for a commission, based on his OTC experience and educational background.

Second Lieutenant John Wesley-Smith was born in 1894 and was a medical student when he was interviewed for his commission in November 1914. He was educated at Giggleswick School where he had been in the OTC and he was studying at Leeds University, again in the OTC. He was fluent in French and German.

Second Lieutenant Thomas Devereux Sinnott was born in March 1887. He was at Ampleforth College and was living in Harrogate in early 1915. He described himself as a worsted spinner and was recommended personally by Colonel Bottomley. He did not go to France with the Battalion as he was seconded to the Divisional Staff as grenade officer.

Looking across the officers there are some common traits. There was predominance of the legal profession in particular and of office based occupations in general. The senior officers, while willing, were some-times over fifty years old and often in poor health. They did have considerable peacetime Territorial service among them – indeed Captain Cross and others were in continuous TF service from 1900 to 1918 – but many had a gap in recent years. It is a great credit to these men that they came forward to be of service despite their age and in-firmity. Many of the senior officers had some connection to the junior; in some cases family, some were from the school that Colonel Bottomley had attended, some were later graduates of his college, some well enough known to be personally recommended for comission by him. This was consistent with the style of the TF at the time, the 2/6th was heavily populated with men who worked for Colonel Hastings in civilian life – these local and social links were important in the way that TF units were recruited and managed. The younger officers were from good schools and most had OTC certificates but little to fall back on in the way of experience. While their qualifications were little different from most subalterns joining their first unit they also lacked the support of an experienced cadre of NCOs as these had largely remained with the 1/5th. Together these men would be required to raise and train and lead 1,000 fighting men.

Beginnings

The Battalion began its war diary on 28 September 1914. It was named the 5th (Reserve) Battalion under the command of retired TF Colonel RAA Bottomley. At this stage it was simply the nucleus for a battalion. It had four officers and ten NCOs plus all the Home Service men and any surplus recruits from the 5th, which was over its war establishment. The officers' mess was at 37 St Mary Bootham in York, a small hotel at the time, which was convenient for the training ground on Bootham Field. Training was a rather grand description for what they were doing.

Arthur Green wrote home to his parents on 4 October 1914. He was billeted at 37 St Mary Bootham:

> Our duties are to build up a new battalion for overseas service
> as a reserve battalion to the 5th at Strensall (who are probably

shortly going to India) . . . we have about 300 men with us now.

Our men here have not even got rifles or equipment so the work is drilling and route marching. During the last 10 days I have had 6 route marches most of them about 10 miles, fully dressed . . . . The recruit officers are numerous, 8 at present, more to come and one can't learn much military work from them and the Colonel and adjutant are too busy to tell one.

Our digs are good, there are other guests in the house in addition to us but we all go into one dining room for dinners etc. where we have single small tables or tables to suit the parties. We have very good bedrooms and a common smoke room and one very good garden at the back. My bed room mate is an old Marlborough boy, nephew of the Colonel and a very nice chap.[2]

At the end of September 1914 all of the rifles had been removed to give to troops going overseas and the officers and men were short of the most basic items. The supply of the TF had previously been the responsibility of the County Association. Now with the BEF deployed and the reservists coming in – 7,000 in the West Riding in the first three months of the war - and the First Line TF units expanding to war establishment, the requirement to supply the Second Line was bottom of the list. Laurie Magnus records the challenge faced at the highest level:

We are to imagine this machine, invented in an epoch of peace to raise 18,000 men for mobilized service at home, stretched now to more than twice its capacity and creaking under un-expected burdens, operated by a shifting personnel of recalled officers, part time clerks and [all] inexperienced, however enthusiastic. Voluntary workers, overwhelmed with Army Forms and Returns and the necessary business of accounting, storing trousers by tens of thousands in spaces provided for one quarter of the supply, yet vexed that 'certain articles such as greatcoats, still come in very slowly and boots, puttees and gloves are extremely difficult to get.[3]

Of the twelve officers in the mess in October only four had uniforms; swords were not to be found in York and revolvers were an undreamed of luxury. As officers were responsible for finding much of their own kit there was a run on certain items, uniform could take a month, revolvers were selling for between £4 and £5 and there was a two week wait, swords were going for £3 and it was possible to get a discount of 10 shillings on them. Down the road in Bradford, the 6th (Reserve) Battalion was also forming, later as the 2/6th it would serve with the 2/5th throughout the war. Captain E C Gregory was a subaltern at the time:

> Unlike units of the New Army, the 2nd Line Territorials had to fend for themselves. They received no specially skilled instructors to help with training, they were practically without uniforms and equipment, they had no such luxuries as field kitchen, bands, blue uniforms presented to them by grateful cities; on the contrary everything was made as difficult as possible for them. Their best men were sent to the first line in return for 'unfits'; they were not allowed to recruit until Kitchener's army had obtained the best men; they had to take on training grounds that that were not required by other units . . . The general impression was one of neglect, they seemed nobodies' darlings . . . .[4]

Arthur Green was also feeling that the best use was not being made of him and his men:

> At 5:45 am we turned out to do physical drill, more or less a shirt sleeve parade in which we do an enormous amount of work. After breakfast Corporal and self were placed at opposite ends of the cricket pitch and we spent the time shouting orders across to each other – consequently I can barely speak now, with a throat as rare as bully beef.[5]

In addition, York had now become too crowded. The *Yorkshire Herald* in September 1914 reported 3,500 members of the West Yorks in the city, 2,500 New Army men in the cavalry barracks and the 5th Cavalry Reserve had 1,500 beds in the Race Course Grandstand. By October there were another 7,000 men at Strensall, which had expanded with tented accommodation.[6] The barracks, schools and public buildings were full and the unloved 5th (Reserve) Battalion had to move out.

1915 – The wanderings of the 5th (Reserve) Battalion

On 21 October the Battalion moved from York to Harrogate, and took up winter quarters at Beechwood Hotel, Radlyn School, Harlow Villa and Dunloran School. The men were scattered through these hired houses. Although there was a former 5th Battalion drill hall in Harrogate it does not seem to have been available. What any remaining staff or boys at Radlyn School ('for the sons of gentlemen') thought about the

Col Bottomley, Capt Cross and a parade on the Stray at Harrogate, *Ackrill's Harrogate War Souvenir,* *1914*

arrival of several hundred partially equipped soldiers is not recorded. The record of this time is complicated by the periodic use of Harrogate for training by the 1/5th Battalion – then simply referred to as the 5th – although they tended to live at the Majestic Hotel. This period marks the beginning of the relationship with Harrogate. The various billeting locations began to get their own identities; for years later soldiers would identify themselves as having been 'one of the Beechwood Boys'.

The Battalion opened the relationship with their band. On 4 November the *Harrogate Herald* recorded:

> An enjoyable concert was given at the National Reserve Club, Harrogate on Monday, the entire programme being presented under the auspices of the 5th (Reserve) Battalion West Yorks Regt. The Artists acquitted themselves admirably in their respective roles which gave much pleasure to the large assembly which included Colour Sergeant H Horner, Colour Sergeant J A Ellis, Sergeant G Brown and a number of NCOs.

Company, still in civilian clothes, drilling with Long Lee Enfields on the Stray, Harrogate. *Ackrill's Harrogate War Souvenir,* *1914*

2/5th West Yorks training on the Stray.
Ackrill's Harrogate War Souvenir, 1914

Recruits arriving in Harrogate, *Malcolm Neesam*

The significance of the names to the local reader was that these were all
Harrogate men; each edition of the newspaper contained a recruiting
advertisement to invite others to join them. The newspaper itself was
also looking for ways to help. Clothing and equipment remained in short
supply, none of the soldiers had a greatcoat and most were missing
various pieces of uniform. On the day they arrived the *Harrogate Herald*
ran an article on the sort of gifts that would be acceptable for soldiers
in general, including mufflers, balaclavas, mittens cardigans and jackets.
By 11 November specific requests were appearing in the *Herald* for the
Battalion. The men of the 5th (Reserve) West Yorks were described as:
' . . . sadly in want of 200 warm (not necessarily new) overcoats or mack-
intoshes to protect them from the cold they have been feeling.'

Local residents were ordering them from tailors and sending them to
the Battalion. In January a list was published of local people who had
made donations; dozens of pairs of mittens, quantities of socks,
mufflers, scarves and body belts. The appearance of the Battalion
parading on a cold day has not been recorded, perhaps for the best. The
photographs of them arriving in Harrogate show the one company with
uniforms and rifles. Elsewhere 'recruits', lines of men in their own
clothes, clutching their possessions in parcels are shown entering the
Beechwood Hotel.

The move was broadly good as recruiting had been next to impossible

The Beechwood Hotel, Harrogate. *Margaret Power*

in York. This was not simply because of the competition with other units and with Kitchener's army. York was a notoriously bad place to find soldiers; at one recruiting station, of the average enlistment for Kitchener's army of thirty-four men a day in York, 93 per cent were from outside the boundaries. However, the absence of uniform was a real problem for the Reserves and the recruits were slow to come. This did not affect the opinion of one recruit reported in the *Herald* – a Scotch terrier belonging to a Mrs Bastow (possibly a relation of Lieutenant Bastow of the 1/5th) began to attend drill and would

Pte W Brown.
Prince of Wales's Own Regiment of Yorkshire Museum

Pte F W Camp.
Prince of Wales's Own Regiment of Yorkshire Museum

not be sent home. It was adopted as the regimental mascot and provided with puttees. The Battalion also supported recruiting events – spending time at the Hirings in Knaresborough on 25 November, for example. Pictures of happy recruits arriving in Harrogate were published in the *Herald* to encourage others. However the reality was different. According to Arthur Green:

> We have plenty of money in England, what we want is recruits. Day after day letters appear in the *Times* from officers returned from the Front saying that the Army is being taxed to the utmost and it can't stand it much longer without losing nerve and strength. On Thursday we went on a march to Knaresborough, it being their Hirings. The place was crowded, type of man frightfully weak, and after a whole day's work we got 19 recruits.[7]

The recruits they got were not of the best quality, many were in poor health, some of them had to be deloused before any uniform was issued, some were actively diseased and there was an out break of scarlet fever.

All in all, Harrogate was a friendly location for the Battalion – there were a series of entertainments organized for the soldiers and the officers enjoyed an active social life. Colonel Bottomley spoke at a number of recruiting events, church parades took place at St Peter's church and the uplifting hymns were reported in the press. There are also numerous mentions of local people providing food for the troops – and for the

The Band of the 5th (Reserve) West Yorks at Harrogate March 1915.
David Lockwood

officers whose pay was months in arrears and some of whom were living off the gifts of the Patriotic Fund. Colonel Bottomley addressed the Town Council in November, thanking them for the facilities that had been made available to the soldiers and for the general hospitality they had enjoyed. The Band of the 5th Reserve put on another series of concerts for the towns people by way of thanks. The newspapers commented frequently on the good behaviour and bearing of the troops.

There was the traditional Christmas party at Headquarters Mess for the officers and another with the men and a special concert at the Opera House on Christmas Day. There was a Christmas party for the officers' children at which Arthur Green danced with the Colonel's daughter – with some difficulty as she cannot have been more than 9 years old and was, he relates, about 3½ feet tall.

For some of the officers they were entering a society that was new to them. Arthur Green revelled in his new social status; a few months previously he was a junior engineer in the Leeds Sewerage Dept., in late 1914 he was an officer of Territorials and able to move in different circles. He attended the theatre:

> A theatre trip. We officers and friends took up the front 3 rows of the Circle so we had the pick of the place. I being unattached and not taking any friends, was given the honour of sitting on the front row quite near the Colonel and between the Mayor's

daughter and one of the Captain's wives. The Mayor's
daughter is a moderately intelligent young lady with about
£100,000 behind her. I don't know anything about them yet
but that's the sort of people we are open to.[8]

The officers were also of some social standing, Second Lieutenant
Chadwick for example:

My junior subaltern is a man of about 28 years, a very nice
fellow. His Pater runs carpet mills at Kidderminster or rather
this son runs them for a family limited company so you can
guess that he has left behind an income of £400-500 a year to
do this sort of work. His people are in quite a big way and were
up here recently at the Prince of Wales, a top top hotel here
and awfully refined. I believe the old man Chadwick has interviewed Lloyd George on Commercial topics. In fact most of
the people in our Mess are in a good way but they are all
gentlemen and one never sees their money.[9]

It is clear from the letters that the sudden arrival in Harrogate of dozens
of young officers of good family was an opportunity not lost on the
mothers of the town. At some point Arthur Green must have noticed
that his letters home more described a social whirl than a preparation
for war:

Contrary to expectation we are not going to Matlock Baths this
Thursday, two of the captains have been over and found the
billets inadequate and so we expect to remain here over
the weekend. In a way I am not sorry as far as the social side
goes for the people make us quite welcome here . . .
    I dare say you think I am becoming a recklessly dissipated
youth but I'm not anything of the sort. There are houses in
Harrogate I have visited where you are pressed to whiskies and
cigars as soon as you enter and may have as many liquors as
you like and where every opportunity is afforded you to flirt
with the girls of the family and their friends of whom there
usually happen to be two or three present.[10]

He, of course, did not go to houses where this was the practice.

While it was hard to get rank and file, the officer ranks were starting to
fill out and organization was starting to creep in. On 13 January 1915

The officers and NCOs of C Company at Harrogate in early 1915; Cpl George Radford, seated front row extreme left, 2/Lt G Skirrow, seated front row sixth from left. *David Lockwood*

Capt Platnauer's company at the Beechwood Hotel Harrogate. He is flanked by Lt Heaton on the left and Lt AWL Smith on the right.
Lucy Harrison

the *Herald* announced that all of the soldiers of the 5th (Reserve) Battalion had now received their khaki uniforms and presented a smart appearance at church. Also in January the Battalion was reorganized into a four company structure and now started to look more like a conventional Regular battalion. Arthur Green records they moved from eight companies of 120 men each into four of 240. Each company contained four platoons of sixty men in each under the sole charge of a lieutenant. Captain Knowles had 'A' Company. The new 'B' Company was under the command of Captain Watson, Arthur himself was second in command and the platoon commanders included Chadwick and Phillips. Claude Bulmer had 'C' Company, 'D' Company commander is not known.

Following on from this in February the Battalion was re-designated the 2/5th Battalion and gained its place in the war organization as part of the 2/1st West Riding Brigade commanded by Colonel HWN Guiness within the 2/2nd West Riding Division.

The time at Harrogate was brief; in March the Battalion went to Matlock. On 5 March the NCOs of the York and Lancaster Regiment entertained the NCOs of the 2/5th to a farewell social in Harrogate. It is perhaps fortunate that the Battalion left by train rather than marching as the condition of the NCO cadre was unlikely to have been first rate that day. The photographs of the men marching to the station do show all as having their uniforms and boots. However it appears that only the first platoon in each company is armed and none of the men possess marching

order – their large packs or haver-sacks, their larger personal kit is in blankets rolled and carried around their shoulders.

The posting to Matlock was a further set back to training. Even the simplest requirements were unmet; there was no flat ground for the men to drill on and they were accommodated in a number of derelict houses. There was a

Dr Pringle, Medical Officer to the 5th Reserve Battalion throughout the war.
Ackrill's Harrogate War Souvenir, 1915

The departure of the 2/5th from Harrogate, led by 2/Lt Clubb. *Ackrill's Harrogate War Souvenir, 1915*

single café to feed one entire company and it took up to two hours to get the men fed. The moves and the disorganization were already hitting morale – they seemed to be making little progress at getting to war:

> Our colonel is a ripping man but the adjutant never lectures to us and if things don't take a more businesslike turn we sub-alterns are to consider if it is worthwhile to stay here or to transfer, personally I am itching to get into the Royal Engineers.[11]

Luckily this was not to continue, for it was decided to concentrate the Brigade on Doncaster Race Course, admittedly under canvas, but at least it would allow some proper organization and larger scale training to take place. The challenge of bringing all the battalions together allowed the more senior officers to begin to understand the scale and complexity of the organization they were creating. Accommodation, equipment, rations and fodder for several thousand men were required.

Officers of the 2/5th on a jaunt from Matlock 1915. Left to Right, Capt
Claude Bulmer, Lt FG Phillips, Lt JW Stoddard, Capt JL Thompson (on
motorbike) Lt AE Green. *Liddle Collection*

These logistics remained a challenge, some of the company commanders took their personal cars to London to load up with tents and
drive them back to Doncaster.

> Well, we are here at Doncaster on the race course. Our coming
> here at 9.00 am on Friday was managed all right though when
> we arrived here arrangement had been muddled up thanks to
> the Divisional staff and we were for a day hopelessly short of
> food and canvas. Now we are coming round and fairly well
> provided for. We officers have to rough it as far as food goes,
> sitting down to cold meals drinking out of basins and making
> a table out of camp beds but our tents are fairly comfy and not
> too crowded.[12]

They remained at Doncaster for April and May and then moved again,
this time to Thoresby Park, near Mansfield in Nottinghamshire.

Thoresby Park
Thoresby Park itself was not a great location. Letters describe it as
exposed to the wind, dirty and isolated. The tents were pitched among

bracken which was alive with fleas. There was no bathing facility for the
men and only cold water for the officers. The wind was such that on a
number of occasions the tents blew away, as did the cookhouse, and it
would appear that HQ was also affected and a descending tent pole
felled Colonel Bottomley causing him to have to recuperate in London.
A new cookhouse was paid for by the people of Selby. There was also a
contrast with Harrogate in their reception.

> Thoresby Park and neighbourhood belongs to Earl Manvers
> who has a Hall in the wood just across the valley from here –
> we can hear the bells chime the quarters and the church bell.
> Near us and between us and Worksop lies the Clumber estate
> belonging to the Duke of Newcastle, that again is very pretty
> and is barred to the military, officers included. Still we have
> trespassed about 3 miles in and got in front of the Hall . . . pity
> we can't have more of the run of the country round here.[13]

The highlight of the week was a few hours shuttling into Worksop on
Thompson's motorbike to go to a hotel for a bath and a meal. There is
no record of receptions, functions or comforts for the troops here,

Lt Riley QM (right) and an unidentified officer with the Battalion cookers on
20 July 1915 at Thoresby Park. *Don Jackson*

Lt Riley at the new Cookhouse at Thoresby Park, paid for by the people of Selby, 20 July 1915. *Don Jackson*

however the Colonel was keeping up active links with Harrogate. The *Harrogate Advertiser* in July 1915 recorded:

> Recruiting in Harrogate. The Mayor said that an application had been received from Lieut.-Col. Bottomley of the local battalion of the 5th West Yorkshires, which was composed mostly of Harrogate and district lads to the number of 450, who had been away in camp, had been granted a week's holiday and were devoting it to recruiting purposes – previous to going elsewhere to fill the gaps in the regiment now at the Front. Lieut.-Col. Bottomley had written to him to ask if they would entertain the men to dine at the Grove Road School on Saturday next. The estimated cost was £50.12s.6d. He had also been asked to provide 200 seats at the Kursaal for the soldiers, who had not had such an opportunity during the time they had been in camp, and which was equivalent to £5.

However it was at Thoresby Park that the Battalion started to ready itself for war in a more convincing way. As they left Doncaster rifles were issued – admittedly obsolete Japanese rifles. The 'Japanese Rifle' was the Ariska Type 30 or Type 38, largely a copy of the Mauser. These were approved in the service in February 1915 as 'Rifle, Magazine, .256-inch Patterns 1900 and 1907'. Some 150,000 of them were bought. The number and calibre of rifles the Battalion possessed was recorded in the strength returns at the time and fluctuates somewhat. In March 1915 they had 417 .303 rifles, in April they were down to 200 Lee Enfields but had 600 Japanese rifles – for the first time they were able to give a rifle to each soldier. These rifles were not Drill Purpose only but were used on the ranges so the Battalion had at various times been trained on the Long Lee Enfield, the Ariska and the SMLE. Machine-gun sections had been formed and these were now equipped with more than the ingenious wooden models they had previously possessed. There were repeated trips to Clipstone Camp for musketry and bayonet training was carried out regularly.

In 1915 the Battalion still faced a key problem. The fundamental issue was that higher command saw this as a training unit and a recruiting organization and not as a potential fighting unit. It was hard to create a fighting unit when men were constantly being sent away. From their letters, the officers of the Reserve felt themselves to be creating a complete battalion for overseas service. Their primary role in the eyes of the Army was to provide recruits. A check of the war diary shows the drain of men for 1915:

Clipstone Camp, the 2/5th built the ranges here and trained in musketry.
Author's Collection

4 January 1915	30 men sent to 1/5th at York
7 January 1915	18 men sent to 1/5th at York
9 January 1915	33 men sent to 1/5th at York
5 March 1915	20 men to 1/5th at Sutton on Sea
12 April 1915	39 men sent to 1/5th at Gainsborough
8 June 1915	1 NCO and 17 men transferred to Home Service Depot
29 June 1915	99 men to Expeditionary Force
7 July 1915	4 Subaltern officers to BEF
15 August 1915	29 men to Expeditionary Force
19 September 1915	2 Subalterns to Expeditionary Force
11 October 1915	32 NCOs and men to Expeditionary Force
16 October 1915	2 Subalterns to Expeditionary Force
31 December 1915	2 Subalterns to Expeditionary Force

Over the twelve months the 2/5th provided 300 men to the 1/5th, 18 men to Home Service and transferred 10 officers. An examination of the number of trained men in the Battalion reveals that in June 1915 304 out of the 747 Other Ranks in the Battalion were recruits – a little over 40 per cent. By December 1915 450 out of 546 Other Ranks were recruits, 82 per cent. After six months the Battalion was smaller and had a smaller proportion of trained men. It was getting further from readiness for France. This was not lost on the men; through 1915 there was a significant fall off in morale in the Battalion. The period at Doncaster had raised expectations that they were to have a real role and might expect to go overseas. Thoresby Park started to look less like preparation and more like a holding pen for units with no particular purpose. On arrival at Thoresby Park E C Gregory commented:

> There were the same old rumours of immediate service abroad but now' blaséness' had grown into scepticism and only the very youthful paid any attention. However there was no real spirit of discontent as yet.[14]

However by the summer the spirit of discontent was rife. In August A E Green commented on:

> the utter incompetence of the major and several senior captains – I am resolved not to go out to the front with this battalion, there are only 2 officers you can rely on, the rest are washouts.[15]

However the very absence of talent had benefited some of the more junior officers – Green again:

> I am distinctly lucky in getting a captaincy for it is a terrific rise in position and I am really too young and inexperienced for the job. Watson having been frequently off parade and slack I have had a good chance to practice 1st in command.[16]

The Battalion would stay at Thoresby Park from May until October 1915, training and sending men to the Front but getting no nearer as a unit. In October, the Division was suddenly ordered back to York where it stayed until November. This concentration was interpreted by the men as the precursor to being sent overseas and prompted some of the officers to action. On 24 November in Ripon Cathedral Lieutenant Hedley Heaton married Miss Margaret Smith, second daughter of the Bishop of Knaresborough. Lieutenant A W L Smith, as a fellow officer and the bride's brother, was best man. The officers as a group gave the couple an oak grandfather clock. The list of presents filled half a column of the *Ripon Gazette*.

In fact the change of location was simply another false dawn. By the end of 1915 the enthusiasm for soldiering was gone from the officers replaced by dull routine.

> This week has been a sort of feeding up one, or else I am getting tired of this sort of thing. Things don't seem to go here – I think it's all because our best men have gone at various times to the Front and we are left with a weak residue and lack of numbers. It is very disheartening and you can never see much progress anywhere, not even in things that matter.[17]

Throughout this time the *Harrogate Herald* kept up its tracking of the affairs of the Battalion and its officers. The paper's editor, W H Breare, who acted as a combination of gossip columnist, information clearing house and unofficial gazette to the Harrogate men at the front. Those wanting to keep track of old friends as they moved about the Army could refer to it; photographs of Harrogate men serving were published with updates on their activities and soldiers at the front received copies regularly. An example from December 1915 helps the officers' mess of the 2/5th keep track of a former colleague – Second Lieutenant Allen:

> I was glad to receive a call from Lieutenant Allen, one of the sons of Mr Christopher Allen. He is the brother of Fred Allen, of the Canadian Force, who married Miss Annie Knowles, the

assistant stationmaster's daughter. Lieutenant Allen first went out with the 1/5th West Yorks. Then he was made Second Lieutenant, and sent to the 2/5th. Next he was sent back to his old regiment, and now he has been transferred for ultimate duty elsewhere. I was much impressed with Lieutenant Allen's smart appearance and keen intelligence. We certainly have great reason to be proud of our Harrogate soldier lads, and we are.[18]

Nicholas Charles Bernard Hesse Allen was the godson of Princess Alix of Hesse who became Tsarina Alexandra wife of Czar Nicholas of Russia. She was staying at Lieutenant Allen's mother's hotel when he and his twin were born. Allen is not home under the best of circumstances. Enlisted as a private in the 5th (Reserve) in October 1914 he was commissioned in April 1915 and went to the 1/5th. However he did not excel and his company commander Captain J C Peters was very unhappy with him. By September he was instructed to resign his commission.

> His character is generally unsatisfactory, he has no sense of duty and no influence over his men and it is considered unsafe to leave him in charge.[19]

1916 – Salisbury Plain and Somerleyton

The rather aimless feeling the pervaded the Battalion started to fall away rapidly at the end of 1915. The leadership that had overseen the creation of the Battalion moved on in December . There was a flurry of inspections in November as the hand over process got underway.

> A new Divisional commander was appointed in December, namely Major General W P Braithwaite CB, whose name will always be associated with the fame of the 62nd and who was to become Lt General Sir W P Braithwaite KCB for his services.[20]

And with the new Divisional commander came the assurance and action they had been hoping for.

> The whole staff, both of the Brigade and the Division, was now altered . . . . The announcement was made that very shortly the whole Battalion would proceed to Salisbury Plain to complete

their training and equipment – 6 weeks was given as the time required – and would then proceed abroad.[21]

Colonel Guiness, who had led the 185th Brigade retired and was replaced by Brigadier General De Falbe. On 4 January 1916 he inspected his new command and two weeks later they were in Larkhill Camp on Salisbury Plain completing their training for embarkation. This made joining the war seem imminent to the men, the normal procedure being a period of sharpening up and then off to France. Superannuated officers and those in ill health were cleared out – Cross and Watson fell victim to the Medical Board. This provided opportunity and Hedley Heaton became adjutant on 18 February 1916. This secured his captaincy. He was a good adjutant, he knew the junior officers well and his position as a relation (by marriage) of the Colonel made him a trusted subordinate, thus he could form the bridge between the different levels of the mess. He would show himself to be personally brave but his contribution to the Battalion from this date would be meticulous planning, communication of orders and organization that would keep the 2/5th together as a unit.

However, national events intervened and the Division's move to France was cancelled on several occasions. In early 1916 the Battalions were required for a 'mobile column' which would be deployed to Ireland to deal with the disturbances culminating in the Easter Rebellion. During February there were orders to the Battalion for 'emergency moves'. A 'mobile column' made up of most of the Brigade was formed and trained in March and April and inspected by the Divisional

Lark Hill Camp Salisbury Plain, home to the Battalion in early 1916.
Author's Collection

C Company 2/5th at Lark Hill May 1916. Starting front row, sixth from left
Claude Bulmer, Col Bottomley, Headley Heaton, Lucius Smith, Geoffrey
Puckridge. *Lucy Harrison*

Commander in May 1916 so this was a serious issue. Gregory
comments:

> A real thrill occurred at the end of April during the Irish
> Rebellion. The battalion was formed into part of a mobile
> column which 'stood to' for days all ready to move to Ireland.[22]

One cancellation was due to the greater need for individual replacements than for whole units. The confusion over roles remained – at one
point it seemed they would return to being a training unit again.
Battalion orders for the 2/6th in March 1916:

> The GOC has received instructions that the recruits now being
> posted to the Division are in exchange for trained men who are
> to join the 49th Division overseas. It is with great regret that
> the GOC has received those instructions for it means the
> temporary postponement of the departure for active service of
> the Division, which has only recently received the approbations
> of the Field Marshal commanding the Home Forces . . . The
> cause is the shortage of men in the West Riding of York avail-
> able to maintain the regular units, the 49th Division and this
> Division up to the requisite strength.[23]

The effect was devastating on morale. Gregory:

> So again, depression came upon all and one morning shortly
> after nearly the whole of the officers went up to the orderly
> room to ask to be transferred into the Machine Gun Corps,
> who at that time were asking for officers willing to transfer from
> the infantry.[24]

A Divisional order came out forbidding 62nd Division officers to
transfer, but many of the men went when the call came out for the RFC.
The order transferring trained men to 49th Division was cancelled in
May 1916 but the sense of purposelessness was back and pervasive. On
the march the Battalions would sing:

> When the war is nearly over
> When the war is nearly over
> When the war is nearly over I'll be there

During the later part of the year the bombardment of the coast by
German ships and the raids by Zeppelins had increased the perceived
threat of invasion. The redirection of a TF Division on home defence
was therefore a reasonable response. From June until November the
Battalion would stay in Somerleyton, Lowestoft on air raid duty:

> The reason given was that the Division was the only efficient
> one in the country and therefore it must be retained for Home
> Defence. This bogey of a German invasion could not be
> eradicated and but it was unfortunate that the 62nd Division
> should have to suffer for this obsession. Practically every
> excuse under the sun had been invented for its retention but
> this was about the last straw. 'John Bull' might well write an
> open letter asking if this Division had been forgotten. This
> letter led to the Division nicknaming itself 'John Bull's
> Division' . . . the men became stale and it was difficult to keep
> up any interest, let alone enthusiasm in military duties,
> although everything was done to make training as varied as
> possible.[25]

However, it seems most likely that the incoming Brigade Commander
of 185th Brigade and the new Divisional commander were agreed that
a high proportion of their troops were not ready for the front and
that there was huge ground to be made up. The 2/5th had been

reinforced from the 3/5th at the start of January 1916. They were a mixed bag; Gregory describes the ones received from their reserve battalion as weedy and unfit. Arthur Green also comments on the undersized and poorly prepared recruits, some of whom were lousy. When the Battalion was inspected by Lord French in January these 'unfits' were paraded separately, and one assumes, some distance away. The Derby recruits however (recruited under Lord Derby's scheme whereby men could enlist but delay mobilization) were better but their arrival in March postponed the date of departure as they required further training. However the most detailed evidence for the unfitness of the Battalion lies in the letters on Colonel Bottomley's file concerning his departure. Brigadier General De Falbe writes:

> I have to report for the information of the general officer commanding, that in my opinion Lt Colonel R A A Bottomley Comn'd 2/5th Btn West Yorks Regiment does not possess the qualities and experience necessary for the successful training of a battalion for active service.
>
> He lacks the power of organizing, is indecided (sic) and prone to leave matters to his subordinates without exercising the supervision necessary to ensure the work of the battalion is being carried on efficiently.
>
> In taking on command of the brigade I found the books of the battalion badly and inaccurately kept and ascertained that book inspections were never held. At more recent inspections I find that although the company books are now better kept, those of the QM are still in an unsatisfactory state. The QM has been on the sick list for the past 4 months but until I insisted no steps were taken to replace him and the work of the QM stores, in the hands of a young officer without experience was allowed to carry on, apparently unchecked.
>
> The Regimental Transport, partly owing to the Transport officer going sick, was allowed to deteriorate and at a recent inspection gave clear evidence of a lack of care, cleanliness and discipline.
>
> The drill of the battalion is indifferent. Both officers and NCOs selected to train the recent influx of Derby Recruits are to a great extent ignorant, and this ignorance is evidently due to a lack of training and proper grounding in the details of drill, without which it is impossible to train others.
>
> The strength of NCOs is consistently below establishment. The shortage was pointed out to Colonel Bottomley about 3

months ago and he stated that the junior ranks were not qualified for promotion, and that owing to the slackening in recruiting the number available to select from was limited. This was the case, since then however little or no effort appears to have been made to instruct junior NCOs and to qualify them to fill vacancies in the higher ranks.

The general standard of efficiency in the Battalion is low and this appears to be due either to easy going methods and a disinclination to impose authority or to inability on the part of the commanding officer.

Shortly after taking command of the 185th Brigade I was required to report on the commanding officers, and I reported (on 27.1.16) on Colonel Bottomley as 'fit' in the belief that certain faults of training and organization which I had observed and pointed out would be remedied. This expectation has not been fulfilled owing I believe to Colonel Bottomley's want of initiative and power of command.

Having regard to the above I regretfully feel compelled in the interest of the service to ask that Colonel Bottomley may be required to resign and that an officer of wider experience and more force of character may be appointed to command.

Colonel Bottomley was informed of this report and given an opportunity to respond. His dignified and measured response was forwarded to Southern Command:

Sir

As permitted by your letter informing me of the report upon myself and enclosing copy which you are forwarding to the GOC the Division; I have the honour to submit the following remarks which I shall be grateful if you will forward with your report.

Upon your report Sir, I can say nothing, for no doubt you have considered any difficulties and extenuating circumstances before expressing this opinion and therefore excuses I will not offer.

As the report stands Sir, I fully appreciate that it means an absolute end to anything in the way of military service in the future. I should therefore esteem it greatly if, in view of such past services as I have rendered not altogether unsatisfactorily (as I believe will be found recorded at the War Office in the reports of the Brigade Commanders when I commanded the 6th Battalion West Yorks Regiment (Bradford)) such modification could be made that which, resigning command of this unit, I might be permitted to join the Territorial Force Reserve of Officers so that possibly some work of a military type might still be open for me during the war.

The final word came from Southern Command:

> I concur with the preceding minute . . . I recommend that Lt Colonel R A A Bottomley comd 2/5 West Yorkshire Regiment be transferred to the Territorial Force Reserve and a successor be appointed to the command of the battalion on which latter subject I am making a specific suggestion.
>   I understand that ill health has been a contributory cause of his lack of energy and this added to his plainly expressed desire not to be cut off from being of use to his country in a time of national (illeg) leads me to hope that some suitable employment of a less responsible nature may be found for Lt Colonel Bottomley who, according to his lights, has always done his best.

The sad sequel to this memo is that there is no record of his ever being found such a role. His letters to the War Office result only in a final, rather brutal reply:

> . . . there are so many senior officers returning from the front that preference is given to them, and it is regretted that there is no third line unit for which you could at present be considered.[26]

This verdict on Colonel Bottomley's command of the 2/5th is not entirely fair. In his letter of resignation he pointed to the Annual Inspection Reports. Both the 1906 and 1907 reports have survived. The 1907 report can find few faults other than some variation in numbers:

> A good Battalion in all other respects, as might be expected when an able and energetic Commanding Officer is well backed up by his subordinates, has the advantage of no detachments. The training of scouts has been a subject to which close attention has been given with excellent results.

He had 798 men in the Battalion and so was 254 short. However he had a full cadre of NCOs. Of his men, 682 had fired their annual weapons test and 499 of them were either Marksmen or first class shots, Signalling and scouts are described as good and the machine-gun section had its qualifications from the School of Musketry at Hythe. Clearly Colonel Bottomley knew his business in training troops.

After leaving the command of the 6th Battalion (previously the 2nd Volunteer Battalion) Colonel Bottomley was a military representative on the Territorial Force County Association so he had oversight of all training, recruitment, logistics etc. These bodies ran the TF as a distinct force from the Regulars so he was clearly in demand in the TF hierarchy. He had been out of circulation in the TF for maximum of three years, probably less, when recalled to the 2/5th so he was quite up to date with training and organization.

A review of the strength returns in the 2/5th for the period of his command does show him to be seriously short of NCOs; at times he had less than half his establishment. At this time when Kitchener's Army was advertising for time expired soldiers and for TF NCOs to come into the New Army, there were few left for the 2/5th. Colonel Bottomley had the choice of making up men he knew not to be of the right quality or doing without. A British battalion is led by its officers but managed by its NCOs. It will have been very hard indeed to organize and train this battalion on the resources allowed to Colonel Bottomley. A review of the junior officers shows them to be keen, well educated but in-experienced. New officers learn much from their NCOs of whom there was a shortage, and from more experienced officers, of whom there were few.

When Colonel Bottomley left the Battalion only a third of his men were registered as being trained – at times he had had up to 1,000 recruits to deal with. In July 1915 all his trained men were transferred and he had to retrain from scratch – he had just got the first men through to being trained soldiers and he had managed to get them modern rifles to replace their Japanese ones when he was relieved. The criticized Transport Train at times consisted of only nine horses, making logistics very difficult – for example the tents used at Doncaster were collected from the depot by officers in their private cars.

It seems likely that the stress of bringing the 2/5th up to the standard of the pre-war Territorials in these circumstances broke Colonel Bottomley's health, however, he was the CO and, however hard he had tried, it was not enough.

Arthur Green wrote home on 14 May 1916:

> We have just had our biggest shock and we would have preferred anything to it.

After having our photos taken today the CO took us into the Mess and asked us to accept a photo each as the particular reason was that he was shortly to leave us and another is that he is to be replaced by another man – we don't know who – or when but very soon. It has absolutely staggered us all and it seems most unfair that after seeing the battalion through heaps and heaps of troubles, things most of us never realized, someone else should step in, put a bit of polish and then take all the credit. It is awfully hard but harder for the CO than anyone. We shall never get such a gentleman and such a courteous and perfectly manly man to work under and never such a one for understanding those under and about him and above all capable.[27]

The officers presented the Colonel with an inscribed silver cup which remains in his family today. It is inscribed 'To Lt Colonel R A Bottomley TD from the officers of the 2/5th West Yorks Regt as a token of their love and respect, May 1916'.

A specific recommendation for replacement was made and a new Colonel was appointed to sort the Battalion out. Lieutenant Colonel J Josselyn took command on the 20 May 1916. John Josselyn CMG DSO OBE TD (as he would become) was born in London in 1872. He was a solicitor in Ipswich when he returned to England from India in 1910.

Silver Cup given to Col Bottomley by the officers on leaving the Battalion.
Rodney and Audrey Bottomley, T H Johnson

He had a long TF career, beginning in the cadets, then at age 17 in the Suffolk Yeomanry and commissioned in the Madras Volunteer Guards and Madras Artillery Volunteers before returning to England as a major in 1910. He could not carry his rank across so reverted to captain in the 6th Battalion Suffolk Regiment. However, he was taken on as a brigade major with 186th Brigade and so when the appointment for colonel of the 2/5th came up he was well placed to take it. He was already in Larkhill and had General Braithwaite's personal recommendation. According to his records he had spent some time in France – ten days in March and April 1916, when he was part of Southern Command Staff, but the exact role is not recorded. He was preferred above Major Dale of whom De Falbe said, 'although a conscientious and painstaking officer is not possessed of the necessary experience'.[28]

Colonel Josselyn

Colonel Josselyn was starting from a poor position – the move to Somerleyton near Lowestoft to respond to an air raid threat, was not popular. No unit had ever been known before to proceed to the Plain

Col John Josselyn and family. *Audrey Mylne and Carol Wright*

and not go aboard from there. The 62nd Division was the first Division to break this record. In Gregory's words:

> Perhaps when the history of the war is written in its entirety we shall know the truth of this retention of the 62nd Division in England for over two years: but whether it was justified or not it was a cruel position to place all those men in, the bulk of whom in the early part of the war had come forward voluntarily to serve their country. Owing to no fault of their own they had had to endure the taunts of their comrades and the ridicule of their families and friends. At least five times they had been on the point of going abroad and as many as four final leaves had been granted.[29]

They had also had their first deaths; Private John Roughton of Friskney in Lincolnshire died on 4 July 1916 and on 9 July 1916 Private John Donaldson succumbed to a tumour in 1st Eastern General Hospital in Cambridgeshire.

Taking matters in hand, Colonel Josselyn got to work very quickly. First he re-equipped the Battalion. They had finally received some new rifles – SMLEs – at the beginning of May and they were still getting used to them, however it would be July before there were enough for all. New clothing and equipment was issued to all – including steel helmets. The 62nd Division was the first to arrive in France with all its troops so equipped. The officer group was strengthened; new officers arrived from outside the Division, one from Devon Regiment, one from the Hampshire Regiment, one from a London Regiment and another with South African experience. Unfit men and those still undergoing recruit training were posted to the Third line Battalion. By the end of July the 2/5th fielded 1,052 trained soldiers, a full complement of 51 Sergeants and 980 rifles. At the end of July they were inspected by the King. Arthur Green records with excitement the performance of the 2/5th and 'B' Company on the day:

> We had a good week this week, Monday we had a preliminary inspection by the general, Tuesday a day of rest and rehearsal, Wednesday the inspection of the whole Division by HM the King. The Division is split up over this part of the world into 3 groups each about 10 miles from the others so the inspection was in a central spot and we had to march to this – 10 miles in proper kit, rifles and ammunition I have never known the men do such splendid things before. They were absolutely

marvellous and made a great name for themselves and we are awfully proud of them. They had a rest of about an hour before marching past and every man re-polished all his buttons and belt and cleaned his boots, grooms cleaned their horses and everybody set out brand new and clean – that's soldier's spirit. Then after 14 miles march we came upon the King stood in a small spot on the road side. He was surrounded by staff, General French, Lord Scarborough, General Mends, generals galore. It was fine show and we marched past like old troops and put on as much 'side' as it was possible to do. Jove! but it was grand and the Brigadier absolutely raved over it all after-wards – he was so delighted he could scarcely refrain from patting all the men on the back. The King specially compli-mented us and our band which on key bugles played *God Bless the Prince of Wales* and *Rule Britannia* and the Brigadier issued an order afterward proclaiming us the best Battalion in the Brigade and the CO told us that we were the best company so you see we got on well.[30]

Sadly the troops had seen this all before. In October they were described by Gregory:

The men – in their own language – were 'too fed up for words' by this time and hardly the heart left even to grouse.[31]

So that when, in December, the order was received to be ready for embarkation by 5 January the whole thing seems to have come as a surprise.

Chapter 3
The Cost of Learning

New boys

The 2/5th was at last on the move. The Battalion pulled out of its various billets in Bedford on 5 January and headed in two parties for Southampton. Hedley Heaton records that they had a rough crossing to Le Havre with many of the men badly seasick and a night under canvas in Sanvic to recover. They then entrained from the freight depot there for Frevent. This was their first experience of the French railway trucks (40 Hommes, 8 Chevaux) which would be a feature of their travel over the next two years. Officers were spared this by the provision of some Second Class compartments. The journey was slow, relieved only by the YMCA canteens at various halts along the way. At 2 p.m. on 8 January 1917, after a twenty-two hour journey, the Battalion dis-embarked into snow and sleet at Frevent and marched the five miles into billets at Fortel. These billets were not ideal and the men got an unpleasant surprise at being crowded into barns and outbuildings. The rear party of 3 officers and 100 men arrived the next day and they all shuffled round and began to organize training routines. Arthur Green wrote home:

> How amusing it is to barge into a French household and ask for accommodation, beer, bread and candles. These French houses are very casual and pretty filthy. All our men are in a huge barn and simply buried in straw and enjoying themselves immensely. . . . The officers have 3 rooms at one end of the farmhouse – one bedroom for self and orderly, one mess room and sleeping for the rest of the officers and the other room does for the officers' servants, cooks etc. We are quite comfy and the meals we get are very good, cooked by 2 men who have spent part of their lives as stewards on board ship.[1]

Billeting map
showing the
location of the
2/5th in Fortel,
8–21 January
1917.
*National Archives
WO95/3079*

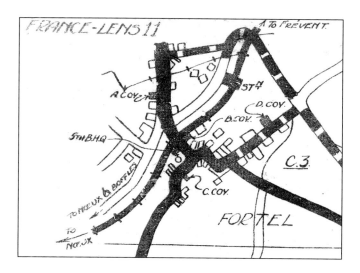

Captain Green may have been misled that the men were taken with
the French accommodation. Private Rowling wrote to Mr Breare at the
Harrogate Herald at around the same time:

> Just a line to let you know that I have arrived here safely, and
> after travelling in the 'corridor trains', otherwise trucks, have
> landed within sound of the big guns. You will understand I am
> unable to mention what place we are at, but it is practically all
> alike round here – dirty, and not a bit like home. At present we
> are billeted in barns, etc. The weather is anything but pleasant,
> wet and cold; but of course we cannot grumble, except to
> ourselves. I haven't come across anyone I know yet, but there
> is plenty of time. There are several local boys in my section, so
> if you send the *Herald* to me I can pass it on. There is S
> Ridehalgh, J McNichol, of New Park, and one or two more.
> Wishing you and Mrs B a happy and prosperous New Year.[2]

Lieutenant Riley also kept the people at home up to date on their arrival,
his particular responsibility as quartermaster comes to the fore in his
remarks:

> At last we have left England for active service. The battalion
> marched out on January 5th, and now we are well up the line.
> The men are splendid and as keen as mustard. I intended
> writing you from England, but everything was such a rush that

> I could not find time. We have plenty of hard work here, but
> still so far as my duty goes not so hard as in England. You see,
> I have no records to keep here. The feeding of the men is
> splendid. Fresh meat every day and plenty of bread, butter,
> jam, potatoes, etc. We had quite a good crossing, and very few
> men were sick. If you could send a few spare copies of your
> publications, etc., now and again to me, I will see that they are
> distributed to the men. Must close. Wishing you every good
> wish for 1917. PS – We managed to bring the band along with
> us, too.[3]

He was clearly on a different crossing from Hedley Heaton.

Training was broken almost immediately by some excitement. An
ammunition train was wrecked about five miles from Fortel. The local
Transport Officer's requests for men to clear the ammunition had failed
and the French workers were understandably reluctant to use the line
while it was covered in spilt ammunition. The 2/5th was approached as
they were training nearby. The Battalion asked for volunteers; 'A' and
'B' Companies comprising 300 men went up to the accident. Between
5:00 p.m. and midnight they transhipped 90 tons of spilled ammunition
much of it shells weighing up to 120 lbs. The letter of thanks and
commendation from the Third Army was happily copied around the
Divisional HQ and back to Brigade and then Battalion level – all
countersigned. The Battalion was informed that the 'Field Marshal
Commander in Chief' had received a copy with great satisfaction. It set
a good tone for their start in France.

First blood – 2/5th is introduced to the trenches and to shellfire

The settling in period was over and on 23 January the Battalion moved
to Couin to begin instruction in trench warfare. Couin is a village fifteen
kilometres east of Doullens and the chateau there was used as a
Divisional Headquarters for much of the war. At this time it was a rear
area with a number of field ambulance units operating from it. The
procedure for new units was for officers and then company sized groups
of men to be brought into the line for a few days for a tour with a more
experienced battalion. In the 2/5th's case they were attached to a unit
of the 19th Division. The accommodation had again taken a turn for
the worse – partially completed huts – and the weather was still bitterly
cold. The realities of life in France were now starting to come home to
the officers and men alike. In the last weeks of January, while each pair
of companies was in the line the other provided working parties or

trained intensively. Rations were becoming harder to obtain, the conditions on the roads were poor for the men marching in and out of the line and there was little fuel to warm the incomplete huts in the camp. In the diaries, the adjutant, Hedley Heaton grows increasingly annoyed as he describes the arrival of rations up to two days late. Arthur Green chronicled the move up and these were his impressions as they moved closer to the enemy:

> Last Monday we began our trek, there is about three inches of snow and this region is frost bound (the other night we had 16 degrees of frost) and the forecast says it will last over the weekend. The first day a goodish march of 15 miles, mainly on good roads, the kitchens travelled with us and we got a meal on the roadside. A good part of the way was spent on main roads and we got a glimpse of old motor buses used to convey troops up to the trenches. We had our band with us and they helped the marching. The next day we put in nine miles and we passed miles and miles of ammunition columns. We were also interested in several Taube planes which hovered around. The sky was a mass of little white specks of smoke where our anti aircraft shell were bursting round him. It is one of the prettiest sights I have ever seen to see the tiny fleck of a plane gliding and turning in and out among the shells which have just burst.[4]

Individual specialist officers also went into the line; Lieutenant Hutchinson (Lewis gun officer), Lieutenant Bickersteth (bombing officer) and Second Lieutenant Gray (signals) all spent time as 'understudies'. Although there was one slight wound the Battalion was unscathed by its first experience of the front line. Arthur Green went up with his 'B' Company on 26 January:

> The last six days I've spent in the Trenches. As a matter of fact being in the trenches is a good deal safer than being out of them if you are near the line. Thompson, Bulmer and myself went by old London motor buses, reached the town near the trenches at 4pm, had tea, and were sent to respective Battalions. After walking about a mile of communication trench (10 feet deep) got to BHQ, spent the night here, had 3 rooms, kitchen and servants places about 300 yards from the front. Next day went to Company holding part of the front line, they had HQ dugout 10 feet below, bunk beds, telephone, office etc.

Floor and walls in wood or wood lattice, roof held up by stiff struts and beams, coke fire and a good hot meal. My job to understudy to company commander – a fine Scot, a DSO – other officers mainly MMs risen from the ranks.[5]

As the Battalion moved into its trenches it lost its first man in France – not to action but to illness. Charles Bacon from Leyburn in Yorkshire died back in Le Havre. He had been left behind sick in one of the five British hospitals there when the Battalion landed. He was buried in St Marie cemetery in Le Havre.

On 31 January the Battalion came a little closer to the war. The 2/5th moved to Mailley Wood and from training and experiencing the line into reserve and real work. This sort of move sounds very straight-forward, however the scale and complexity of a battalion move is considerable. On this day, it involved a column of almost 900 men led by headquarters, then the band, then 'D' Company with its 150 or so men, a field kitchen, pack animals and its Lewis gun handcarts. Then there was a gap of 200 yards and then 'C' Company with its attendant train, a gap, 'B' Company, a gap, 'A' Company and then after a further gap any remaining Battalion transport. They were following an Engineer unit 500 yards ahead.

The war diaries are full of movement. In England the Battalion moved location seven times during 1915 and 1916. In France it moved every few weeks and companies would move every few days. This was a mammoth event. The fighting companies would take up 590 yards of road and Company HQ a further 60 yards. This was not all – the 1st Line transport took up a further 210 yards, HQ transport 115 and every machine-gun section 30 yards – totalling more than 1,000 yards to accommodate the column. As each unit moved at 100 yards per minute it would take more than ten minutes for the Battalion to pass any cross-roads – a considerable traffic control problem. This was also not a simple column of marching men; it had a one-horse cart for Battalion HQ, two water carts, six carts for small arms ammunition, three general purpose carts and four field cookers — all pulled by two horses. There were also four spare horses, eight pack animals and nine bicycles to be looked after. In addition, as the war progressed the signallers and extra Lewis gunners acquired hand carts for their stores and the amount of equipment travelling with the Battalion increased. Each time the Battalion moved Hedley Heaton, and whoever was serving as the trans-port officer, had to work out how to get this column organized and moving.

Working Parties

Mailley was in the Beaumont Hamel sector and the men were brought up from Mailley to work near Beaumont Hamel itself and on Hawthorne Ridge. This ground was heavily fought over in the Somme battles and was a mess of shell holes, wire and water filled trenches. The old 1916 battlefield had eventually been captured and now lay behind British lines. The Battalion was detailed to assist the RE Signals in laying cables in the area of Hawthorn Ridge. As they had only been in France a month the men would not yet have developed the experienced soldier's ability to judge incoming and outgoing shellfire and assess the risk. The first party on the Ridge quickly took casualties from shellfire, Edgar Metcalf and Percy Skelton of 'A' Company being fatally wounded. They were evacuated to the casualty clearing stations at Varennes where they are buried. After this, daylight work was stopped and more men were moved up. Despite the cover of darkness and mist, on 6 February 'C' Company lost Douglas Tucker, William Wilkinson, William Cawthorne, and Ernest Longford.

These early casualties were a great blow to the battalion, especially as the men had been together for a long time. Percy Skelton was aged 21, eldest son of Mr and Mrs E. Skelton, 102 Regent Avenue, Harrogate. He had worked for three years at Mr Ridge's chemist, and then at 'Rayswi' Factory before joining up on 24 July 1915, at the age of 19. His mother received the following letter:

Dear Mrs. Skelton, I regret very much to have to report the death of your son. I joined this battalion in August last, and I was given command of the platoon of which he was a member. I found him to be always a very good and nice boy. He would have done anything for me, and stuck to

Pte Percy Skelton of Harrogate, killed 2 February 1917 by shellfire on Hawthorn Ridge.
Ackrill's Harrogate War Souvenir, 1917

me through thick and thin. He was one of the best I had in any command. I was quite near him when he was struck. One bit of shell went into his throat and another into his head. I am thankful to say he was knocked unconscious at once, and did not suffer much pain. The sight of it made me quiver. He was the first to be wounded in my sight. We were being shelled pretty heavily at the time but I had to go through it and bandage him at once. I did not think then that he would live, but I can assure you that our Red Cross did all in their power for him. They are really a very fine body. You have my very deepest sympathies, and again I assure you that everything was done to save your dear son.

I remain yours sincerely,

G.F. Stuart, Lieut.[6]

Learning the trade – Patrolling and rehearsals

While the working parties were out, preparations were being made for the Battalion to move into its own sector of the front line. On the night of 13 February, they took over the front line from units of the Durham Light Infantry and the Bedfordshire Regiment. Calling the position a line is something of a euphemism. They took over a series of reinforced shell holes and defended posts loosely connected via a network of support trenches. This was a particularly dismal area of the sector. Ten Tree Alley was on a ridge line with the German lines only seventy yards beyond it. It was impossible to move between the posts in daylight. Each post was a reinforced shell hole where the men spent twenty-four hours up to their knees or waists in slime. The bottom of each post was water filled and crusted with ice. Any man wounded was liable to sink in the mud or would have to wait hours until four stretcher bearers could struggle up in the dark to assist him. After a few hours most of the weapons in each post were useless and clogged with mud, the ready ammunition filthy. After twenty-four hours men had to be pulled from their holes and half carried to the support positions where they rested before attempting to make the trip of a few hundred yards to safety in Y Ravine. The trudge back down the Wagon Road was marked with unburied corpses and destroyed equipment.

However, Company HQ for 'B' Company in the support position was not bad – Arthur Green:

> Now enjoying the security of a Bosche dugout, who was good enough to leave behind a store of stacks of bombs and bully beef in a new part of the line . . . we did not allow the Bosche

enough time to get comfy here, he has not burrowed down as far as usual – he builds much as we do but in an upside down way, first a flight of steps or staircase panelled with wood, then a room big enough for 7 or 8 to get in, another 8 or 10 steps down and another room and two or three galleries with small bedchambers and bunks off it so leading out after 20 to 30 yards, up more steps into open air. He has an eye to comfort.[7]

A rough handling on the first patrols

The Battalion now had to start putting its training into action – it had to dominate no man's land, learn about the enemy position opposite and defend its own line against their probing attacks. In both attack and defence, inexperience showed.

On arrival in the trenches the Battalion pushed patrols out into no man's land. This was their first experience of patrolling and despite limited objectives was severely punished. German units spent longer in each sector than British ones and the men positioned on the German side of Ten Tree Alley would have known the area very well and probably known that a new unit was opposite them. A party sent to investigate an enemy post was quickly driven in by machine-gun fire. The enemy then fired a series of bombardments into both front line and HQ positions displaying an accurate knowledge of where these were to be found and demonstrating that they could retaliate effectively to any aggressive action. In patrols and shelling in the first twenty-four hours the Battalion lost seven men killed: Thomas Durdey, Hubert Lister, Thomas Pocklington, Harry Turpin, Percy Chadwick, Walter Chapman and Alma Walkington. Henry Wildman died of his wounds. Battalion records show another eighteen men wounded.

Lance Corporal Harry Turpin had worked at Rowntree's before the war and had joined the Battalion in March 1916. He had two brothers serving elsewhere in France. Walter Chapman, from York, had been a pre war territorial and was killed during the bombardment, he was also an employee at Rowntree and Co. Alma Walkington was from Kirkhammerton and had been one of the early recruits. Hedley Heaton writes in the war diary on 15 February that 'except in the case of the right company no information was obtained'.

The exercise was repeated on 17 February. One of this day's patrols was led by Second Lieutenant Girling. They moved out near Ten Tree Alley and were quickly spotted. Heavy shellfire came down, Second Lieutenant Girling was wounded in the foot and the situation deteriorated rapidly. Private Wesley Taylor, who was part of the patrol, got back to the trenches to get a stretcher and returned to him with

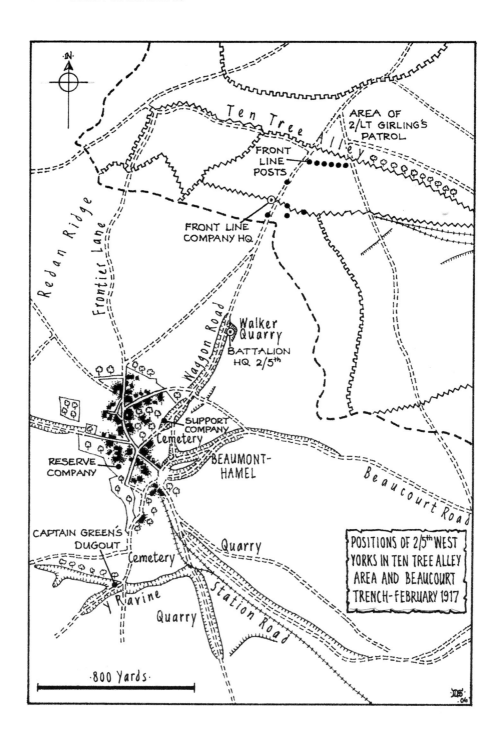

POSITIONS OF 2/5th WEST YORKS IN TEN TREE ALLEY AREA AND BEAUCOURT TRENCH—FEBRUARY 1917

Private Plumb. They were unable to get him safely out of the shell hole on the stretcher and while trying to do so Wesley Taylor was himself wounded by shrapnel and had to return to the Company position. Plumb abandoned the stretcher, picked up Second Lieutenant Girling on his back and carried him to safety. At the same time Corporal Marston's Lewis gun section was shelled and a gun put out of action and left in the open. Corporal Marston recovered it and got it into action again. The patrols were suffering heavily and the Company runners, including Private Pickthall went out to find and guide them in. These men won the Military Medal for their actions.

The first few days 'solo' in the line had not gone well. The ground was exceptionally difficult. There were few dugouts in the front line, little cover from shellfire and the men were not experienced in the business of moving about no man's land without attracting attention. The shelling and patrol actions of 17 February cost the lives of Robert Stabler, James Fairclough, James Halliday, Alfred Moss, John Mullins and Abraham Warn. From the point of view of morale these losses were also serious – these men are commemorated on the Thiepval Memorial to the Missing – patrols were returning with soldiers having simply disappeared and with no obvious gain.

A further six men were wounded and Bertie Brown was to die of wounds taken in these actions. As is commonly the case, raw troops had made up for their inexperience with bravery.

These deaths soon appeared in the newspapers at home. Lance Corporal Alfred Moss's death was announced in the *Harrogate & Claro Times* on 5 April 1917. He was 21 years old and was the second son of Mr and Mrs Moss of West Terrace, Burley-in-Wharfedale. He was formerly employed by Messrs. Brown and Sons, Grocers, Beulah Street, Harrogate. Bertie Brown's passing was marked in the *Harrogate Herald* on 28 February 1917 when his wife received the news that her husband, previously reported dangerously wounded, had died in hospital. Corporal Brown was formerly in the employ of J. Hunter and Son, pork butchers, of Harrogate, and left a wife and three young children.

Henry Angus Girling was evacuated to England on 25 February 1917 and went to Reading hospital with an infected wound to his left foot. It did not respond to treatment and his foot was amputated in July 1917. He returned to service at the West Yorks Depot and after the war he emigrated to South Africa. He died there in 1976.

The loss of Post 10

After this fairly tough initiation, matters did not settle down. On night of the 17/18 February the incoming 2/8th Battalion proposed that the relief was postponed due to mist. However the mist thinned as evening came on and the 2/8th began to move up. While they had been in reserve for the last few days they were also tired, had been shelled and were unfamiliar with this area. The relief went badly. The centre company relief got lost and never showed up and the business of getting out of the line took until after dusk on the 18th. It then became clear that something else had gone wrong. The 2/8th right Company believed it had relieved all of the posts, but the men of Post 10 were missing. Navigating around this position had already proved a problem. The posts had nothing to distinguish them from other shell holes so white tape had been laid between them. This was soon broken up by shellfire or sinking in the mud. Sentries were nervous about German patrols moving around them and tended to shoot readily, further complicating movement.

The story emerges from the records slowly and in pieces. On 22 February Fifth Army Command sent a brief note to Divisional HQ:

> It is understood that the enemy captured a post held by the 62nd Division about the 18th of February. Will you please forward to Army Headquarters a full report on the circumstances under which this post was lost.

A series of replies came from Brigadier De Falbe. The facts of the matter:

> About 06:15 19/2/1917 an enemy bombing party of about 10 men raided the above post held by the 2/5th Bn West Yorks Regiment apparently having crept close to it without having been observed. The sergeant in charge of the neighbouring post reports that after throwing bombs they jumped in and came out again almost immediately with 6 prisoners, one of which was wounded. The remainder of the garrison, (3 men), were killed. The raiders then separated a little from the prisoners and were fired on by the neighbouring post, who claim to have killed three. They then retired.
>
> It is to be noted that the post in question should have been relieved on the night of the 17/18th, by the 2/8th West York Regiment but owing to a guide losing his way this relief was not carried out. It is probably that the garrison of the post was exhausted and were not keeping a good lookout.
>
> A patrol subsequently went to the post and found it blown in by shell fire.

This did not reflect well on the 2/8th. The question of why the relief had not taken place was raised. The reply showed considerable confusion in the lines that night. Major Nigus of the 2/8th reports:

> On the night of the 17th/18th February A Company [2/8th Battalion West Yorks] under the command of Major F A Lupton guided by 2 guides of the 2/5th Battalion proceeded to relieve the posts of the 2/5th West Yorkshire Regiment. Both these guides lost their way and Major Lupton ordered the whole company to return to Battalion Headquarters.

Major Dale [2/5th] told Major Bell [2/8th] what was happening and Major Bell halted the Company and sent for Major Lupton. There is no record of their conversation but Colonel Josselyn ordered Major Dale and Captain Heaton – his second in command and his adjutant – to get 'A' Company up to the line. As they started off to do so it became clear that only two platoons of 'A' Company were now present so a further platoon of 'D' Company had to be added. Lieutenant Moore [2/8th] went off to find the missing two platoons. By the time the whole group got to the support line it was too light to get forward to the advanced posts. On the next night, 18/19 February, relief for the three forward posts were sent out under guides from the 2/5th. They relieved only two posts. Major Nigus continues, 'and it is stated that an officer of the 2/5th West Yorkshire Regiment (name said to be Stuart) reported to Major Lupton that the relief was complete'.

On the morning of 18 February the 2/8th had been trying to sort out the platoons that had wandered off and re group the companies in the right place. They had real difficulties relocating the men of 'A' Company 2/8th in the front line – finding them only by marching in the open on a compass bearing. As the parties were reunited, two men of the 2/5th arrived from Post 10 and reported that they had not been relieved. It was then too light to get to them. A relief patrol had to wait until the night of the 19/20 February, by which time the post had fallen.

Brigadier De Falbe forwarded these reports adding:

> When the 2/5th Battalion took over the line from the 97th Brigade the ground was white with snow and frozen hard and the moon was still up. Tracks through the snow showed clearly. Before the 2/8th West Yorks relieved, the thaw came, all tracks in the snow disappeared, there was thick fog and the moon had

waned. The difficulties experienced by the guide can therefore hardly be exaggerated.

The action taken by Major F A Lupton 2/8th West Yorks in ordering his company to retire, when the guides temporarily lost their way, was a very grave mistake. The double journey through heavy mud exhausted the men and the time loss prevented the relief being completed until the following night.

Authority was still not satisfied with these responses. There was further probing on why the sergeant in the neighbouring post did not do more to assist and why there was a twelve hour gap between the raid and the report of it which made Major Lupton go up to the post to see what was happening. The reply was simple – the sergeant did not fire as the enemy sap was only twenty yards away – there was no time on the way in, and on the way out the raiding party had prisoners. He was then attacked himself and had to defend his own post.

The sergeant appears to have attempted to have the raid reported immediately. His first messenger was shot dead, while the second had a bullet through his helmet . . . he decided to wait until it was dark before making another effort, hence the 12 hour delay.[8]

Major Lupton, no doubt realizing how grave the situation was, did go up to the post, with only his orderly, to establish where exactly it was and what was happening. He never returned. Second Lieutenant Holland of the 2/5th went out on the night of 20 February to see if he could find either the men or Major Lupton. He found the post bombed in, the men gone and no sign of Major Lupton. Major Lupton's body lies in Queen's Cemetery Bucquoy; he is assumed to have been killed on 19 February.

Over the period of the relief and the search for Post 10, Arthur Ayscough, John Banks, Robert Bell, Arthur Cammidge, Thomas Ellwood, John Holdsworth, Percy Radband and James Wilkins died in action. Once again the Battalion was unable to recover the bodies. Harry Gamble was wounded and evacuated to Bertrancourt where the field ambulances were and where he died of his wounds. The *Harrogate Advertiser* on 3 March 1917 recorded that he was in his 21st year, and was previously employed by his father, who was a carting contractor. He lies in Bertrancourt Military cemetery. William Wise also died of his wounds and is buried at Varennes where there was a concentration of three casualty clearing stations at the time.

The final act of the Post 10 affair took place not in France but in the *Harrogate Herald* in March 1917.

Pte Harry Gamble of Knaresborough, died of wounds 19 February 1917. *Ackrill's Harrogate War Souvenir, 1917*

> Private George Holgate, West Yorks, son of Mr E Holgate, of 131 Cold Bath Road, Harrogate, is, we regret to say, a prisoner of war at Dulmen, West Germany. Nothing has been heard of Private Holgate for several weeks, and it was a relief the other day to the family to learn that he was alive and well, although he had had the misfortune to be taken a prisoner of war. In reply to enquiries from his sister, Miss Holgate, Lieutenant Hanley Hutchinson wrote: 'In reply to your letter of 7th March, I much regret that since my last note to you (enclosed to you with T Ketson's), I have heard nothing of your brother. I still think that he and Lance Corporal L Jewitt were taken prisoners; if so, they will be with you again ere long, I hope. One dead body of another of my men was found near, and, as no signs of your brother or his gun were found, I am all the more convinced that he is alive. Enquiries have been made, and will be made of course, with pleasure, and I am only glad to think you have written to me. Anything I can do will be done gladly. Your brother was an excellent fellow in every way, and he is a great loss'. Since that letter was received, Mr Holgate got a card from his son from the Dulmen internment camp, saying he was well. Private Holgate, who is 22 years of age, was in the employ of Messrs Hudson Bros, ironmongers, Harrogate.[9]

It is assumed that both men survived to return home as there is no record of their death in captivity. There is an eyewitness 'Other Rank' account of this period of initiation into trench warfare. Sergeant George Radford was serving in 'C' Company at the time. His records have

Sgt George Radford, wounded on 17 February 1917.
David Lockwood

survived and show that he was wounded on 17 February and therefore could have been involved in Second Lieutenant Girling's patrol.

Born in 1895 off Heslington Road, York, George was a physically fit, strong 19 year old at the start of the Great War. With a feel for adventure, he volunteered for service in 'Kitcheners New Army' and because of his physique, was accepted immediately and sent to train at Aldershot Depot as a Physical Training Instructor. At some point in early 1917 he was cut off from the Battalion with his section without food and water, he with three other comrades, survived for a number of days on remnants of water retrieved from the bottles of dead comrades, eventually escaping to safety. In February 1917 he carried out his own patrol. He took two men with him he was given the task of locating the position of a German machine gun that needed to be 'knocked out' before an attack on the following morning. Crawling out into No-Man's land they were able to pin-point the offending machine gun so that our artillery, on being given its position, could obliterate it and its crew. Almost back to safety in our own lines, George and his men were directly hit by a single shell. In the instantaneous flash and explosion, George recalled seeing that his two companions, his rifle and his lower left arm had disappeared. With shrapnel also in his neck and the serious arm wound, he fell into the crater. Struggling to put a temporary dressing on his shattered arm he lost consciousness as snow began to fall. Throughout that night and all of the following day when the attack took place, he lay in the shell hole and in moments of consciousness piled snow on the stump of his arm. After twenty four hours unattended,

The hospital in High Street Oxford where Sgt Radford was treated.
David Lockwood Collection

he was found by two Canadian stretcher bearers who were
collecting the wounded from that day's attack. They
were amazed to find George still alive after so long exposed and
George recalled they carried him away with a huge snowball
like a 'Christmas Pudding' still on his arm. His presence of
mind to use the snow had saved his life. He was taken to a
casualty clearing station and laid outside in the falling snow
with numerous other wounded, all awaiting attention. His last
recollection before being taken inside was to warn the medical
orderlies to be careful as his coat pockets contained hand-
grenades.[10]

On 20 February, John William Winterburn was killed in action while
the Battalion was in reserve at Y Ravine. Back at Thoresby Camp,
Winterburn had been servant to Arthur Green and to Geoffrey Skirrow.
He had been a drummer in the 2/5th's band which was a constant source
of pride to the Battalion. The 2/5th was regarded as having the best band
in the Brigade but these men also served as stretcher bearers – a
hazardous occupation. Captain Green kept a photograph of him among
his papers with his date of death noted on the back. Remarkably the
exchange of letters between his widow and John Winterburn's comrades

has survived. Later in the war letters to the bereaved become formulaic, 'much loved, missed by all'. The letters from the Battalion at this time reflect the shock of officers for the first time dealing with the loss of their soldiers and reveal the close relationships that had formed between officers and men. Arthur Green wrote:

> My dear Mrs. Winterburn - I am bitterly sorry to have to inform you that your husband has been killed while doing duty in the trenches, though you may by now have had the official notification. We are all, officers and men, absolutely staggered at it for 'Tiggy' was one of the most popular of our men. He was proceeding with another man on a message for me, when a shell burst near by, and from that moment he was unconscious. This was on Tuesday afternoon, the 20th Feb. I am most distressed at it, and all our sympathy is with you in your grief and with your family. I have lost a servant who was prepared to go through thick and thin with me to the end – a thorough, sound, and lovable man, with no equal as a worker. You have lost a husband who, I am sure was all a husband should be. There is not a man or officer in the company who does not give you his whole-hearted sympathy, and who would not do anything to show how well we valued 'Tiggy'. We can scarcely believe it, for it was all so sudden, and day by day we miss him more. He was buried about 4 o'clock on Tuesday. Now, Mrs. Winterburn, I had made a lifelong friend of your husband. Now that he is gone I want you to feel that I am your friend, and that if you want any help I am ready to help you all I can. If I could do more I would. The postcard I enclose was written by your husband, but never posted, I am sending you some letters, which came for him when we got out of the trenches. Again with our fullest sympathy,
>
> yours very sincerely,
>
> Arthur E. Green, Captain.

Drum Major Procter wrote:

> Dear Mrs. Winterburn, - On behalf of myself and the whole of the band, I desire at this the earliest opportunity of expressing to you our very deep regret and sympathy in your great and irreparable loss sustained by the death in action of your

beloved husband. Words cannot describe the shock and horror with which we were struck when the news reached me an hour or two after. I am sure you understand our feelings a little as 'Tiggy', as he was called, was always the popular favourite of the band. The remainder of the band were not in action, but were behind the lines on fatigue work, and Will should have been with them, only that he chose to be true to his master, Capt. Green, and went to the trenches with him, so you see he died a hero and faithful servant. He is buried a little way behind the firing line and so long as we remain in this part of the line we shall endeavour to look after his grave. I feel I cannot say more at this juncture, as I am too full about it all, as the regiment has suffered very badly this week. Trusting that God will give you the grace and strength to bear this great burden,

I remain, yours very sincerely,

George Procter, Drum-Major[11]

His widow wrote to Captain Green:

Thank you very much for your kind letter of sympathy in which you informed me of the death of my dear husband. It came as an awful blow to me as your letter and one from Drum Major Proctor are the only intimation I have had yet. I heard from one of the Yew Park lads, who had written his mother but I could not believe it, but know (sic) I know it to be only too true.

The only consolation I seem to have is in knowing that he died doing his duty and that he is buried decently. I cannot express myself in thanks just what I feel for the kind sympathy extended to me by yourself and the other officers and men in his company. It is as you say, the kiddies and myself have lost the dearest father and husband that one could have wished for and I am sure you will miss him as he valued the kindness you have shown him greatly.

I remain, yours sincerely

Mrs JW Winterburn[12]

Private Winterburn is buried in Ancre Valley Cemetery.

Pte JW Winterburn of Harrogate.
Liddle Collection

On 22 February and out of the line,
Arthur Green wrote home. The first
two pages of his letter are a series of
requests for equipment, holdalls
and bags for kit and food, a small
tooth brush, a replacement hair
brush. He then goes on to sum-
marize their first few weeks in
action, first the period in Ten Tree
Alley:

Now about our trench experiences. We moved up about
10 days ago as far as I can remember. The frost was still on
and everything was quite hard.
You may have gathered where
we are. My dugout was
absolutely full of German bombs and had not been in British
possession for more than a week and we could see parts of the
attack going in, which have been spoken of in the com-
muniqués. There are of course no real trenches here for we are
more or less behind the Bosche first line defences – we really
held a series of shell craters for our front and support lines and
the Company HQs were lucky if they could work into a
German dugout. But of course the Bosche knew where his old
dugouts were and didn't forget to pay them a certain amount
of attention.

We were up in the line seven days but on the second the thaw
set in and then the mess started. The whole of the ground has
at one time or another been turned over with shells and was all
ups and downs and once the thaw came it was a worse mess
than anything I have ever come across. We wore thigh boots
all the time but I can't describe the mud – some men's greatcoats (where they had slipped down which was frequent) were
50lbs in weight at least.

He then describes conditions in Y Ravine, near Beaumont Hamel:

Mrs Winterburn's
letter to Capt
Green, March
1917.
Liddle Collection

After being relieved from the trenches we (B Company) were sent into some trenches in the rear in reserve. There we had 3 huge dugouts for the whole company, getting 70 men in one of them. They were recently Bosche and contained bedsteads and all sorts of crannies and chambers. There we spent our time in sleeping and eating and got about 18 hours out of the 24 in sleep. Of course in the trenches proper there is not much sleep as the officers have to go touring all round day and night and reconnoitring has to be done so one is pretty tired at the end of it all.

Then the Battalion went into rest at Bolton Camp, Mailly Wood & Forceville where they were engaged in road building.

After 2 days in reserve we were again relieved about 12 midnight and in the rain we came out to march to a camp about

6 miles back. We got in at 5am and again got a trek at 11am next morning for this place, which is almost out of the sound of our guns and here we are doing working duties and trying to get clean.

Arthur Green's final view of this period:

We did extremely well, stood a good deal of shelling, beat off 2 German attacks, great things for a battalion newly out here.[13]

Colonel Josselyn was also keen to encourage his men. On the day that they came out of the trenches Battalion orders contained a note to all ranks:

The Officer Commanding is proud and much gratified to be able to tell all ranks that the Brigadier congratulated the Battalion on the good work done by all ranks during the recent tour of duty in the line.

The OC always expected that all ranks of the Battalion would face every hardship and do their duty in the face of the enemy without flinching but the conduct of all ranks under the exceptional hardship and unusually trying conditions of the weather, of the situation and of hostile activity have exceeded his expectations. He can only say in commending their devotion to duty and bravery of all ranks that he is proud of all and feels more than ever the honour of his position as their commanding officer.[14]

While this may have been the official view, and that of 'B' Company, the Battalion had lost a considerable number of men for such a short period in the line. The 62nd was the last Division to come out from England and was a rare thing on the Western Front in 1917 – an entirely inexperienced unit. This became clear in the post 10 affair. While some errors were made most of the problems occurred because it took the new battalion too long to carry out basic tasks and they did not have the experience of finding their way in the devastated areas that more hardened troops had mastered. They had yet a great deal to learn.

The patrol war extended – the pursuit of the withdrawing Germans

Despite the very active German patrolling and shelling encountered by the 2/5th in mid February, they were in fact covering a withdrawal. The

Battalion was back in the line in Gudgeon Trench on 26 February. Gudgeon Trench was an old German position a little to the north of Miraumont. On their left the Duke of Wellington's advanced into Orchard Alley with little resistance and sent out patrols, finding no enemy. The 2/5th then advanced at night and pushed out further patrols, which found neither the expected friendly forces, nor any enemy – the Germans had gone to the Hindenburg Line. In these patrols Charles Flatt was killed in action and his grave lost in the fighting. Frank Owston died of his wounds and Francis Learoyd, a pre-war reservist and territorial who was over age for enlistment, succumbed to his injuries in a hospital near Doullens.

> It is with a keen sense of regret the villagers of Staveley have received the news of the death of Lance-Corporal Frank Learoyd (West Yorks), who formerly carried on the business of joiner and cabinetmaker in the village of which he was a native. Mrs. Learoyd last week received intimation of her

Pte F Owston of Harrogate, died of wounds 26 February 1917.
Ackrill's Harrogate War Souvenir, 1917

L/Cpl Frank Learoyd of Stavely, died of wounds 26 February 1917.
Ackrill's Harrogate War Souvenir, 1917

husband having been admitted to hospital and wounded severely in the head by shrapnel. On Wednesday a telegram arrived stating that he had succumbed on Monday. Corporal Learoyd, who was forty-six years of age, had been a very popular organist at Staveley Church for nearly twenty years; was assistant overseer for the township, and a member of the Staveley Lodge of Oddfellows, for which he had also acted some years as secretary. He was well known in Harrogate and Knaresborough, and formerly was a member of the old 1st West Riding (P.O.W.) Volunteer Band, which had its head-quarters for the left half battalion in Harrogate. He joined His Majesty's Forces two years ago from the National Reserve, and served his business apprenticeship with Messrs. Hudson and Rainforth, of Harrogate. Much sympathy has been manifested with Mrs. Learoyd and her three sons in their sad bereavement.[15]

On 1 March, still in Gudgeon Trench, Major Dale, the Battalion second in command was visiting B Company Headquarters. He was hit by a shell and killed along with two men from B Company, Thomas Binns, and Edgar Turner. Major Dale was a pre-war Territorial with the 5th Battalion, a solicitor from York and one of the founder members of the Battalion. He is buried in Queens Cemetery, near Bucquoy. Thomas

Binns' and Edgar Turner's bodies were never recovered. In March 1918 Major Dale was awarded the OBE to recognize an act of bravery while not in contact with the enemy. He was recommended for the Albert Medal but – 'In lieu of this honour he was awarded the Order of the British Empire First Class for an act of gallantry in averting a disaster during the throwing of live bombs'.[16]

The Battalion moved out to

Maj AP Dale, son of the late Alderman RP Dale killed by shellfire near Gudgeon Trench.
Ackrill's Harrogate War Souvenir, 1917

Maj Dale's grave at Queens Cemetery, Bucquoy.
Author's Collection

Miramont on 2 March, where it was in support but still well within range of the enemy guns. There was an air of confidence about them as they were moving into enemy territory. Arthur Green wrote on 6 March 1917, 'We are still pushing ahead, a bloodless gain - nothing like the usual July 1st push and losses'.

The assumption among many of the soldiers was that now the Germans had finally broken and were on their way back to Germany, there would be a pursuit . Things seemed to be going very well and the theme of Arthur's letters is that open warfare had returned and the Germans were on the run. Writing of this period when back in camp, Green records:

> We are still on the advance, no time for trenching. Every night we move to a new position and try to make oneself look like ground during the day, pot at any Bosche that shows himself and another creep forward the next night. Supplies move by night. If the Bosche are shelling it holds up the food when in

the trenches we are not able to get hot food, that is one draw-
back but there are worse when thick mud comes up to the knees
and threatens trench feet. In some places Bosche stew is still
warm, we don't eat Bosche stuff as a rule it may not be safe.[17]

It was not only the food that was unsafe. There was also some excitement as the engineers were called in – the dugout selected for Battalion
HQ proved to have been booby trapped.

Charles Benson and James Knowles died at this time. Charles Benson
had fallen ill and was in a general hospital back at Le Treport, near
Dieppe. James Knowles died of his wounds while the Battalion was still
in the line and his grave has been lost.

The attack on Achiet Le Petit – preparations and training for the real thing

The Battalion was withdrawn from the line on 7 March to prepare for
the attack on Achiet Le Petit – their first formal operation. While
the men were refitting and recovering, the officers were working on the
scheme of attack. Between then and 12 March the orders were worked
out and a model of the enemy positions built. The attack was rehearsed
in daylight and amendments made to the objectives. It was practised in
the dawn and in the dark. While it was important for the men to understand their role in the attack much of the work was also to allow the
officers to understand how the Battalion was working within itself and
with the flanking battalions to achieve the objective. Time and again in
the reports of attacks the difficulties of ensuring that the unit's flanks
were covered are highlighted. This gap in operations also would have
allowed the officers to reflect on their first spell holding the line and to
consider some improvements in their tactics. However the attack on
Achiet Le Petit was cancelled – something far bigger was on the way.
Now that they had worked hard at their training, they would have to
wait a while.

They spent the wait in road building around Station Road in
Beaumont Hamel and the roads to Achiet Le Petit. This was a common
activity for any battalion – it was possible to buy post cards showing this
activity to give people at home an insight into what they were doing. For
the 2/5th however it was carried out in a very cold spell while again living
in run down huts or under canvas. Again Hedley Heaton was not at all
happy about the men's living conditions as their huts became very wet
when the snow melted.

The *Harrogate Herald* continued to fulfil its support role; as the men
came out of the line into rest they got their post and Private Chris

Horner sent in his thanks and news and seems to have found himself a more comfortable billet.

> Have received the parcel containing the shears and scissors, and I am writing to thank you very much for the same. They are real good ones and just what I wanted, and have come at an opportune moment, as the Battalion is out of the line at the present time and have plenty of time to make good use of them. Have had good reports from home about the way the war is going on, and we are all in good hopes of soon being back in Blighty, when I may get an opportunity of thanking you personally for the utmost of trouble you have taken over this request of mine. Am writing this well behind the line, where we are billeted in dugouts and getting quite used to living in semi-darkness. This is quite a good rest for the Battalion after the strenuous time we had in the line, but we are working hard now making roads and railways, over which we hope to advance. In closing, may I thank you once again for your kindness and wish your Harrogate and Knaresborough papers continued success.[18]

Training continued and had dangers in itself, a bombing accident wounded Captain W H Marston, 'C' Company, and Lieutenant Bickersteth and nine other men on 1 April.

Captain Marston was a serious loss as he was one of the most experienced soldiers in the Battalion. He was 43 years old and had served with the King's Royal Rifle Corps for twenty-one years. Previous to joining the 2/5th he had held a non combatant role and an honorary commission but he applied to relinquish this and requested a role in a line regiment in June 1916. He was made temporary captain the next month and ordered by telegram to Somerleyton to join the Battalion in July 1916. On 1 April 1917, he was leading bombing practice and had four bombs left over which he, Lieutenant Bickersteth, Sergeant Page and Corporal Holmes were disposing of. His exploded prematurely and amputated his right hand. The Battalion level enquiry cleared him of wrong doing but Brigade criticized him for throwing grenades in a volley. Captain Marston returned to service and was still serving in Northern Command in April 1919. Though Lieutenant Bickersteth's wounds appeared minor he seems to have developed lung problems. He was examined by numerous medical boards and occasionally passed fit but never returned to active service. William Shepherd died a few days later, at Varennes on 3 April but not as a result of this accident.

Reconnaissance at Bullecourt

Whatever the detail of the retraining and reorganization in March, its effects were soon felt. When the Battalion returned to line on 3 April it was tasked with the preliminary reconnaissance for the attack on Bullecourt. The move up was completed without incident and the battalion took up a position in the lines east of Croisilles, facing Bullecourt. Battalion HQ was 500 yards south of St Leger. It was here on 5 April that Battalion HQ took a direct hit from a shell, Colonel Josselyn was knocked out and Bernard Greaves, HQ signaller, was killed. It also wounded two other men. Bernard Greaves was a Knaresborough Grammar School old boy and a member of the Wesleyan church in Knaresborough. One of the wounded men was Signals Sergeant Robert Ainsley who was hit in the neck. He recovered and applied for a commission in November 1917, returned to England in February 1918 to enter training and was finally commissioned back into the 5th Battalion in 1919.

Bullecourt formed a salient in the Hindenburg line. The wire in front of it was very thick and designed to channel attacking forces onto hidden machine guns. However, it was believed to be lightly held with reserve troops and would fall to a vigorous assault once the wire had been breached by artillery. On the night of 5 April the Battalion pushed its outposts out to 500 yards from the Hindenburg line, in front of the fortress village. The line of posts was occupied by two companies and

Pte Bernard Greaves of Knaresborough, killed 5 April 1917 while acting as a signaller in Battalion HQ.
Ackrills Harrogate War Souvenir, 1917

over the next week they rotated through them as though in a conventional trench line.

As the Battalion waited in front of Bullecourt, Major Peter, late of the 1st Battalion Royal Welch Fusiliers, arrived to be second in command. Major Peter was a pre-war regular soldier, who had enlisted in 1896 in the 2nd Volunteer Battalion Lincoln Regiment and had served in South Africa. He then enlisted in the 7th Dragoon Guards and served for fifteen years attaining the rank of SSM. He was still serving when the war broke out and was commissioned second lieutenant in the 1st Battalion Royal Welch Fusiliers and went to France in April 1916 where he won the MC[19]. His influence started to show very quickly when he took the patrolling in hand and it was done in a much more professional manner. This can be seen in particular in the details and quality of the written orders issued and the order and structure brought to the patrolling. There are no repetitions of a vague 'patrols were pushed out' – the location of posts, patrol routes through them and the results of patrols are recorded in detail.

Having established the line it was now up to the Battalions' patrol commanders to find out how strongly the enemy position was held and what effect the barrage was having in preparing its fall. A different group of officers and NCOs now entered the war diaries forming the first of 2/5th's long list of redoubtable patrol commanders. Lieutenants A W L Smith and Geoffrey Skirrow were tasked with assessing the damage done to the defences of Bullecourt by the barrage. Therefore, on the night of 7/8 April, Lieutenant Smith, 'C' Company, left his trench at 3 a.m. His patrol report reads:

> Starting point U19.b.6.6. Object in view to reconnoitre enemy wire and ground between our posts and wire. On leaving our line the patrol proceeded North East until it struck a track at U19.b.10.8 Patrol proceeded along the track until it came in touch with the wire at U14.c.2.2. Patrol proceeded North West along the wire for 200 yards to U14.c.2.3. The wire is 15 ft thick and 4 ft high. Other rows of wire were observed behind the trench but the patrol is unable to state how many. The entanglement is put up with five rows of screw posts 3 ft apart. The wire is quite undamaged by our artillery, their shells have apparently dropped 15 yards short all along the line. The patrol returned at 5:15 am.

Finding the role of observation and recording somewhat dull, Lieutenant Smith sent back to the trench line for a Lewis gun and used it to break up a working party he had spotted on the enemy side of the wire. Sergeant Major Coulter of 'D' Company was also out that night. He inspected a further 300 yard of wire and found no damage at all, indeed few shells seem to have come anywhere near the wire. He was back in at 4:30 a.m.

The artillery had another day to improve its performance and then 'C' Company went out into the wire again. Lieutenant Smith went out and did find a 2 foot gap in the wire, which had already been plugged. While the shells did now seem to be landing in the wire he found no significant damage. The Brigade war diary notes that he was attacked in no man's land. The patrol came under rifle fire and, under cover of this, an enemy section moved towards it. Lieutenant Smith and Lance Corporal Cust waited until they were fifteen yards away and then hailed them with bombs while the rest of the patrol withdrew. Cust was awarded the Military Medal for this action. For these two patrols Lieutenant Smith was awarded the Military Cross, the first decoration for an officer of the 2/5th.

Not to be outdone, Lieutenant Skirrow, also of 'C' Company, went out on the night of 8/9 April. He seems not to have been content with visiting the wire and returning but stayed out all day under intermittent rifle fire and bombardment to observe the enemy defences. For this patrol he was awarded the Croix de Guerre. These positions were very close to the wire. This was re-emphasized on 8 April when the Battalion took eleven casualties from British guns near 'A' and 'C' Company HQs

as a shell exploded prematurely. Fred Fawcett, Christopher Hotchin and John Whatley died as a result of this and their graves were lost in subsequent fighting.

On 9 April Second Lieutenant G F Stuart went out, ordered to find out if the Hindenburg Line had been evacuated. Hedley Heaton notes in the war diary that the position remained strongly held. Although these patrols did not lose

Lt Geoffrey Skirrow – awarded the Croix de Guerre for patrolling near Croisilles on 10 April 1917.
Harriet Bennett

Lt AWL Smith awarded the MC for
two patrol actions near Croisilles
between 7 and 9 April 1917.
Lucy Harrison

Lt Smith's MC.
Lucy Harrison

any men dead there were some losses. At some point at least one man
went missing. Sergeant Pinkney was taken prisoner and did not arrive
back in York until December 1918. Harry Pinkney was born in 1880
and enlisted on 16 November 1914, regimental number 200915.
Previously he was a clerk with the LNER in York. He was held at
Cassebruch POW camp in eastern Germany where his portrait was
painted by a Russian fellow POW.

These forays were not just good patrol work. The patrols were
bringing back information that the enemy defences were largely undam-
aged and that the defenders were actively patrolling and repairing them
in spite of the British barrage. These reports were made on the day
before the first full-scale assault on Bullecourt was launched.

Sgt Harry Pinkney, captured in April 1917 while on patrol near Bullecourt. *Brian and Sue Mullarvey*

In the wings – the 2/5th at the first battle of Bullecourt

The First Battle of Bullecourt went very badly overall. The basic plan was that the bombardment would break the wire allowing infantry in and the lightly held positions would be abandoned by the enemy. Where the wire was unbroken the Australians would use the tanks instead of a barrage and, advancing behind eleven of them, smash their way through. The Australian infantry were in position in no man's land well before Zero Hour

Cassebruch POW camp where Sgt Pinkney and other 2/5th prisoners were held. *Brian and Sue Mullarvey*

on 10 April but they were on their own. The tanks had been held up in a snow storm and could not get up to the front line until well after daylight. The attack was cancelled at 4:15 a.m. and there was a rush to get the men back under cover before they were spotted.

The experience of the 62nd Division was somewhat different. They were committed to the attack knowing that this was their first action and, believing the Germans to be preparing another withdrawal, it should have been a good place for them to start. Further, their involvement was contingent on Australian success or a German withdrawal. The 185th Brigade was to send forward strong patrols at the same time as the Australians advanced at 4:30 a.m. on 10 April to find out if the Germans were still there.

The Brigade commander, De Falbe, was well aware that the enemy was still there and the wire intact. In later years he commented on the '. . . excitement of higher command believing Bullecourt evacuated, we on the spot know the enemy is still holding the line strongly'.[20]

The 2nd Heavy Artillery Group that was firing the shells supposed to destroy the wire had not only failed in the sector that the 2/5th had checked – the wire all around Bullecourt was untouched. However, that would not have been a problem if the advance of the 185th Division had been cancelled at the same time as the Australians. But it wasn't.

On 10 April the orders were received that the Brigade were to 'occupy' the Hindenburg line. This is a very different from sending out patrols to find out if it is held. The 185th Brigade expected to enter and hold the German trenches. The 2/5th was to remain in its positions and assist by fire. As ordered, the 2/7th and 2/8th Battalions sent out patrols in force at Zero Hour. No message came from the Australian 4th Division to the 62nd to prevent it. In addition the orders given to the 185th Brigade were confusing as to the circumstances in which the patrols were to be out and what the Battalion were to do if the patrols found the position defended. Six strong patrols went out and were at the wire by 4:45 a.m. There was a strange silence from the right – no sounds of an attack or tanks. There were no gaps in the wire. The German posts opened fire and drove the patrols back into a sunken road where they were shelled to pieces by their own artillery. The two battalions of West Yorks lost 162 men and a deep suspicion of the Australians was born.

The 2/5th were well aware that things were not going well. They had inspected the wire themselves and therefore had no illusions about how poor the artillery was. The quality of shells fired at this time was pretty poor. The artillery was firing shrapnel rather than high explosive to cut the wire but without the accuracy or the fuses to make it effective. The advance of the 2/7th and 2/8th was clearly visible to the men of the 2/5th and they saw for the first time what the prepared and professionally commanded machine guns of the 120th Wurttumberg Regiments could do to an infantry advance. At least one Battalion officer – Lieutenant Skirrow – was at Brigade HQ during the attack and able to see the big picture, which was probably as depressing as witnessing the action itself.

The 2/5th lost two men on the 10th, John Atkin and Charles Shepherd, far less than the other Battalions, and had three other men wounded. On 11 April there was a repeat performance. However this time Divisional HQ intended to make sure that the Australians were actually in Bullecourt before they moved. At 8:00 a.m. the message came that the Australians had entered the village and patrols were sent out prior to ordering the full battalions into the attack. These patrols found an enthusiastic defence behind intact wire – exactly what the reconnaissance patrols from the 2/5th had reported. A further report came in saying the Australians were not in fact in the village and the 62nd Division attack was not launched. Sadly further along the line Australians had entered the lines beyond Bullecourt where, un-supported, they took terrible casualties. The Australians believed that the attacks were to have taken place at the same time and that the 62nd had been late moving and left them unprotected.

The Battalion remained in the line until 12 April. Despite the failures of the previous two days it was again responsible for a series of patrols that amounted to an advance and occupation of the Hindenburg Line. It is hard to see what the purpose of these patrols was given that their reports had been ignored in the battle planning so far. The war diary records:

> Orders were received over the telephone that strong battle patrols were to be sent out to occupy Hindenburg Line at dusk – these were sent out and strongly opposed by machine gun fire and were subjected to an enemy barrage – the enemy trenches were found to be strongly held. The battle patrols were with-drawn under Brigade orders (verbal) and two other patrols were sent out to report on the wire in front of the Hindenburg line. 2/Lt A Holland A Company was in charge of one of these patrols and he did excellent work. He thoroughly inspected whole of the wire on our front and with rare exceptions found the wire intact, where it had been broken it had been repaired.[21]

Casualties for these patrols on 12 April amounted to five, of whom one, Joseph Forth, was killed in action.

Taking stock – the first four months in the field
By the time of First Bullecourt the 2/5th Battalion had been in France
for ninety-four days. It had spent nineteen days in the front line and
witnessed its first major battle. It had lost one officer killed and forty-
nine of the men were dead. Yet it was still a relatively inexperienced
unit. It had made big steps forward in company and platoon level
operations but had yet to work together as a battalion. Its specialist
units, Lewis gunners and bombers, had been intensively trained, its
musketry more intensively developed than most Territorial or New
Army battalions, but there are no records of officers attending training
courses, so frequent in the later months, or of higher than company-
level training with the exception of a few days in late March. In being
given a supporting role at First Bullecourt they had been very lucky,
however it must have undermined their confidence in their artillery,
their Commonwealth allies and their own leadership.

Chapter 4
2/5th at the Battle of Bullecourt

The Plan – massive artillery preparation and the use of tanks

The 62nd Division was tasked, in conjunction with the 3rd Army on its left and the Australian 2nd Division on the right, with the capture of a section of the Hindenburg Line including the villages of Bullecourt and

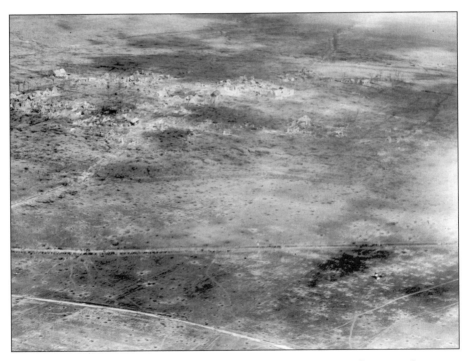

Reconnaissance photograph of Bullecourt before the first attack.
Photograph courtesy of the Imperial War Museum, London Q57678

Hendecourt. The 185th Brigade task was to capture the village of Bullecourt including the front and support line trenches.

During the week preceding the attack the village was again bombarded but this time by heavy artillery – there was to be no repetition of the wire cutting problem. Nor was there to be an opportunity for the enemy machine-gunners – there would be a creeping barrage that opened at Zero Hour on the enemy wire and then worked ahead at 100 yards every three minutes to keep the enemy in their shelters until the advancing infantry were upon then. The effect of this barrage can be seen on the aerial photographs. The photographs taken by the RFC in April show a ruined and burning village but it is still recognizable; some building have roofs, the lines of the road are clearly visible. The wire entanglements are also there. From the photos taken around the time of the second assault, the village had been shelled into dust, all land marks were gone and the photo interpreters have had to enhance the enemy trench line to make any sense of the photo.

To deal with strong points and to ensure that any remaining wire would be crushed more tanks would be deployed. The Division would

Reconnaissance photograph of Bullecourt during the bombardment.
Photograph courtesy of the Imperial War Museum, London. Q55670

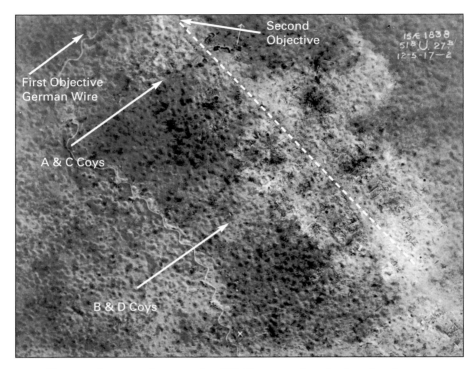

Reconnaissance photograph of Bullecourt after the bombardment.
Photograph courtesy of the Imperial War Museum, London IWM 55678

be supported by eight tanks of No. 12 Company, D Battalion Heavy
Branch Machine Gun Corps under the command of Lieutenant
Colonel Lloyd. Their orders were to assist the division to 'capture the
village of Bullecourt and the hostile system of trenches from U28.b.8.8
to U21 and U20b'. To keep any surviving infantry firmly in their
dugouts the machine guns of the 212th Machine Gun Company would
provide a barrage for twenty minutes after Zero Hour on the German
front line and then move forward to support the posts established in the
village.

There would be a considerable amount of support available from
trench mortars. The 4th Australian Division had allocated nine medium
trench mortars (three batteries of three) to be at the disposal of the 2/5th
and 2/6th Battalions.

There would be no shortage of supplies. On the night before the
attack the dumps were topped up, into the immediate supplies dumps
on the railway embankment went four trench mortars, 100 shells for
them, thirty-two rolls of barbed wire and as much small arms ammu-

nition and as many grenades as the four Battalion pack mules could carry. The dump already contained 2,000 Mills bombs, 250 rifle grenades, 20,000 rounds of small arms ammunition and 200 Stokes mortar bombs. This preparation was not without cost; James Judge and Samuel Rawlings, members of the Transport Section were killed while carrying supplies to the Brigade dump. In 2005 the site of this dump was still littered with Mills Bombs and rolls of barbed wire.

However, Bullecourt's defences were formidable. The German front line was a deep trench all round the salient, double in places with dugouts under the parapet. A further trench ran through the centre of the village on the line of what was formerly a street and then the Hindenburg Support Line ran to the north of the village – giving it three easily defensible positions. None of these positions had been penetrated by reconnaissance patrols. There was a belief that there were concrete bunkers in the front line but there was no detail on the depth of the dugouts. The ground itself was difficult. It sloped up to the north, so units coming in from west and south could be fired on by machine-gun posts in the second and third lines. These posts had been located and shelled but the effect was unknown.

Leading role for the 2/5th and 2/6th Battalions

Between the battles the Battalion was in rest and training in the villages of Sapignies and Behagnies. There was a great deal of training for the specialists – bombers and Lewis gunners in particular. The news of decorations also came through prompting Lieutenant Riley to write to the *Harrogate Herald*. Although this was not published until 9 May, after the battle, it was clearly written between 28 April when Lieutenant Smith's medal was announced in the war diary and the Battalion being put on thirty minutes notice to move on Sunday 29 April.

Lieutenant T Riley, of the old Beechwood Boys, writing to Mr. W H Breare, says:

I am sending you the names of five men who have won the Military Medal and one officer who has won the Military Cross during the recent big advance. Military Medals - Lance Corporal T Marston, 201879, C Company; Lance Corporal J W Cust, 201511, C Company; Lance Corporal J Ewbank, 201557, D Company; Private Wesley Taylor, 5294, C Company; Private F C Plumb, 201499, stretcher bearer, Headquarters Staff. Military Cross – Lieutenant A W L Smith, C Company, son of the Bishop of Knaresborough. Lieutenant Smith wiped out a German party almost single-handed, and is one of the most respected officers of the battalion, having served with us from the old Beechwood days. You will be pleased to learn that the band are great favourites out here, and in great demand. They are under my care, and have many and varied duties to perform, and I have never yet come across such a lot of fine fellows. They are always ready for any work no matter how dangerous or what hour of the night or day. The Harrogate people should indeed be proud of their battalion. I should like to give you all the details of how our men have won the good name they have had. I am afraid the censor would object.

The first time I come on leave I shall call and see you. Then I hope to give you a few details of how our men have conducted themselves. We have won numerous trophies, and I hope to let you have one for exhibition if the authorities will allow. The best trophy was won by the band, and we had a very lively time too, getting it away from the trenches. All my staff are in the very best of health, and looking forward to a speedy return of peace. We get many rumours out here, and these, in conjunction with what we see, convince us that the Boche is having a most terrible time. He smashes up all the villages, blows up roads and places every manner of obstacles in our way, but we still get at him and they are of small avail. Our CO, Lieutenant Colonel Josslyn, TD, and our adjutant, Captain Hedley F Heaton, have had a most trying time, but I am pleased to say keep wonderfully fit. I shall be pleased to hear from you and know how the Harrogate people are faring during these times of short rations, etc.[1]

Private Parkinson also took the opportunity to keep the *Herald* up to date:

Just a few lines to thank you for your continued kindness in sending me the *Herald*, which never fails to come safely. We have been up the line again, but at the time of writing I am glad to say that we are in rest billets – ruined houses. I am glad to say the weather has improved a lot these past few days, which makes things much better for all concerned. I should be glad if you could send me an old pack of cards if you have any, for me and the lads, as we could have a game or two at nights, which I have not had the pleasure of having since I left England. I hope the weather is better with you and that you had a better

Easter than I had, which I spent in the trenches in very bad weather; but I have pulled through merry and bright again. In conclusion, I hope you will grant my request, and that you are keeping in the best of health.[2]

The *Herald* was quick to respond, reporting on 9 May that:

I have dispatched this week three golf clubs and one dozen balls to Driver W Smithson; safety razor to Trooper A Lawrence; playing cards to Private W Parkinson; a parcel of woollen comforts to Gunner J Schofield; safety razor to Bugler W H [Harry] Kirk.[3]

Bugler Kirk was also in the 2/5th, the units of the other men are not known

On 1 May the men went to company training and the officers gathered to hear the orders for the forthcoming operation. This time the 2/5th was one of the attacking battalions. The orders for this attack were comprehensive and clear. Their start position was on the left of the Brigade, on the north-west side of the main road into Bullecourt from Ecoust [see map]. As the moonlight was very bright, the forming up line was moved back 200 yards so that they would get into position, move up to the start line at zero minus eight minutes, then over it and directly into the attack. Immediate cover would be provided by Lewis guns on the start line itself until the enemy wire was masked by the attacking battalions.

The Battalion would move up in two waves on a two company front. The Divisional History records that Frank Knowles and 'A' Company were on the left and Arthur Green

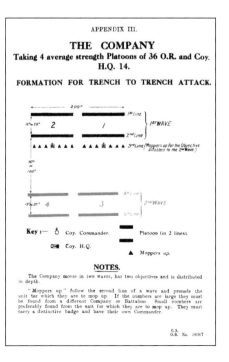

'Text Book' formation of the 2/5th for the attack on Bullecourt. Instructions for the training of platoons for offensive action 1917. *Imperial War Museum*

and 'B' Company on the right of the first wave. Claude Bulmer's 'C'
Company on the left of the second wave and John Wesley Smith's
'D' Company on the right.

The formation for the attack was conventional, manuals at the time
show how each company would attack in two sets of lines [see illustra-
tion] with men assigned to mop up enemy who might emerge behind
them as they advanced. The enemy front line trench would be occupied
by 'A' and 'B' Companies. 'C' and 'D' would then pass through them
to occupy the second and third trench lines. These trenches would be
blocked and defended on the flanks and posts would be put out 200
yards beyond the objective to break up counter attacks. Specific parties
were assigned to capturing key trenches on the left boundary with the
186th Brigade to ensure that there were no gaps.

Also, in a specific instruction 'the greatest attention will be paid to
maintaining touch with the Second Australian Division on the right'.[4]
This would be the responsibility of the right Battalion – the 2/6th.
They were on the other side of the main Ecoust road; the boundary
between the two Battalions followed the road up into the village. Their
objectives were the right portion of the same three lines of trenches.
Their exact starting formation is unknown but as with the 2/5th, 'A'
and 'B' Companies were in the first wave, 'C' and 'D' in the second.
Because of the need for close coordination the 2/5th and 2/6th had
their headquarters in the same dugout. At the first Bullecourt engagement all the Battalion HQs were separate and the command post of
the 2/5th was over 2,500 yards from the action. This time the HQs of
all four Battalions were within 100 yards of each other, on the outskirts
of Ecoust, and 700 yards behind the start line. They were surrounded
by the trench mortar units and on the route back to the Advanced
Dressing Stations and so on the natural route for walking wounded
from whom information could be gleaned if company runners did not
appear.

Concerns before the battle

This attack appeared well planned, used all the available support arms
and followed a substantial barrage. There was every expectation that the
120th Württemberg would be pushed out of the village. However, even
before the attack there were worrying factors, inside and outside the
Brigade. First, the Australians would not be attacking in an unbroken
line on the right of the 2/6th. Their intention was to penetrate the
German line further north and east and then bomb down the line to
meet the 2/6th. Once the first objective was taken they were also to assist
in the capture of the village from the east.[5] The 2/6th therefore was

dependent on a speedy success on the right if they were not to be
exposed on their flank.

Within the Brigade, there may have been problems for Colonel
Josselyn. On 5 April, Battalion Headquarters had a direct hit from a
shell – one signaller was killed and the CO himself stunned. Some
months after the battle it would come out that his spine was damaged
in the blast and he was in considerable pain, but refused to leave the
Battalion before its first major test.[6] The second factor in the Brigade
was the lack of confidence of at least one Battalion commander in the
plan itself. Very unusually, Colonel Hastings of the 2/6th wrote to
the Brigade commander with comments on the plan. He did this on 17
April pointing out: 'The strength of the 2/6th Battalion West Yorkshire
Regiment is probably too small for the task set it, if the village should
be strongly held.'

At the time the 'trench strength ' of the Battalion was less than 400
men; 'A' Company 85, 'B' Company 60, 'C' Company 105, 'D'
Company 90. The 2/6th Battalion had been reduced by casualties –
particularly the destruction of a platoon when a billet was hit by shellfire, by losses in patrolling and also by high rates of illness resulting from
the conditions in the line at Ten Tree Alley. Colonel Hastings did a line
by line appreciation of the plan showing how many men would actually
be able to assault each section of the objective, an example being:

> One platoon of A Coy on the right is to clear the trench on the
> east of the village. This trench is 500 yards long, has at least a
> dozen dugouts and three machine gun emplacements – a severe
> task for 25 or at most 30 men.

He proposed more limited objectives, a faster move up, leapfrog by
the supporting battalions and more support on the east side of the
village. The reply came on the 18th from the Brigade Major R N
O'Connor:

> The Brigadier recognizes that your Battalion is much below
> establishment but considers it to be strong enough to carry out
> the task allotted to it . . . the Brigadier does not propose to
> adopt either of the alternatives suggested by you.[7]

Colonel Josselyn and Colonel Hastings had now been in the same
Brigade for at least eighteen months and had been commanding their
battalions together for a year. Colonel Hastings was a long standing
Territorial going back to the 2nd Volunteer Battalion which became 6th

Battalion West Yorks, where he had been second in command to Colonel Bottomley and then CO himself. He commanded the 6th for four years, retiring in October 1913 and was quickly recalled to raise the 2/6th in September 1914. This was more than a Battalion to him, it contained soldiers he had served with since he was a young man, and many of his pre-war employees whose families he knew. He was understandably reluctant to put it into more hazard than was needful.

The concerns of individual soldiers were more personal. Private Pelham Pearson wrote home on 24 April to reassure his sister:

> We expect going into the line any day now and shall go over the top, well there is no telling what will happen until the thing is over. I trust in God to bring us back safe but if it is His will that I do not I ask you all to take it as such and not to grieve. I shall be happy and things happen so swift there is no pain, and another thing, don't think we are downhearted or dispirited or have a rotten time out here. We have some happy and pleasant times out here.[8]

The Attack - Initial success

On 2 May at 6:10 p.m. the Battalion left Behagnies and marched for three hours. They then paused, had a hot meal and moved off again at 10:30 p.m. to Longatte where they met their guides. These guides from 2/7th led them by platoons to tapes on the left of the Ecoust – Bullecourt road. The forming up was complete by 2:45 a.m. despite some shellfire.

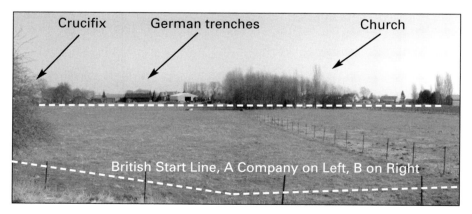

View from the centre of the start line to the first objective – the German front line. *Author's Collection*

The 2/6th was also in position and in touch with the 2/5th at this point; however of the 2/5th Duke of Wellington's on the left there was no sign. The enemy opened a barrage at 3:30 a.m. causing some casualties to 2/5th.

As planned, eight minutes before Zero Hour the Battalion moved off and up to the start line and at 3:45 a.m. red flares were seen and the Battalion set out to Bullecourt. 'A' and 'B' Companies crossed no man's land quickly and found the wire well cut. They moved up the trench south of the Crucifix and captured an officer and thirty-one men there while the barrage was still landing on the machine-gun emplacements. The first objectives were captured within minutes, seemingly lightly held. The initial German response was counter battery fire. At 4:10 a.m. enemy artillery destroyed the guns and ammunition dump of the supporting Australian trench mortars.

'C' and 'D' Companies moved up, passed through 'A' and 'B' Companies and began to establish posts. Resistance began to stiffen with machine-gun fire from enemy posts east and west of them; a trench mortar battery also found the range and bombarded them. However 'D' Company, maintaining contact with the 2/6th got out beyond the church and established a post there [see map]. By 5:00 a.m. the Battalion was half way through the village. By 5:15, on the left, Second Lieutenant G B Foster of 'C' Company had reached a point just in front of the third objective and had a post overlooking the Hindenburg support line. All that was needed was for the rest of the Brigade on the right and the 2/5th Duke of Wellington's on the left to catch up with him and the village would have fallen.

Nothing of the sort took place.

The fight in the village
By 6:35 a.m. the fight had turned very nasty and, with casualties very heavy among the officers, the 2/5th began to lose control of the battle and stalled.

While the wire was generally well cut, it was not so at the western corner of the village. It is likely that Captain Frank Knowles, commanding 'A' Company, was killed here early in the battle. His company moved on into its objectives but as it was ordered in the plan to hold a line of posts, the platoons did just that and do not seem to have moved further to support the beleaguered platoons of 'C' Company. 'C' Company commander – Captain Claude Bulmer – was wounded after 5:00 a.m. and got back to Battalion Headquarters at 6:00 a.m. There was now no senior command on the left. Second Lieutenant Foster, 'C' Company, was isolated and sent back a pigeon post:

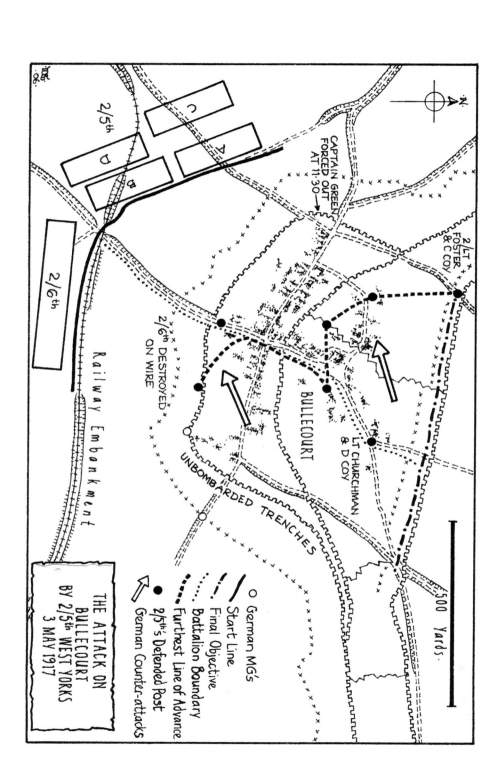

THE ATTACK ON
BULLECOURT
BY 2/5th WEST YORKS
3 MAY 1917

○ German MG's
Start Line
Final Objective
Battalion Boundary
Furthest Line of Advance
● 2/5th's Defended Post
German Counter-attacks

2/5th

2/6th

Railway Embankment

CAPTAIN GREEN
FORCED OUT
AT 11·30

2 LT
FOSTER
& C COY

2/6th DESTROYED
ON WIRE

BULLECOURT

UNBOMBARDED TRENCHES

LT CHURCHMAN
& D COY

500 Yards.

N

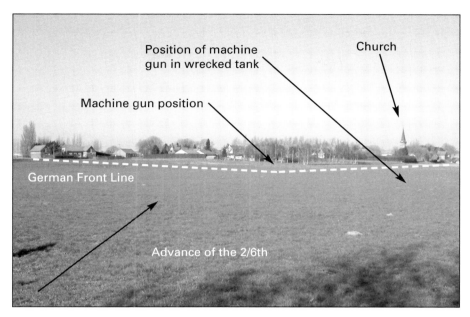

Area advanced over by 2/6th West Yorks, taken from the railway embankment. *Author's Collection*

We are in communication trench at point U21d5.5 post above road [To the North and rear of the village]. There are 3 Boche machine guns on our left and 1 on right. We failed to reach our objective having advanced beyond the village but we tried to return to this position with 10 men in support of either flank. Send rifle grenades to oust machine guns. We are being shelled by enemy. Village held by machine guns and snipers. I have 40 men now including (3 words illegible) and 4 2/6th West Yorks.

On the right, B Company had taken its objectives and been passed through by D Company under Lt Wesley-Smith. D Company, still in touch with the 2/6th, got beyond the church and possibly into the open beyond the village. Lt Churchman and Second Lieutenant Annely led this part of the attack and were both missing at the end of the day. John Wesley-Smith broke his leg at the enemy wire and was evacuated by a passing tank. D Company, lacking most of its officers, ceased to be an organized part of the battle.

Captain Arthur Green commanding 'B' Company was already wounded in the first assault, and was again before the end of the day.

CSM Rathke DCM, decorated for his part in the fight in the village, 3 May 1917.
Ackrill's Harrogate War Souvenir

Of his officers, Lieutenant Wilcox was shot through the thigh and captured. Lieutenant P Clubb had a lucky escape as a piece of shrapnel passed through his haversack and his field pocket book, knocking him down and bruising him, but not seriously injuring him. By 6:30 a.m. Captain Green was the senior officer surviving and took command of the line of posts that the Battalion had established, assisted by CSM Rathke. He came out of the line on at least one occasion to re-supply with bombs and small-arms ammunition and returned to conduct the defence. The 2/5th went to ground in the shell holes in the village, prepared to hold onto what it had taken and waited for the flanking units to catch up and reinforcements to pass through them. Rathke won the DCM for his actions.

The destruction of the 2/6th
The Germans had, according to their usual policy, held the front lines lightly, created strong points with good fields of fire and held troops in reserve for counter-attack. Their plan now went into action, using the gaps between the 2/5th and the 2/6th and the Australians. By early morning the 2/6th on the right had been destroyed. The barrage on the positions to be attacked by the Australians did not land until 4:15 a.m. The 2/6th moved out into no man's land at 3:45 a.m. There was no way the Australians could occupy the enemy troops to the 2/6th's right – which left them completely exposed. At Zero Hour, 'A' and 'B' Companies ran 200 yards to the enemy wire. The noise and dust disorientated them and they became tangled up with 'B' Company of the 2/5th and had to pause to find their way again. As they moved forward, it became clear that the machine-gun post in an abandoned tank at the southernmost point of the village was still in action. This was a commanding position anyway and the extra height from the tank meant the 2/6th was clearly visible and enfiladed.

It seems that 'A' and 'B' Companies of the 2/6th were effectively wiped out in the seven minutes that were allotted for them to get across

Lt AWL Smith,
wounded at
Bullecourt is
visited by the King
in hospital in
Manchester.
Lucy Harrison

no man's land and into the village. 'C' and 'D' Companies passed
through them and continued the attack. 'D' Company only had two
officers to begin with and lost one near the railway embankment. The
rest of 'D' reached at least the church (where they were seen by Captain
Green) but the Company commander, Captain Gregory, was wounded
and with further massive casualties 'D' Company ceased to be a fighting
unit. Lieutenant Armistead fought on at the head of 'C' Company until
wounded and forced back. The 2/6th had all 12 company officers killed
or wounded and 287 men killed wounded or missing out of the 393 who
went into the attack. They never saw the Australians. No help came
from the right for them, nor could they help the 2/5th.

The 2/5th is driven out of the village

The situation for the 2/5th was very poor. The 2/6th had been unable
to hold a position much to the east of the main road; the Australians
had not arrived in the village leaving the enemy free to move his
reserves. The counter-attacks began to come in from the east taking
each post in turn. In the easternmost posts and those beyond the
church there were no survivors but soon the enemy ran up against
the rough line in the village where they were held by the Lewis guns of
'C' and 'B' Companies. However this line, short of bombs and rifle
grenades, began to crumble under the attack and could not be held
without reinforcement. The 2/7th Battalion was in support, in the
original plan it was split, with some companies supporting the 2/5th
Duke of Wellington's on the left. Only one Company moved forward
to the aid of the other West Yorkshire Battalions. The men of this reinforcement company from the 2/7th West Yorks at 6:30 a.m. saw

other men retiring on their left and did so themselves. There were no reinforcements on the way.

The trench mortar unit that the 2/5th expected to call on for immediate support had been blown up – all its guns were out of action leaving only the Brigade's own trench mortar battery. They lobbed 150 shells into the village but were too far back to really help.

The 2/5th Battalion was also increasingly short of machine-gun support. After joining in the initial barrage, the 212th Machine Gun Company shouldered its guns at 4:30 a.m. and moved up into close support. Second Lieutenant Newman in command had lost one gun before Zero Hour but he pushed the remaining ones forward. On the left he put No. 4 gun and acquired a German machine gun as well. He set up No. 3 gun in a shell hole in the centre, No. 2 gun in the crater on the road, and subsequently further forward into the village itself. However, by 5:45 a.m. No. 3 gun was shelled and out of action, by 6:00 a.m. No. 1 gun was bombed out and lost, No. 2 gun was pushed out of the village and was back in the crater at 6:00 a.m. Although this last gun remained in action it was not in a good position and unable to help the bulk of the 2/5th's posts.

Unable to use these supporting arms and with artillery occupied elsewhere, the remaining arm to call on was the tanks. The records of the Brigade list the fates of the tanks involved in the village. Tank 791, under Lieutenant W S McCoull entered the village on the eastern side and by 5:45 a.m. was on his way back to the rally point. His tank was hit by shellfire and while evacuating it he and all his men were killed. Tank 793, Second Lieutenant Knight, went in by the western side. He drove along the trench in the middle of the village but saw no infantry and was driven back to the southern trench. Exchanging his wounded with another tank he went back for a second pass in Bullecourt but was back on the starting point by 7:55 a.m. so he must have left the village by 7:30 a.m. Tank 598, under Second Lieutenant Lawrie got into the Hindenburg Support Line above Bullecourt but was hit and burned out. Tank 596, under Lieutenant Westbrook was also in Bullecourt, taking on machine-gun posts inside the front line between 4:10 and 5:00 a.m. He returned to the start line with a punctured radiator, all but one gun out of action and he and his crew wounded. The three machine gun posts of 212 MGC had a ringside seat for the tank actions. They saw two tanks working up and down the German front line on the left at 5:00 a.m., one tank engaging machine-gun posts in the centre at 5:45 a.m. and one on the right of the 2/5th position engaging at 5:30 a.m. Lieutenants Bickerdike and Armistead of the 2/6th called on tank support for their push eastwards – it is likely that this was Lieutenant Westbrooke's tank – but this action was complete by 6:00 a.m. As Lieutenant Bickerdike and Second Lieutenant Newman were leaving the village at 8:45 a.m. they passed one tank out of action and another stopped to take on wounded. These were the last reports of tank actions. It seems that the gap from parapet to parados in the larger German trenches in Bullecourt was too great for the tanks. Also, as the tanks involved were Mark Is and IIs they had little protection from the armour piercing bullets recently issued to German infantry. In short, the tanks were not coming to the aid of the 2/5th.

As the morning passed, the remnants of the 2/6th were forced out either back to the railway embankment or into the 2/5th positions where they joined in the defence. On the left, contact had been established with the 2/5th Duke of Wellington's who had got into the enemy trenches but this was broken by machine-gun fire and the Duke of Wellington's withdrew. The 2/5th was now completely isolated. Captain Green had established a block on the trenches crossing the Ecoust-Bullecourt road and attempted to reinforce the posts in the centre of the village. He was now down to forty men and no bombs. He was forced back to the railway embankment by 11:30 a.m.

The description of his actions in Brigade Orders, in the staccato style of the time, reads:

> In the attack on Bullecourt on 3rd May he captured the first trench with half his company, organized the defence of the whole trench with the remnants of the company on his right. Established posts in the centre of the village with his other half company. When attacked by bombers on right flank himself held the block for some time, and finally, on the unit on his left being driven into his trench by German bombers and retiring organized the defence of his left flank, endeavoured to reach his posts in the centre of the village, which were cut off, collected men of several companies into an organized body and withdrew then in good order at 12:00 noon. All this when he himself had been wounded at the first assault.[9]

CSM Rathke's citation reads:

> Although himself wounded, he collected and successfully led a small party against a strong enemy bombing attack upon our trenches. His promptitude saved the situation at a very critical

time. With great determination and coolness he remained at his post, indifferent to his wounds until his company was relieved.

The impact on the 2/5th

The Brigade return on 4 May shows only eleven other ranks from the 2/5th killed.[10] However as matters became clearer they show a further 110 wounded, 1 shell shocked and 138 men unaccounted for. The Battalion war diary shows 257 casualties among the men. Among the officers Captain Knowles was missing believed killed, Second Lieutenant A Wilson was definitely killed. Lieutenant C H Churchman was missing, as were Second Lieutenants E G Annely, and H Wilcox, who was known to have been wounded. Captains Bulmer and Green were both wounded, Lieutenant A W L Smith and Lieutenant J. Wesley Smith were wounded, as were Second Lieutenants G B Foster and C S Almond. Phillip Clubb was wounded but on duty. Assuming that the full twelve company officers went into action, ten of them were now out of action. On 26 May the fighting strength of the Battalion was only 290 rifles – 40 in HQ, 'A' Company at 59, 'B' Company at 66, 'C' Company at 59 and 'D' at 66. This represents somewhat less than 30 per cent of their strength in April.

British analysis of failure by Divisional and Brigade staff

The outcome of the attack was carefully analysed. In a document originally entitled 'Reasons for Failure' but in later drafts re-titled as 'Conclusions' these were set out by the 62nd Division. The report acknowledges the difficulties presented by the Australian plan of assault:

> The danger of this course was obvious; as some 300 yards of the Hindenburg Line was left un-attacked and with no barrage on it from zero plus 33 to zero plus 60 a period of 27 minutes. It was considered however that a bombing attack down the Hindenburg Line would overcome resistance, with the assistance of the 2/6th working in an easterly direction.[11]

It also prepares to place the blame within the 62nd:

> The importance of gaining touch with the Australian Brigade was impressed on the OC 2/6th West Yorks Regt and complete liaison existed between this Battalion and the 22nd Battalion

of the 6th Australian Brigade which was attacking on the left of the 2nd Australian Division.[12]

This statement seems unlikely. There was a huge gap between the units in the line and between their headquarters. An observer standing upright on the top of the railway embankment at the extreme right of the 2/6th would be hard pressed to even see the area where the Australians were putting in their attack and runners would have to cover several thousand yards to pass messages between them. In summary the reasons for the failure of the attack as far as the 62nd was concerned were:

1. The gaps left in the line of attack between the 2/6th and the Australians. 'Bombing up both front and support lines for 350 yards is an operation requiring at best a considerable time.'
2. 'The number engaged were not sufficient having regard to the condition of the defences and the strength of the garrison.'
3. The hour fixed for Zero made control extremely difficult owing to the darkness.
4. The direction of the wind blew the dust from the barrage into the faces of the infantry, making it hard to see or coordinate movements.[13]

It would appear that Colonel Hastings got it right. The casualty records for the Brigade were compiled by Major O'Connor; possibly he reflected on the Brigadier's response to Colonel Hastings's concerns as he totalled up the many hundreds of casualties. The Divisional History was very clear in its verdict:

> The failure of the 62nd Division to capture Bullecourt was due largely to a fault which certainly cannot be charged to the gallant troops who stormed the village . . . Neither could the Divisional staff which had laboured to make all arrangements complete as possible be blamed. It was due to an error in tactics . . . the Australian Division did not launch its attack side by side with the 2/6th West Yorks, thus some hundreds of yards of the enemy positions was left free to enfilade the 2/6th West Yorks; which indeed happened.[14]

By the time the Australians, who did reach their objective, were ready to turn left the Yorkshire Battalion was already cut to pieces.

Jonathon Walker, historian of the Bullecourt battle, commented:

The 62nd West Riding Division lost 191 officers and 4,042 men – a devastating introduction to the western front. If the purpose had been to blood them it had succeeded, but their inexperience and at time irresolute attacks had been mercilessly punished by a tough professional enemy. But what hope could there be for a second line territorial division when a crack Division like the 7th could not shift the enemy from Bullecourt.[15]

For the Australians of the 6th Brigade it was also a disastrous day. The defeat of the West Yorks on their left meant that flank was exposed. On their right the Australian 5th Brigade had been shot to pieces and had withdrawn allowing the Germans to concentrate all their forces on the 6th who continued to hold into the next week as the position was slowly expanded. It would take until 17 May to secure it. The AIF felt that it had a grievance against the 62nd for the lack of coordination at First Bullecourt and this did nothing to help.

The official view
The reactions of higher command were unsympathetic. The 185th Brigade would assault again later in the month when the 2/7th would attempt to take the Crucifix, another costly failure. General Gough accused the Division of 'lack of fighting spirit' and 'ill discipline' and the 62nd was certainly under a cloud. This was emphasized over the next few months by the changes in senior officers. The 185th Brigade commander De Falbe was replaced by General Viscount Hampden. During the summer, Colonel Hastings of the 2/6th was removed and appointed an area commandant in Arras, he was over age to be commanding at the Front and his DSO and Mention in Dispatches may have done something to mollify him.

Survivors
For the officers involved, it was some time before they could collect their thoughts. E C Gregory of the 2/6th, who was commanding a company that day, wrote:

All personal accounts from those who actually participated in the engagement are very hazy and indistinct. Everyone has a vague recollection of a village hailed upon by shells of every size and kind, machine gun and rifle bullets, with clouds of brick dust rising high into the air as the shells crashed through the air with a deafening roar into the village. Our barrage was severe but equally so was the enemy's. It seems impossible that anyone could survive in that village and it gradually became a shambles.[16]

Arthur Green writing from hospital in England to his parents a few days later:

On the whole we did apparently have a bad time. Of the 4 company commanders who went into action Wesley Smith broke his leg at the enemy wire and was taken back in a tank, Bulmer was wounded in the leg and is in hospital in Park Street, Knowles is reported killed and I am here. A few others were injured in various trivial ways. The men rather suffered too.[17]

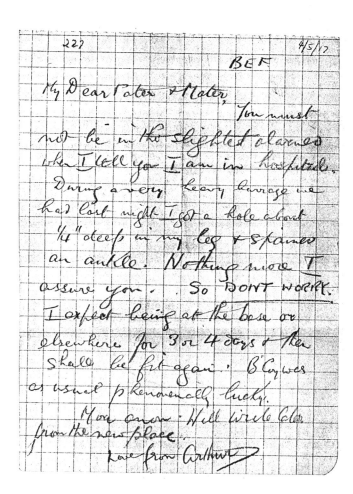

Capt Green's letter to his parents telling of his wounds.
Liddle Collection

John Airey, still on duty, wrote to Arthur Green to give him the full picture of the losses:

> Knowles is killed almost for certain, Wilson too. Churchman, Annely and Wilcox wounded and missing but prisoners we hope. Wesley, yourself, Bully [Bulmer], Lucius [Smith] and Almond wounded – all the rest safe but battle worn . . . . The army commander has said that the 'although the attack was successful the lack of discipline in the division prevented its being pushed home and held.[18]

Perhaps the last word should go to Colonel Hastings. In 1938 when the official history was being written by Captain Falls he received a draft of the chapter on his Battalion at Bullecourt. His enraged nine page response has survived.

> Bullecourt was not a village but a fortress which consumed three British divisions before it was captured, into which on the night of the 3rd May the skilled 7th Division did not penetrate so far as earlier in the day, the <u>"inexperienced"</u> West Yorkshire men had done. Why so strongly stress <u>FAILURE</u> on the May 3rd <u>morning attack</u>?[19]

The Wounded

Those who were sent back to England wounded tend to fall out of the story. In looking at the fates of the officers and men for whom records survive the seriousness of their injuries becomes apparent. Claude Bulmer was hit by multiple pieces of shrapnel in the right leg. Although he had a medical board in June 1917 his wounds were still bad and it was estimated he would not be fit for another five months. In

Lt Wesley Smith, Company Commander wounded at Bullecourt. *Ackrill's Harrogate War Souvenir, 1917*

fact he would never be listed as fit again. John Wesley-Smith was disabled by the gunshot wound to his right leg. He would endure six operations to remove bone and drain the wound which left him with a permanently twisted foot. He also was never fit again, though he lived until July 1966. Arthur Green's wounds are only described in his letters as a sprained ankle and a 'neat hole a quarter inch deep in the leg', however they would keep him in England until September 1917. Lieutenant A W L Smith was shot in the upper left arm and took shrapnel wounds to his left leg. He was treated in a hospital in Manchester where he was visited by the King. It is unclear whether he returned to the Front; he did not return to the Battalion.

It is difficult to trace the wounded men who were evacuated to the casualty clearing stations and then home to England as in most cases neither their medical nor personal records have survived. However, some of the 2/5th's wounded again used the *Harrogate Herald* to let friends and relations know what was happening. Less than a week after the battle Mr Breare's information service was working hard:

> Private W. Rowling (West Yorks), youngest son of Mrs Emma Rowling, Antique and Curio Dealer, 1 Montpelier Gardens, Harrogate, has been wounded. He was taken to the No. 2 Australian General Hospital, Boulogne, and probably by the time this is in print will be in England. In a letter home he says it is nothing serious. 'It happened on Thursday morning at 4.30 [May 3rd 1917 was a Thursday]. Our guns had started to put a heavy fire on Fritz, so our chaps could advance. I was waiting in a bit of shelter on the roadside, when a bit of old iron off a heavy German shell gave my head such a clout, and but for my steel helmet I daresay I should have been a 'goner', but God spared me, and all I have is a scalp wound. Of course, it may be a bit in healing, but you must not fret yourself. I have a terrible headache and feel a little deaf. It was awful, hundreds of guns firing at once, but I will tell you all some day. I am comfortable here, but would sooner be in Blighty.[20]

As the weeks progressed the information became more detailed and started to bring in news of other soldiers. Another of Mr Breare's correspondents, Private Parkinson, had also come to grief:

> When I sent some playing cards to Private W. Parkinson, of the 2/5th, who was in hospital at Keighley wounded, I hardly expected to see him very soon, but I am glad to say that he

looked in on me on Monday morning, having been discharged, otherwise granted sick leave, at the conclusion of which he will report to his depot. Parkinson was wounded on the 3rd of May – a memorable day for the boys of the 2/5th – in the left leg and foot. He lay out two days and found himself in hospital May 5th, where he has been until last Thursday. He is the son of Mrs John Parkinson, 13 Pearl Street, Starbeck. A bullet went through his helmet and, as he puts it, he was then 'within two inches of death'. Private Samuel Abbott, of Oatlands, was missing at the same time and Sergeant Wharton taken prisoner. There was talk of amputating the leg, but happily that has not been necessary, though it is still troublesome. He does not look as if you will see him out where you are very soon, if at all. You may be sure, boys, that there is someone in Harrogate pleased to see Parkinson home and that is his mother, who has borne his illness so long and patiently. He is her only son and child. Just those two! May good fortune attend them both henceforth.[21]

The missing

With the many missing it was a long time before the families were certain of what happened. Distraught parents were soon writing to Company officers in the hope of getting some news. In June, Arthur Green received a letter from Mrs H Abbott:

> Dear Sir
> I hope you will excuse the liberty I am taking in writing to you. I am very anxious to know if you can give me any information about my son Private Harold Abbott (200557) B Company 2/5th West Yorks who has been missing since the first week in May. I have had your address given as my son's officer and I do hope and pray you will be able to give me some information about him, the suspense is really awful.[22]

A few days later, a letter from letter arrived from Irene Reason in reply to Green's informing her that her husband was missing.

> It was most kind of you to tell me my husband had his steel waistcoat on. I wasn't afraid of him being without it and it has been my one hope and comfort for the last month. I only hope now that he is a prisoner, that will be bad enough but I know he will make the best of it and there will be the consolation of

having him home again. I am anxiously awaiting every post in the hopes of having some word.[23]

Slowly the truth was assembled from the chaos after the action.

Mr. and Mrs. J. W. Abbott, of 45 Mount Street, Oatlands Mount, Harrogate, who previously had an intimation that their son, Private Harold Abbott (West Yorks.) was missing on May 3rd 1917, have now received an official message in which the Army Council say that they are 'regretfully constrained to conclude that he is dead and that his death took place on that date.' Their Majesties' (the King and Queen) message was enclosed with the document. He joined up soon after the war started and was with the Beechwood boys. He went to France in January 1917. Before enlisting he was employed by his father, who carries on an upholstery business on the Tewit Well Estate. He was 21 years of age. A York corporal had previously informed Mrs. Abbott that the worst had happened and that he helped to bury him, but the deceased's belongings not having been returned, the mother still clung to the hope that her son's comrade was mistaken. [24]

Sergeant Oliver W Goundry, son of Mrs. M J Goundry, Gate Bridge Mill, Galphay, Ripon has been reported wounded and missing in France since May 3rd. He joined the West Yorks. Regiment in November 1914, and did his early training in Harrogate, going to France in January 1917. He was wounded at Beaumont Hamel on February 14th. Any news concerning him will be gratefully received. A letter from his officer states: - Your son went into action on the morning of May 3rd and has not been seen since. We are almost certain he was taken prisoner, as his party was cut off in the rear. I understand he was seen by someone to be

Pte H Abbott.
Ackrill's Harrogate War Souvenir

slightly wounded soon after the attack started, but he would not go back, preferring to stay with his men. I am unable to tell you how much we miss him. He was undoubtedly one of the best and bravest soldiers in the battalion. I was with him when he was wounded at Beaumont Hamel, and it may interest you to know that he was wounded when dressing another man's wounds. He had been in my platoon since last July, and I valued him immensely, not only as a N.C.O., but as a personal friend.[25]

The hopes of these families were in vain; these men were all killed in Bullecourt, none has any known grave. Some parents were forced to follow up the slightest rumours to find out what had happened, using the *Herald* to advertise to soldiers still overseas.

Mrs Graham, of 1 Northumberland Court, would be pleased to be put in communication with Private Robert Brown, 200337, 2/5th West Yorks, who is in hospital in France, and is said to have seen her son, Private E A Graham, when he was wounded, and attended to him during the attack at Bullecourt on May 3rd. News from any other source would be equally welcome to the anxious mother.[26]

Pte E A Graham.
Ackrill's Harrogate War Souvenir

Mrs Graham may well have found Private Brown as there is a more detailed entry a year after the battle, but the outcome was what she had feared.

Mr. and Mrs. Arthur Graham, 1 Northumberland Court, have received a communication from the Records Office in which the authorities are constrained to presume the death of their son Ernest Arthur Graham, of the West Yorks., who was reported missing on the 3rd May 1917. A comrade, Robert Brown, informed the Red Cross Society that Graham was severely wounded by a shell as they were attacking at Bullecourt on the above date. He was put in a shell hole and bound up as well as possible by the men who had to advance and leave him in the hope that the stretcher bearers would fetch him, but it was feared he was not found.[27]

The prisoners

The war diaries do not contain a final accounting for the battle. A few days after the engagement 138 men were unaccounted for, however some had been evacuated by other units and some had lain out for some days after the battle. The Battalion did not recover the bodies of the men lost in Bullecourt itself and it would be many weeks before the Germans had sorted their prisoners out and opened communications, either directly or through the Red Cross. It is likely that 80 to 100 men were captured at Bullecourt.

One officer was captured alive at Bullecourt. Lieutenant Harry Wilcox was a school master who enlisted in the ranks and served from March 1916 to January 1917. He was commissioned in January 1917 and joined 'B' Company in the 2/5th. He was shot in the thigh on 3 May and was unable to retire with the rest of 'B' Company. He survived his time in Karlsruhe POW camp and returned to England where he spent his time as an instructor at Bulford until he was demobbed in December 1919 and returned to teaching.

At the end of the war the City of York held a dinner for its returning prisoners of war. Compiling the invitation list was done most thoroughly and the date of capture and unit of all the men were recorded. From York alone there were eighteen 2/5th men captured – Henry Boyes, Harry Davison, Jacob Deeprose, Frederick Godson, Ernest Godson, Robert Greenwood, William Horsemen, Albert Hustinik, Samuel Kershaw, George Moss, George Nichols, Harold Peckitt, Walter Slater, Harold Robinson, Frank Thomas, Edwin Thompson, Wilfred Trowsdale and Joshua Ward

In addition Sergeant Wharton and Corporal Hall of Harrogate were captured. News of Corporal Hall's survival got through to Mr Breare by July:

> Mrs Sherwood, of Craydon Street, has just called to give me the happy intelligence that her brother, who was missing, Corporal A Hall, is a prisoner at Dulmen, Germany. He has been missing since the 3rd of May. So there is one more family made happy.[28]

It was not until after the war that their experiences started to be told. In 1919 Corporal Hall talked about his capture.

Repatriated Prisoners

> Corporal Hall, son of Mr George Hall, painter, of Harrogate, was captured at Bullecourt on the 3rd May. It appears that the object of the Hun was to march the prisoners backward and forward, starve and ill-use them, and then parade them before their people as samples of Englishmen, Hall being one of the 1,800 treated to this exhibition. They were kept working behind the lines from 6:00am to 6:15pm with only one meagre meal a day. Whilst the English in this case, however, had an 8 hour day, the Russians had 6 and the French 10. After a spell of processions to and fro from Fort MacDonald, they were sent to Germany. Disinfection, inoculation and examinations were the order of the day, Hall being inoculated no fewer than five times. After five weeks he was sent to a NCOs' camp – Eaton Moor, a much better camp than the average, where he remained 14 weeks. His next habitation was Bokeleh Camp, 25 kilometres from Bremerhaven.
>
>   It was a bit rough here at first, but improved towards the finish. The prisoners had no scheduled work and passed the time in knitting, unravelling mufflers or any woollen things, and making socks. Washing was difficult, as no soap was to be had. Whilst here the English were fortunate, and able to get passes through the agency of the Danish Ambassador, but the French and Russians had to take 'French leave'. He had the good luck to get parcels from England within a fortnight of their being dispatched, and Hall gave every credit to the postal authorities for this excellent dispatch. The only things that were missing were tobacco and cigarettes.[29]

The sudden loss of so many prisoners raised concerns for their well being in Germany, which was under a tight blockade designed to starve the country. There was great concerned for them. Margaret Heaton in Ripon was particularly concerned about the welfare of the men of the 2/5th – Her brother was Lieutenant A W L Smith, her husband was the adjutant and her uncle was Colonel Bottomley. She wrote to Captain Green while he was convalescing in Fowey to give him news:

I have not heard much news of the wounded. Wilfred, [Lieutenant A W L Smith] I went to see yesterday and he actually met the train, walking on both legs and looking ever so fit, but his arm will be some time before it is any use to him. He expects to be sent to the command depot in Manchester any day.

Colonel Bottomley wants us to raise money in Ripon for our prisoners who get help from the Depot at York. I don't quite know how to set about it as I am not keen on holding a public meeting. I think I shall get the Dean's wife to organize it and then have a certain number of interested people to have house to house collections weekly. I do think the prisoners really have more call upon our sympathy than anyone.[30]

The West Yorks Regiment made its own arrangements to ensure the welfare of the men. At one point over 30,000 rations per month were being sent through intermediaries in Switzerland to West Yorkshire prisoners in camps throughout Germany and Austria. On his return to England, Corporal Hall wrote to the committee that had organized this relief:

Dear Sir

Now that I am back in England I feel it my duty to write and thank you for your kindness in ministering to the prisoners of war. I can tell you sir there was not a man in Germany as well attended as a West Yorkshireman . . . . I hope it will be some satisfaction and repayment to you sir to know this and the good you have done to all of us you will never realize.[31]

The Dead

The losses of the Pals Battalions on the Somme brought home to the army the impact of having units drawn from the same town when something went wrong. While the 2/5th was not a Pals battalion the dead of the first six months are concentrated in a few towns. The bulk of the dead came from York and Harrogate, followed by Lincoln, Leeds, Selby and Ripon. Of 120 men lost, York accounted for 42 and Harrogate for 28. Ninety-eight of the men had enlisted somewhere in Yorkshire. Many of the drafts received while at Somerleyton had been from Lincolnshire and they represent a further twenty men. The 2/6th was heavily a Bradford Battalion and the 2/7th and 2/8th had roots in Leeds so the impact of this battle on Yorkshire was huge.

Captain Frank Knowles, York solicitor, died leading 'A' Company on the left of the attack. He was an only son and his mother, a widow, did not long survive the shock of his death. She received a letter from one of 'A' Company's surviving officers:

> Dear Mrs Knowles
>
> It is with sincere regret that I write to inform you of the death of your son Captain F H Knowles who fell in action whilst leading his men in an attack on May 3rd.
>   I cannot express how much we, his fellow officers and friends feel this loss to the Battalion. In Captain Knowles we have not only lost one of our best officers but also a true friend. At all times he has been a cheerful companion. I belong to the same company and the men have asked me to convey to you our heartfelt sympathy in your sad bereavement. I hope that it may be some consolation to you that he fell while leading his company. His fine example will never be forgotten by us.[32]

Frank Knowles has no known grave and his name is on the Memorial to the Missing at Arras.

Second Lieutenant Arnold Wilson of Bradford was also killed, though there is no record of which company he was part of or where he fell. He also is commemorated on the Arras Memorial to the Missing. He had started the war as Private 1583 in 'F' Company the 5th (Reserve) West Yorks. He transferred to the 6th Battalion and was with the BEF in France from April to August 1915 when he was wounded in the face, arms, legs and chest by shrapnel. The official letter to his father, a Wesleyan Reform minister, concerning the commemoration of his son, received a dignified reply. His father wrote:

> We shall be glad to receive the plaque and scroll in honour of our son who after being wounded to the verge of death nobly offered his services again for the front notwithstanding permanent disablement.[33]

Second Lieutenant Ernest Annely was a fairly new addition to the Battalion, having reported on 10 April. He would remain missing until October 1917 when his body was found in Bullecourt itself and buried. However continued fighting around Bullecourt erased his grave and he is commemorated at Arras. He left a wife in Sheffield but his records have been destroyed and no more information has come to light.

Lieutenant Churchman, an officer of the Suffolk Regiment attached to the West Yorks, was from Abbey Springs, Sproughton near Ipswich. It was some years before the picture of what happened to him became clear. In December 1917 a report was sent to his father, Sir Arthur Churchman:

> In an official list received from Germany it is reported that the disc of Lt C H Churchman . . . was removed by an English soldier, J Taylor 2/5th Battalion West Yorks, and transmitted to a field commissariat on 29th August 1917.
>
> Statement from Pte Taylor a prisoner of war at Zerbst gives the following information 'we were attacking Bullecourt on the Somme on 3 May 1917, I was close to him all the time and saw him immediately after he was hit and as far as I can say the wound was fatal. I was taken prisoner of war shortly afterwards'.

In January 1920 his wrist watch and charm were sent to his father. A further letter from the War Office in September 1921 stated:

> An identity disk belonging to the late Captain C H Churchman West Yorkshire Regiment has been returned to this country by the German Government through diplomatic channels.[34]

Of the men, most of their records have been destroyed. However a few letters have survived. To Lieutenant Clubb of 'B' Company fell the task of writing dozens of letters to the bereaved. One such went to May Pearson, sister of Private Pelham Pearson:

> Dear Miss Pearson
>
> I expect that since you wrote me on the 23rd you will have heard that your brother was killed on May 3rd.
>
> My Quartermaster sergeant wrote to your mother and told her all he had heard from one of our sergeants who was with your brother after he was wounded
>
> I suppose you have heard that we did an attack on the 3rd and that we got rather a bad time. Your brother was in my platoon and I saw him on the tape line but after that all was confusion indescribable. I am awfully sorry to say that he did

not get back. I am not going to use words of consolation because I realize nothing makes up for such a loss. Everyone is a fatalist out here – by persuasion and I should like to say how sorry I am that fate willed your brother should go so soon. He is a man I held in great esteem for although like most of us he was quite out of his element, yet he did his job from start to finish. The average Englishman is peaceably inclined and I think he, like many others has done a fine thing in coming forward as he did. It will be no consolation to you but perhaps a little comfort to you that he lived and died a man, doing a man's work.

Believe me, yours very sincerely

Philip Clubb[35]

Some families experienced a double agony. CSM Horner was listed as killed and the announcement was made in the *Herald*.

Mrs Howard Horner, of 9 Newnham Terrace, Harrogate, has heard through a letter sent by Sgt Drummer Procter, that her husband, CSM Horner, has been killed in action. He leaves a family of three children.[36]

However a few weeks later he was re-listed as missing.

Sergeant Major Howard Horner, of the Beechwood Boys, is missing, and I should be glad if you lads could send me information regarding him. All we know, up to the present, is that private letters from comrades reported him slightly wounded in the wrist on the 3rd May. He did not want to leave the trenches, but his officer insisted. His friends next heard from the Red Cross, the War Office, and York that he was wounded. Nothing has been heard since. Whether he has been shifted from hospital to hospital or taken prisoner we do not know, but naturally his wife and friends and, indeed, all of us are anxious to hear something regarding him, and we are confidently hoping for the best.

I have had many friends of missing soldiers, especially those who were missing on the 3rd of May, to see if I could give them any help or encouragement. I am glad to say that I was able to send them away more cheerful than when they came and decidedly hopeful. I received this early news of the postcards having come from missing prisoner soldiers after seeing friends of Sergeant Major Horner. I hope the good news of missing men turning up as prisoners will bring still further comfort and hope to those who have not yet heard from their boys. In the case of Petch, the usual rumour came through by means of some boy's letter to friends suggesting that Petch had been killed. I hope all you boys will be very careful in sending any such information. It is best not to mention mere rumours or surmises. Say nothing if you do not have direct evidence. You see, though you may write to somebody in confidence, it is bound to get out, and it is whispered from ear to ear and it grows. The consequence is the relatives are anxious and distressed. I know how these rumours arise, and I am sure they are given in good faith. You are told that a boy is missing. Somebody else is likewise informed, and perhaps he will say, 'I hope he is not killed'. Well, that word killed sticks, and in passing from mouth to mouth it gradually becomes converted into a statement that such and such a boy has been killed. So you will be very careful in your letters, won't you, even in those to your most intimate friends?[37]

This hope was short lived. By July it became clear that CSM Horner had been killed on 3 May. The *Herald* recorded the details of his military career:

He was the youngest son of James H Horner, of 22 Devonshire Place, Harrogate, and leaves a widow and three children, who reside at 9 Newnham Terrace, Harrogate. CSM Horner had a good record of service, having for the past 25 years been in the old Volunteers, the Territorials, and on active service, first joining in January, 1892, when the headquarters were St James' Hall. He was promoted to colour-sergeant in 1905 and later made CSM. He attended all camps in connection with Volunteer training. He was with the Territorials in training at Scarborough when the war broke out, and signed on with many of his comrades for a certain period. At the expiration of this time he volunteered for further service, and went out with the Beechwood Boys in January last.[38]

As Colonel Bottomley had taken an interest in the prisoners so Captain Cross was doing his best with the families of the missing and killed. He wrote to the widow:

> Dear Mrs Horner, As promised, I have been making enquiries regarding your husband, and the enclosed letter (which kindly return) has just come from Captain Heaton, who followed me as Adjutant. I am sadly afraid the worst has happened; over a month has gone by and the only evidence available confirms our worst fears. I need hardly say how deep my sympathy is for you and your children, and as you will, I hope, understand, this is much more than a mere expression of feeling. From early in 1900 to last year I had the privilege of being intimately and closely associated with your husband, and two men cannot soldier together for such a length of time without getting, as it were, an inside knowledge of each other. Your husband more than merited the regard and respect he was held in from the Commanding Officer to the last joined recruit. For the long period I was an officer in the company of which he was so great an ornament, I acknowledge with gratitude the unselfish help he gave to one and all, and especially to me his former company commander, and other officers who followed have on every possible occasion told me what a tower of strength he was. He

L/Cpl Walter Smith.
Ackrill's Harrogate War Souvenir

Pte W Mackintosh.
Ackrill's Harrogate War Souvenir

knew his work, he helped everyone, he was unselfish in the extreme, he was patient and painstaking, never lost his temper, never used a foul word or expression, and always did far more than mere duty imposed on him. Such is the record of my old friend and comrade, Howard Horner. He was better than most and inferior to none. Any further information I can get I will see reaches you without delay.

Again with much sympathy,

Yours very truly, E P Cross.

Between 3 May and 25 May when the Battalion would next be in action, fifty-nine men were listed as killed in action or having died of wounds, presumable from the Bullecourt engagement. On 3 May the attack on Bullecourt cost the lives of:

Harold Abbott	Joseph Angus
Archie Baines	Ernest Baul
Martin Bratley	George Brown
William Brown	Maurice Challoner
George Clark	Samuel Clark
Herbert Deighton	Albert Dixon
Frank Driver	Edward Flanagan
Thomas Flanagan	Isaac Franklin
William French	Oliver Goundry
Ernest Graham	William Harrison
Archibald Hewson	Harry Horner
James Henry Howard Horner	Lawrence Jackson
George Judd	Harold Judson
John Philip Kirk	William Lazenby
Walter Mackintosh	Thomas Marshall
Arthur Medley	Arthur Miller
Pelham Pearson	Robert Prest
Harold Reason	William Reaston
William Reddish	James Redshaw
Ernest Reed	Fred Richmond
Lawrence Rush	James Seymour
William Simmonite	Leonard Smith
Mark Smith	Walter Smith
Sydney Whitaker	Reggie Wilcock
William Wortley	

L/Cpl F Richmond.
Ackrill's Harrogate War Souvenir

Pte E Reed.
Ackrill's Harrogate War Souvenir

Sgt Percy Wrightson.
Ackrill's Harrogate War Souvenir

Pte C F Horner.
Ackrill's Harrogate War Souvenir

In the casualty clearing stations and hospitals, Frank Betson, Percival Wrightson, John Green, Ernest Blakey, Christopher Horner, Edward Carey, George Ware, John Mason, Joseph Eccles, and Peter Ogone succumbed to their wounds.

The wounded in mind

The further losses which are unrecorded are of those men who were shattered mentally by their experiences. The welfare records for York, listing the aid offered to families in the area in the 1920s have a standard term where children are being fed and housed despite having an able bodied male in the house ' Father a destroyed soldier'. Among the destroyed soldiers of 1917 was Colonel John Josselyn. On convalescent leave in September 1917 Arthur Green attempted to visit his old colonel but he could not be admitted. Mrs Jossleyn wrote in explanation:

> My husband is now in hospital in London. He has really been very seedy ever since he returned to the battalion but would not go sick. At last on August 28th the doctors insisted, and to make a long story short, after passing through numerous hospitals he has arrived here diagnosed 'as severe shell shock from a wound'. The doctors say when that shell knocked him out in April his spine was hurt and he ought never to have been allowed to return to work. They say he must have had extraordinary strength of character to have kept going so long. He is now in bed and allowed to see no visitors but myself and even his letters I have to read first so that he shall have nothing in the least to bother him.[39]

Colonel Josselyn did recover and went on to lead a Brigade in Russia. In January 1918 he was awarded the DSO and in June 1918 received an OBE for an act of gallantry not in the presence of the enemy. By the end of the war he had been Mentioned in Dispatches three times, he had also received the Croix de Guerre and a number of Russian decorations. On his return to England he applied to lead one of the new Territorial Army Brigades, but no appointment was given him.

Chapter 5
Rebuilding – Back to patrolling

Reconstructing the Battalion

The months immediately following the Bullecourt battle were a hard period, the scale of the losses will have been apparent at every parade – in May the 2/5th could field little more than 300 men. Whatever the truth of their performance at Bullecourt, the Battalion also felt itself to be in disgrace. There was certainly a need for time to reorganize and get over the shock but the men may have regarded being set to grass cutting and labouring as a comment on their abilities. For the officers the review of their performance was more direct. The war diary for 9 May records:

> GOC Fifth Army addressed all COs and Adjutants of the Division on the recent operations in front of Bullecourt. Discipline and fighting spirit were the points upon which he laid particular emphasis.[1]

Though the officers obviously resented the implications of this, there may have been some agreement with it in private. While the ethos of a Territorial unit might work well back in England, many were realizing the need for a much greater level of professionalism in France. Lieutenant John Airey wrote to Arthur Green in June:

> The army commander has said that 'although the attack was successful the lack of discipline in the division prevented its being pushed home and held'.
>   The CO is on leave, so is Riley – and Major Peter is setting us right from top to bottom; no sparing anyone's feelings, but perfectly soldierly and fair. I am sure he has touched the real weak spot which we always recognized was present but had no one to alter. Parades are dead punctual and everyone, SMs,

QMS's Orderly sergeants and corporals, NCOs and men are being taught their true orbit . . . .

You can scarcely realize what a different battalion we are to what we were exactly a fortnight ago. Peter is insisting on Company commanders being company commanders . . . I bet that within a fortnight we'll be a better disciplined and organized unit than ever we were.[2]

During May and June, Major Peter's reforms started to take root. The Companies were reorganized to have three platoons each rather than four making them easier to handle and reducing the number of officers required. There were a large number of promotions among the NCOs and a re-allocation of them and the company officers, to achieve a good mix of experience across companies. There was also a large investment of time in training; at one point in 'B' Company only Lieutenant Clubb seems to have been left as all the other officers are away on courses.

New officers arrived. In May, Second Lieutenants E Kermode, A

2/Lt E M Kermode DCM, MC and Bar, DSO, the most decorated officer in the Battalion. *Prince of Wales's Own Regiment of Yorkshire Museum*

Kitson and H B Samuel reported and in early June Second Lieutenants R F White, W K Whittle, A J Watson, N H Smith and A S Fairbank. On 22 June Second Lieutenants H Tasker, L F Veal, F V Preston, W Robinson and T E Gibson reported for duty, followed by A E Reynolds on the 26th. These replacements were needed as wastage did not stop – Lieutenant Lupton went home wounded on a patrol near Bullecourt.

This influx of new officers changed the balance of the Battalion. Before, the bulk of commands were held by Territorial officers. Among the senior Battalion officers going into the Battle of Bullecourt only the recently arrived Major Peter had any combat experience, the CO was Territorial and the company commanders and junior officers had come out from fresh from England.

The surviving records show that these new subalterns were somewhat different. Arthur Kitson had seen action as a private soldier in France with the West Riding Regiment, having been out since February 1916. Second Lieutenant Samuel from Bayswater had trained as a barrister but since September 1914 had been in 13th Battalion London Regiment. Reginald White had been wounded with 1/5th West Yorks

Capt R F White
O/C HQ
Company and
Capt Riley in
Favreuil 1917.
Don Jackson

in September 1916. Angus Fairbank had been wounded with the 1/6th at Thiepval in February 1916 and was commissioned in October of that year. Second Lieutenant Tasker had served in France in the ranks with the 1/5th. Second Lieutenant Gibson had also been in the ranks though the details of his service have been lost. Second Lieutenant Reynolds had already seen service with the Royal Artillery, then transferred to the 1/5th and was wounded at Thiepval in September 1916.

Lieutenant Veal – being a Harrogate man and one of the Beechwood Boys – had his commission announced in the *Herald*.

> Second Lieutenant Leonard F Veal, who joined the 1/5th West Yorks after the outbreak of war, as a matter of fact, in September, 1914, as a private, and was billeted at the Beechwood, where the 2/5th were, has earned his commission. He went to France, and was in some stiff fighting. He was sent home to train for his commission, after the advance on the Somme last July. He came to a Scottish camp, and very soon was appointed cadet adjutant. Before joining the Colours he was with Messrs Maxwell Grayson, wine merchants, of James Street.[3]

So, of the new officers whose records have survived, all had experience in the ranks, had been in France before and most had combat experience. This represented an influx of experience, since while some of these men may not themselves have led platoons under fire, they had been under fire themselves and had seen how to manage and lead under those conditions. They also largely maintained the Yorkshire character of the Battalion, though their backgrounds are very different from the 'Young Gentlemen' of 1915. While Reginald White and Horace Samuel continued the dominance of the legal profession, among the other officers are the son of a gardener and a former wool salesman.

It was not only experience that arrived with this intake but also proven bravery on the battlefield. Second Lieutenant Edgar Marsden Kermode arrived and was posted to 'C' Company; he was destined to be the Battalion's most decorated officer. From a wealthy family in Shipley, Kermode was originally in the 1/6th Battalion West Yorks. He enlisted on 25 September 1914 and went to France on 15 April 1915. He was soon in action; the *Regimental Journal* records his winning of the DCM:

> On the 19th of December 1915, a gas attack of a violent nature was launched by the enemy on the Ypres salient. The casualties of the 1/6th Battalion were about 100, of which 18 were

killed by shellfire. The citation reads 'for conspicuous gallantry when he volunteered to assist the wounded of another company and went across the open under heavy shellfire. He saved at least one life.'[4]

Digging and patrolling

This new officer group set about putting their commands in order. While many days were spent on company training, the reorganization was interrupted both by further periods in support and by the constant need for working parties. These parties were by no means without risk. On 26 May, while wiring and digging near Bullecourt, the Battalion took twelve casualties from shellfire. The position was obviously very exposed as of these, seven were killed in action or died of their wounds. Lieutenant Clubb of 'B' Company records what the position was like:

> The battalion did a working party on the night of the 26th, in a very advanced position. We had 5 casualties in our company. I was not there as I was not fit to go. You'll be awfully sorry to hear that old Hewson went west. He was wounded in 3 places; throat, heart and stomach. He died in a very few minutes. They got his effects out but it was too unhealthy a place to recover the body. It was all they could do to get the other wounded away, namely Thompson S and 3 new men. Thompson died of wounds yesterday at the CCS, Andy and I saw him buried, also a new man died of wounds, I have written to the people concerned. I am very sick of the whole business.[5]

Along with Company Sergeant Major Charles Hewson, Thomas Hornsey, Henry Milner and Harry Spencer were killed outright. John Hackney, John Hudson and Samuel Thompson died of their wounds.

Pte John Hackney,
Ackrill's Harrogate War Souvenir

These were the last casualties the Battalion suffered until September 1917.

On 25 June the 22 officers and 356 ORs of the 2/5th went into the left sector at Vaux-Vraucourt. Conditions in this part of the line were poor. While there was some patrolling carried out it seems rather half hearted and most of the men spent most of the time digging and improving trenches. There were no raids or fighting patrols and they came out of the line into support and then into reserve without incident or casualties, simply tired. Second Lieutenant AG Wilson, who had just arrived at the Battalion after being wounded with the 1/5th, noted in his diary:

> It was amazing how hard all the troops worked on the wiring and on the trench building, as the Bn were holding an advanced 'region' which had only recently been captured from the Germans in the battle of Bullecourt. By the time the battalion went out of the trenches for a week we had constructed a splendid strong belt of barbed wire defences.[6]

2/Lt AG Wilson, wounded and commissioned, seen here while recovering at Clipstone in July 1917.
Prince of Wales's Own Regiment of Yorkshire Museum

In July, there was a further brief period of patrolling but the records are confused – contradictory as to who led the patrols and what their purpose was. Certainly, Second Lieutenants Anderson, Robinson and Reynolds were out in no man's land, There is also the first patrol by Second Lieutenants Kermode and Simpson – a partnership which recurred throughout the next year. What was going on during these patrols is recorded by Lieutenant A G Wilson. His diary recalls:

> On 4th night ordered to take a large foot patrol in No Man's Land. Sgt and 14 men. Went on long 12.00 to 3.00am reconnaissance into No Man's Land. Very dark and Very lights often gave no help. Very slow silent progress and we did not bump into enemy patrol. I lost my revolver when crawling and had to make a diligent search in the dark. After a long search actually placed my hand on the barrel of the revolver.
>
> My sergeant approached me, having mustered the full patrol about half a mile from our trench system. He said 'we must return this way, Sir,' and to my surprise the patrol was facing due EAST – direct to the German lines. This night was clear, with all the celestial star system showing bright. I had studied the stars for several years and there to the SE was my favourite constellation 'Orion' in all his glory. I told the sergeant 'You sit down and listen to me,' I said firmly. 'If you go the way you suggest you will all be shot or prisoners before dawn'. I pointed out Orion to him and said that the position is south east and leads straight to the German lines. He didn't trust my decision – 'we must go in exactly the opposite direction,' I ordered. We then mustered the patrol and slowly made our way back and after half an hour found ourselves challenged by a Scots sentry. We were only 300 yards from the West Yorkshire trenches.[7]

On 25 August Second Lieutenant Preston patrolled the Hendecourt – Bullecourt road and saw a German wiring party but no action was taken. On 16/17August, Lieutenant N H Smith took out twenty other ranks between the Bullecourt – Fontaine and Bullecourt – Hendecourt roads:

> Patrol proceeded for 100 yards along the road running north-west in U21.c. and then due east to the Hendecourt road. The roads are hardly recognizable and the ground covered was

nothing but shell holes. Very lights were seen . . . [but] no enemy were seen or heard.[8]

On 29 August a patrol led by Second Lieutenant Whittle had the same result. Again, the Battalion records do not tally exactly with those at Brigade but the picture brought back was of a rather empty no man's land with patrols of both sides unmolested.

Major Peter takes over the Battalion

This changed rather abruptly on 29 August 1917. Colonel Josselyn went into hospital and was then invalided home for shell shock. Hedley Heaton had been taken into hospital on 10 August and would be away until late September. The acting command of the Battalion fell to Major F H Peter.

Major Peter came from 1st Battalion the Royal Welch Fusiliers. While his own records are lost, the Regimental records show that he was an experienced soldier. He had served in South Africa, in the ranks of the 7th Dragoon Guards, for fifteen years in India and he was still serving at the outbreak of war. He was commissioned into the 1st Battalion RWF in June 1916; he was acting captain within two months and was awarded the MC in September 1916. He joined the 2/5th a few weeks before Bullecourt to replace the late Major Dale as second in command. The environment he came from is also important, not only is he an experienced soldier but 1st RWF had a reputation for aggression in trench warfare.

> Some units were aggressive for most of the time during trench tours. These were elite fighting units in which there 'was no thought of abstaining from action for fear of reprisal . . . no live and let live idea'. It is invidious to name some elite units and not others, but these included the 1st and 2nd Battalions The Royal Welch Fusiliers, the 1st Battalion the Royal West Kent Regiment and the 1st Battalion the Gloucestershire Regiment.[9]

The Battalion was now led by an experienced, Regular fighting officer and the change was immediate. From Bullecourt to 29 August the Battalion recorded nine patrols in four months. In the interregnum between Colonels, 29 August to 23 September, there were more than fourteen patrols of which at least two were large fighting patrols. The enemy was sufficiently stirred up to launch two raids on the Battalion – both of which were beaten off with losses. At the end of this period the war diary notes:

We are still sending patrols out and consider ourselves the masters of the 'alleged' No Man's Land.[10]

Back in England

It was not only the Battalion in France that was being reconstructed. The officers and men who had been evacuated were starting to mend. When the less seriously wounded were released from hospital they would be sent to convalescent homes around the country before being examined for a medical board to assess what duties they could carry out. Many took the opportunity to call on the families of other officers and men to bring first hand news. Arthur Green visited the family of Lieutenant Skirrow and was very pleased with his reception:

> My last day in town was a thoroughly busy one. I had lunch at the Skirrows – the people of our own subaltern Skirrow. They live in a charming house in Hampstead in quite a good residential part and there were at home Mr. Mrs. and Miss. They are charming people and gave me a topping time, of course they wanted to hear all about the doings at the Front but they were not much inclined otherwise to talk shop. After a most magnificent lunch of salmon mayonnaise and chicken and trifle we adjourned to the garden where we had liqueurs and cigarettes galore and we simply basked in chairs and cushions until a very late hour. I found Miss Skirrow a very interesting person – young, pronounced but mild opinions, feminine and not very good looking but attractive, rather the sort of person you would expect to be masculine but isn't.[11]

Lieutenant AWL Smith was still recovering in Manchester in June. He wrote to Arthur Green to congratulate him on his decoration:

> Major Peter came over here the day before yesterday from Blackpool and he told me you had won the MC and I was awfully bucked I wish I could have been the first to congratulate you . . . .
> The Colonel RAMC expects I shall be discharged from hospital or probably sent to a command depot for a bit. My arm is not right yet and I have not got back the use of my thumb and first finger but they expect it will be all right by the time my 3 weeks leave are over – so I suppose I shall be back in France before long.

I had a visit from Hedley and two or three from his 'Mrs' [Wilfred's sister Margaret] as well as from the rest of the family who are all up this way. I have enjoyed my time in hospital very much on the whole, especially now that I don't have any pain worth mentioning though I was pretty seedy at first.[12]

Claude Bulmer was recovering in Torquay. He and Green were unable to meet up but he offered some observations:

I can quite understand you going into raptures over the beauties of Fowey and trust you have found some kindred spirits amongst the other convalescents. Bye the bye I can thoroughly recommend the No. 1 Bass at the Yacht Club, top hole stuff, used to knock me over every time. I see comic cuts in the *Daily Mail* says 'enemy active at Croisilles' We know what that means, don't 'we?[13]

Fighting Patrols

In France, on the day after Colonel Josselyn went to hospital, the Battalion launched a campaign of aggression. A joint patrol of Second Lieutenants Kermode and Simpson went into no man's land. The ground over which this patrol took place is difficult. The exit from the front line was in a sunken road which leads gently up hill into no man's land and was in dead ground to the enemy main positions. These were in a deep valley to the north of the railway embankment. As the patrol left the front line they could have walked upright as there is a ridge a few hundred yards ahead. They would then have had to crawl over this ridge and then down the other side as the forward posts that fired on

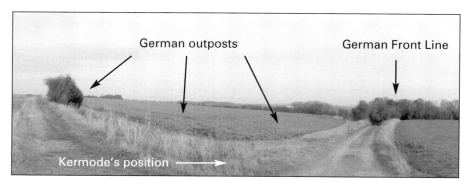

Area of Kermode's attack on the German outposts today. *Author's Collection*

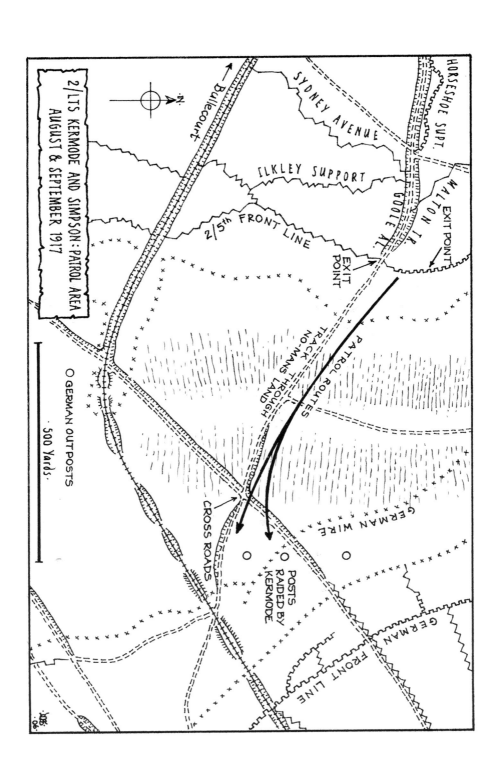

2/LTS KERMODE AND SIMPSON: PATROL AREA
AUGUST & SEPTEMBER 1917

N.

Bullecourt

SYDNEY AVENUE

HORSESHOE SUPT.

WALTON TR.

GOOLE AL.

EXIT POINT

ILKLEY SUPPORT

2/5th FRONT LINE

EXIT POINT

PATROL ROUTES

TRACK THROUGH NO-MANS LAND

GERMAN WIRE.

CROSS ROADS

O GERMAN OUTPOSTS

500 Yards.

POSTS RAIDED BY KERMODE

GERMAN FRONT LINE

German outposts
in tree line

Track Junction
used as
waypoint

No Man's Land

British Wire

No man's land today.
Author's Collection

them were built into the bank of a road, giving them a slightly elevated position and a better view. It would be necessary to be very close indeed to these posts, less than thirty yards, before being able to fire into them. It is worth examining it in detail for the picture it shows of the new style of patrol work.

They took twelve other ranks and a Lewis gun out at 10:30 p.m. [see map]. They examined the track and then went along it until they reached the enemy wire. They followed the track where they disturbed a covey of partridges which took off creating a great noise – much, no doubt, to everyone's consternation. Leaving the patrol Second Lieutenant Simpson and Sergeant Arden ('D' Company) proceeded to reconnoitre the track running north-east. It was free of the enemy although recent boot marks were seen in the mud. The patrol advanced to the cross roads where stick bombs and a circular board painted in red and white halves were found in a recently occupied crater. The patrol then came under heavy machine-gun fire from three German posts.

Once the fire had died down, the patrol halted and observed the movements of the enemy between posts. Second Lieutenant Kermode decided to go closer and got to within thirty yards of one of the posts, picking up a field service cap from the 85th Regiment. He was spotted and fired on by sentries at two posts. He bombed these posts and returned to the crossroads. The patrol then withdrew under heavy rifle and machine-gun fire, which was accompanied by rifle grenades and a trench mortar barrage.[14]

It is hard to recognize the peaceful, deserted, no man's land of the previous days' patrol reports. The reports themselves are different, the level of detail in the reports is different, the obvious aggressive intent of the patrol and the calm relation of the exact position of the multiple enemy who fired on them, show a very different style.

The next night was 31 August/1 September 1917. Lieutenant Birbeck, acting adjutant while Hedley Heaton was away, wrote up the war diary before he retired:

> Patrol tonight – Lt Hutchinson and 2/Lt Airey and 10 ORs of C Company leave U29.d.9.1 at 10 pm to reconnoitre enemy wire in U30d and if possible kill a few of the enemy.

However the enemy was now alert to the different tone of their opposition. This patrol made it to the enemy wire (picking up on the way the 25 July and 3 August editions of *Gazette Des Ardennes*, a newspaper published in occupied France)

where they came under heavy fire immediately suffering four casualties. Hanley Hutchinson was badly wounded and dragged in, two NCOs were killed and one man wounded. They got Lieutenant Hutchinson back to the clearing station, but he died of his wounds at 8:15 p.m. on 1 September. Sergeant Arden and Corporal Eastgate's bodies were left behind in no man's land. Immediately, other patrols were formed to recover them but for the next two nights the moonlight was too bright for the patrols to go out.

Hutchinson's grave at Grevillers, taken by Capt Riley.
Don Jackson

Hutchinson's grave today.

2/Lt Hanley Hutchinson, died of wounds received on patrol on 1 September 1917.
Ackrill's Harrogate War Souvenir

It was not until the night of 3/4 September that Second Lieutenant N G Airey was able to take eight men and scour the last known position for the patrol. Although many shell holes were searched they were not found in the course of over two hours in no man's land. On 4/5 September Second Lieutenant Airey went out again with ten men ostensibly to recce the track running through no man's land but also with the stated intention of recovering the bodies. Again they spent two hours searching and reported various enemy movements but found no bodies.

Hanley Hutchinson was commemorated in the *Herald*:

> Mr & Mrs W H Hutchinson, of The Meads, Ripon, received an intimation by wire on Monday that their elder son, Lieutenant Hanley Hutchinson, of the West Yorks, had been dangerously wounded with gunshot in the abdomen. Later in the day a second wire was received intimating that Lieutenant Hutchinson was dead. The following telegram was also received from the War Office: 'Regret to inform you that Lieutenant Hutchinson, West Yorkshire Regiment, has died of wounds. Lord Derby expresses his sympathy'. The announcement of Lieutenant Hutchinson's death has been received with very great regret in Ripon, where he was very highly esteemed by all who knew him, and his sad death has cut short an exceedingly promising career. Lieutenant Hutchinson was educated at Kent House School, Eastbourne, and at Malvern College, where he remained until he passed his preliminary examination for the law. He served his articles with his father until the last six months, when he went to the firm of Messrs Crossman, Pritchard and Co., of London, where he finished his articles. He passed his final examination and was admitted as a solicitor on the 13th October 1913. He practised in Ripon until the end of September 1914, when he joined the West Yorkshires, his commission being dated September 30th, 1914. He completed a thorough training in England with his regiment, and was appointed machine gun officer. He was a good officer, a smart soldier, and greatly esteemed by all ranks. He first went on active service at the beginning of January this year, returning home for ten days' leave in July last. He returned again to the Front on the 1st August. Prior to the war Lieutenant Hutchinson was deeply interested in the Church Lads' Brigade, and held the rank of lieutenant in the Ripon Cathedral branch. He served in the Cadet Corps at Malvern, where he first obtained the elementary knowledge of drill.[15]

Sylvanus Arden had enlisted in November 1914 and had only recently returned from leave when he was killed. He was about to return to the UK as his application for a commission had been accepted and he was due to begin officer training. Before the war he was a tailor in York and his obituary was published in the *Yorkshire Gazette* on 29 September 1917. No details have been found on George Eastgate's life.

The Battalion seems to have felt that the enemy had gained a point here. Matters clearly could not be allowed to stand. On the night of 5/6 September there was the usual precursor to violence – Second Lieutenant Kermode was in no man's land with eight ORs. A few working parties were heard but nothing to excite him to action and he returned to the trenches. On 6/7 September he returned with Second Lieutenant Simpson, seven like minded individuals and a Lewis gun. They went out at 9:00 p.m. with the objective of raiding posts, killing and obtaining identifications. Leaving the front line they went to the cross roads and waited there for two hours – the Lewis gun had gone wrong and the gunners were sent back for another one. About midnight, Kermode crawled to within fifteen yards of the two posts. Every fifteen minutes an NCO visited these posts. While Second Lieutenant

Capt Riley inspecting a German machine gun. Taken while the battalion was at Favrieul shortly after 2/Lt Kermode's fighting patrol captured such a weapon. *Don Jackson*

Robert Waite.
Ackrill's Harrogate War Souvenir

Kermode was awaiting his moment, Second Lieutenant Simpson with the rest of the patrol observed six enemy approaching from the north-west. He waited until they were forty yards away and then ordered rapid fire both on them and on the posts. Three of the enemy were seen to fall. Kermode then threw three Mills bombs into the posts (one bomb was a dud – very annoying as Kermode himself was Bombing Officer at this time). He then rejoined the patrol who were firing on enemy retiring from the posts. The whole patrol then rushed the enemy position with a bayonet charge but was unable to come up with the enemy who had made good their escape. The patrol then returned to the trenches bringing: one light machine gun (Spandau 1917) complete with bipod, water tube and a belt of ammo; two rifles; one pair field glasses; one Very pistol and cartridges, assorted newspapers, helmets, stick bombs, ground sheets, rations and a water bottle, and one field service cap of 4th Company 1st Battalion 84th RIR (18th Reserve Division) with Prussian cockade.

The period of patrolling and

Capt Riley's dugout, Favreuil 1917.
Don Jackson

raiding was unusually intense and the Brigade Commander was moved to issue a special Order of the Day which commended Second Lieutenants Kermode and Simpson but also, uniquely, named other members of the patrol. With them that night went Lance Corporal H Shepherd and Privates F W Chapman, R Damme, J W Addy and H Dooley. Private Damme was awarded the Military Medal some months later, possibly for this action.

Just to make sure, Second Lieutenant Tasker went back to the post on the next night and set up an ambush but a ground mist prevented him from taking out a small patrol he spotted. Second Lieutenant White was also out that night and the next as was Lieutenant J M Anderson.

The cookhouse in Camp A Favreuil 1917. *Don Jackson*

A beer store in Camp A Favreuil 1917. *Don Jackson*

On the flanks, the 2/6th West Yorks had not been idle – patrolling heavily and raiding on 11 September. At dawn on the 13th the enemy put in a retaliatory raid on the 2/6th which was repulsed, but the 2/5th lost two men in the action – Clement Youngs and Ernest Dalby. Two more men were to die of wounds received in the raid, Joseph Boothroyd and Henry Hawkins. Private Boothroyd was still with the Battalion at the time and they were able to have a proper funeral for him. The only other casualties of this period were not from the patrol war. Robert Waite was killed by a trench mortar bombardment on 10 September and John Apedaile is recorded by Brigade as being killed in a raid on a post of the 2/5th but no mention of this is made by the Battalion war diary.

The Battalion left the line on 14 September 1917 and got into Camp A at Favreuil south of Mory by 2:30 a.m. After a few days rest they returned to the Bullecourt area for a further two trench tours. During the last of these, on 2 October 1917 they found the body of Second Lieutenant Annely, which had been missing since the Bullecourt attack and buried him, though the grave was lost subsequently.

Dominating No Man's Land – a summary of the 2/5th's campaign to control its front

In the space of little over a month the 2/5th had conducted over fourteen patrols led by at least eight different officers, gaining experience of working close to the enemy in no man's land. After the problems at Bullecourt and the reflections on their fighting spirit and discipline, nothing could have worked better to restore their confidence. The credit for this must lie with Major Peter. The Battalion had occupied no man's land pretty much at will and had raided with impunity. On 8 September a note arrived from Major General Braithwaite himself endorsing the favourable comment made by the Brigadier about the raid – 'credit is due to the Battalion and to the leader of the party Lt Kermode'. This was followed by a note from VI Corps to the General stating 'the Corps commander considers that this small enterprise was skilfully carried out and reflects credit on all concerned, more particularly on 2/Lt Kermode'.

In the middle of this campaign, on 23 September 1917, the new CO arrived – Colonel Richard H Waddy. He was a very different type of officer from the previous Territorial commanders.

Colonel Waddy was born in 1886 in Somerset and educated at Clifton College and RMC Sandhurst. He was from a military family with both his father and brother serving. In 1906 he was commissioned second lieutenant in the Somerset Light Infantry and was posted to the Second Battalion. He had considerable overseas experience – in 1908 he was posted overseas to Malta for three years where, in 1909 the Somersets mounted a Guard of Honour in Valetta for the visit of Kaiser Wilhelm of Germany.

In 1911 he was with the Battalion in China providing the guard for foreign concessions put in place after the Boxer Rebellion, which gave him considerable patrolling experience monitoring the Chinese Army. This was followed by a period on the North-West Frontier in India. The 2nd Battalion was one of the units which remained in India throughout the war, however many officers and NCOs were sent home to replace the casualties sustained in France and Flanders. He arrived in 1915 and went to the 3rd Reserve Battalion and then on to France in the summer of 1916 where he was second in command of the 1st Battalion Somerset Light Infantry. On the Somme, he gained experience of battle on the Western Front. He was involved in the later Somme attacks on Transloy Ridge where the Battalion sustained terrible casualties. In December 1916 and early 1917 the Battalion was in and out of the trenches and then in April he took part in the Battle of Arras where the 1st Somersets

Lt Col R H Waddy, took over command in September 1917.
Colonel J Waddy

assaulted the Hyderabad Redoubt. By May, the Battalion had only 220 men but was still engaged in the offensive. Major Waddy, as he then was, took part in all these operations and was in command himself at times.

He was promoted lieutenant colonel on 21 September and set out to take up his new command.[16]

From this point, the 2/5th West Yorks had professional soldiers in command appointments, it also had a CO who had more than a year's experience of France and had commanded a battalion in battle before. At this point the Battalion's fortunes changed and it began a long series of successes, beginning at Cambrai.

Chapter 6
Getting it right –
the 2/5th at the Battle of Cambrai

The innovative approach to the battle

The Battle of Cambrai was to be an experiment. The country behind the Hindenburg Line near Cambrai is flat and open with few natural barriers until the river outside Cambrai and its ancient fortifications. It was good ground to break through. There would be no long preliminary bombardment to churn up ground and alert the enemy to move his reserves into the area. Surprise would be achieved by a short but massive bombardment and a massed infantry and tank attack. High Command regarded the attack more as a test, and as a large scale raid, than a serious attempt to break the Hindenburg Line, however for the troops of the 62nd this was their first major assault since Bullecourt and a chance to show that they had learned how to handle themselves in the attack.

Experience with tanks had moved on since Bullecourt. The enemy was less frightened of the individual tank roaming the battlefield as they had both armour piercing ammunition and field guns in an anti tank role to deal with them. In their fixed fortifications with good communications, German commanders could call down a barrage on an attacking tank with some confidence that they would be able to knock it out before it got close. In particular, if the infantry could be kept back, the tanks alone would become very vulnerable. The formula for Cambrai was to use more tanks than had ever been used before, get them closer, keep the infantry right with them and gas and bombard the enemy into stunned silence while they advanced.

Rehearsals

In October the 2/5th completed its activities up in Bullecourt and pulled back to Barastre Camp where the usual re-equipping and re-training began. At first there was nothing unusual for the soldiers – there was a round of range work and route marches interspaced with the Divisional Concert Party, sports and recreation. However, rather than going back into the line they then moved to Barly. Arthur Green had rejoined the Battalion, now recovered from his wounds, and found Barly a good place to get re-accustomed to the army.

> At the moment we are having a very good time. Some old billets, 8, 9 or 10 hours sleep a night, topping billets for the officers, beds for most of the men and really a tip top time – and what is more it hasn't rained for nearly a fortnight and things are comparatively dry. We work 9 – 1 every morning vigorously and then all play football or some other sort of mob game for the rest of the afternoon, nothing at all to do after 3:30pm until next morning. It is great – in fact so much like home that all the men clean up at 3:30, black their boots and shine their buttons – and we ourselves dine in style every evening, visit and are visited by everyone we know in the Division. The shops are good such as there are of them, and the next village has an imitation Bond Street.[1]

CSM Rathke agreed as he kept Mr Breare up to date:

> I must write and thank you for your kindness in sending me parcels of warm underclothing and waistcoat, and I must also thank the kind friends that sent them to you; and I am sure that all the local boys and others who are out here will never forget the kindness and comforts you have given them throughout this terrible war. I am sure if it had not been for the dear folks at home – that is to say, fathers, mothers, wives, children, and friends – we could never have stood the hardships of the weather, etc. It is a treat to read the news of dear old Harrogate and to know how everything is going on. I am sorry to see the names of so many pals of mine being killed and wounded. Some of them have soldiered with me in the old Volunteers and Territorials since I joined them at the Drill Hall in 1899, and I am sure I feel it very much when I see some of their names appear in your paper. All the Beechwood Boys wish to be remembered to you and wish you the very best of health and every success to your paper.[2]

At Barly the men continued route marching while their officers disappeared for a while. While the troops were on church parade on 4

November, Colonel Waddy with other senior officers attended a demonstration of new infantry tank cooperation tactics. Next day the Company Commanders attended a similar event and on the 6th, twelve company officers and their NCOs spent the day at the demonstration. Captain Green commented of the tanks:

> We (some of us officers) have today had an interesting time watching tanks practising. They are amazing things, they can stand any end up on their heads or on their tails, they can mop up trenches and houses and trees just about as easily as we can fasten our boots and a good deal quicker. After the war perhaps people in England will see them being used for demolition work and very funny they will think them too.[3]

The Battalion then moved to Semincourt where two new elements entered the men's training – tank and aircraft cooperation.

The tanks now had defined roles. There would be wire crushers, to open gaps; there would be the 'males' with their 6-pounder guns to deal with strong points and the machine gun armed 'females' to deal with infantry and trenches. They would be organized in waves so that they arrived at the right moment for the sort of targets expected. They had now clearly become an infantry weapon for close battlefield support rather than an independent arm. For Cambrai, the 185th Brigade had twenty-eight tanks allotted. They would be assembled in three lines – wire cutting tanks followed by fighting tanks on the left and then a further wave on the right. They were divided between Green, Red and Blue, each group being allotted one of the objectives.

> In general the action of the tanks will be as follows: - The wire cutting tanks will act as advance tanks and keep as close to the barrage as they can. The fighting tanks, after crossing the enemy trenches will turn left handed and work along them until the infantry are established in the trench, when they will proceed back to their respective routes.[4]

It was also set down that the tanks would carry small-arms ammunition and bombs to be dumped well forward as re-supply points.

At Wailley and Berneville the Battalion practised company level tactics with the tanks and then carried out a Brigade exercise with aircraft. Again, the aircraft had a new role. They would not be flying high over the battlefield, taking photos and adjusting fire for the artillery, they would be spotter planes in close support of the infantry.

On 12 November the Battalion carried out the exercise. The tanks were marshalled into the advance by Lieutenant H T Barker and Lieutenant Tasker was in charge of getting the message relays working. The aircraft flew low over the Brigade at 11.15 in the morning and called for flares – the Battalion then attempted to send coded messages to the aircraft. The signallers had been issued with sheets that allowed them to send simple messages; 'I am at XXX and am consolidating' or 'I am held up by machine gun at XXX' or 'I need bombs', any of which would have helped had they been able to get messages like this passed at Bullecourt. Message 11 was 'Hostile Battery/machine gun/ trench mortar active at XXX'. This clearly put aircraft into an infantry support role as they were no longer simply correcting the pre-planned fire of the artillery, but providing immediate tactical assistance to advancing infantry. The results of the exercise are not recorded so it is not known if messages were successfully passed.

While the Battalion was engaged in planning this exercise, on 10 November, Acting CSM James Stonehouse passed away from his wounds in a hospital near Etaples.

Thus, the scene was set for Cambrai – the first full scale, modern battle involving all the modern fighting arms of infantry, artillery, tanks and air support. On 13 November they marched to Lechelles and then were crowded into a camp at Ruyaulcourt. By the 18th they were concealed in shacks in Havrincourt Wood, the whole place heaving with concealed soldiers. Here they waited.

The attack itself

The orders for the attack originally ran to only four pages but were considerably amended and extended over the days before the battle. The plan as far as the 2/5th was concerned was fairly straightforward and conventional. The first wave of the attack would be made up of the 2/6th and 2/8th. Both these would have an extra company taken from the 2/5th and the 2/7th. These units would break the Hindenburg Line and consolidate in, and east of, the village of Havrincourt. The 2/5th and 2/7th would form the second wave. The 2/5th would pass through the 2/6th, occupy the rest of the village and set up a line in the open ground beyond [see map].

The Battalion detached 'A' Company to the 2/6th. This company would be under the command of Colonel Hoare and was tasked to act as skirmishers, suppressing the Hindenburg Line outposts until the main attack swept over them. For the rest of the Battalion, Colonel Waddy was clear that the performance of the tanks was not to be a limiting factor as was set out in the orders in capitals:

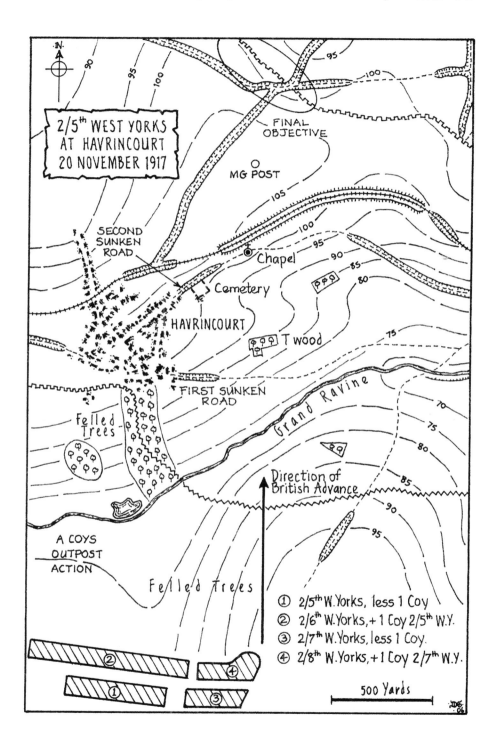

N

90
95
100
95
100
105

2/5ᵗʰ WEST YORKS
AT HAVRINCOURT
20 NOVEMBER 1917

FINAL
OBJECTIVE

O
MG POST

SECOND
SUNKEN
ROAD

100
95
90
85
80

⊙ Chapel

Cemetery

HAVRINCOURT

T wood

75

FIRST SUNKEN
ROAD

Grand Ravine

70

Felled
Trees

75

80

Direction of
British Advance

85

90

A COYS
OUTPOST
ACTION

95

Felled Trees

① 2/5ᵗʰ W.Yorks, less 1 Coy
② 2/6ᵗʰ W.Yorks, + 1 Coy 2/5ᵗʰ W.Y.
③ 2/7ᵗʰ W.Yorks, less 1 Coy.
④ 2/8ᵗʰ W.Yorks, + 1 Coy 2/7ᵗʰ W.Y.

②

④

①

③

500 Yards

ON NO ACCOUNT MUST FAILURE OF TANKS
PREVENT THE FORWARD MOVEMENT OF THE
BATTALION. THE BATTALION WILL SECURE ITS
OBJECTIVE TRUSTING IN ITS OWN POWER OF
OFFENSIVE.[5]

On the night of 19 November they moved out and assembled in
Trescault Trench. 'A' Company formed up in front of the 2/6th
Battalion. The ground, which today is heavily wooded again, had been
cleared by the Germans to improve their fields of fire. It had been left
littered with the tree trunks which made it difficult going for the tanks
and a steeple chase for the infantry.

The actions of 'A' Company in support of the 2/6th
'A' Company moved off from Havrincourt wood at 9:30 in the evening
and went into the outposts of the British front line – relieving the troops
of the 36th Division that had been holding them. They were divided
into four platoons, the two right platoons had a tank each to support
them and those on the left had three tanks. The enemy laid a barrage
down on the outposts between 5:00 and 6:00 a.m. but the Company
moved out into no man's land and let it fall behind them so there were
no casualties. On the right there were difficulties. One tank did not
arrive and the platoon which was to advance up the glade was unable to

Panorama of the battlefield from the German Reserve Line. *Dr M Beggs*

proceed. The other did arrive, breached the wire and the platoon took thirty prisoners and two machine guns – successfully capturing the outposts allotted to it. The platoons on the left advanced with their tanks but took considerable casualties from machine guns immediately in front of them. The author of the battle report from 'A' Company was Colonel Waddy himself – the Company commander and his second in command having both been wounded. Only two officers were casualties on the first day of the battle, Second Lieutenant N H Smith was killed and Second Lieutenant A J Watson was wounded – both of these may have been on the left flank of 'A' Company that morning. 'A' Company was normally commanded by Phillip Clubb but he does not appear to have led it on 20 November.

With the outpost battle still going on the rest of the Battalion began to move. The outposts in front of the 2/6th, and the fire from Femy Scrub opposite, held up the advance of the 2/6th. The 2/8th and 2/7th on the right made better progress and the whole of the 2/5th then began to move forward into the battle, sliding slightly to the right to avoid the positions holding up the 2/6th. The battalion level battle was now on.

The assault on Havrincourt by the 2/5th

The main force of the Battalion was formed up with 'C' Company in a sap ready to spread out into a screen in front of the other two

Second Sunken Road   Final Objective

From the first sunken road to Havrincourt Cemetery, their next objective. *Author's Collection*

East Side of
Havrincourt Village

Parapet formed by
edge of sunken road

companies. 'D' Company was on the right and 'B' on the left. Although no nominal role of the officers has survived from the day of the battle there is a marginal note in the war diary a month before. 'B' Company was under the command of John Airey and 'C' Company of K E S Stewart. 'D' Company was being led by acting Captain Robinson, as 'D' Company's normal OC, Captain Green, was a Brigade liaison officer during the attack so he was not at the head of his men for this assault.

For the main body of the 2/5th, the attack began when 'C' Company scouts went out to locate gaps in the wire and then at 6:20 a.m. the Battalion's first wave went over the top heading for the gaps. The Battalion's tanks had not appeared although some had gone off to their right, skirting Femy Scrub. Touch was established with the 2/7th on the right but the left flank was open as it was anchored on a thick wood on the start line, creating a gap in the line.

The Battalion passed to the side of the 2/6th who had captured most of the objective but were still fighting in the southern corner of the village. On the way they engaged a machine-gun post in Femy Scrub – without their tanks they showered it with rifle grenades until the twenty

Havrincourt
Cemetery

Site of
"T Wood"

Direction of Advance

occupants gave up – and proceeded to their forming up place in the sunken road to the east of Havrincourt. Despite the good cover this gave, enemy artillery found it and 'B' and 'C' Companies took twenty-four casualties here. After thirty minutes the Battalion had reassembled. Still without their own tanks they acquired two surviving tanks from the first objective and went forward.

A machine-gun post in T Wood off to the right, immediately engaged them but a platoon sergeant charged it with a bayonet party, bombed the dugout and placed the captured machine gun in one of the tanks. As they continued up the slope they then came under fire from Havrincourt Cemetery. The cemetery itself is high and walled and forms a very good position; however the ground has a double dip in it at this point, which provides some cover for an attacker. 'C' Company called up a tank and attacked it. Support from the rest of the Battalion was delayed for fifteen minutes while a further machine gun, firing out of the east side of Havrincourt, was dealt with by a tank. They then rushed up to the cemetery and assisted in its capture – taking thirty prisoners. Running east along the top of the cemetery is another sunken road – though not as deep as the one below it – but it had a junction with an

The village of Havrincourt and T Wood.
Photo courtesy of the Imperial War Museum, London, IWM Panorama 308

old railway embankment which provided cover. Here the Battalion paused again, sorted itself out and acquired another tank as the earlier set had now disappeared. Immediately to their front another machine-gun post opened up. The post was close to the final objective in an area of support trenches. With the help of the new tank the post in the trench directly to the north was smothered. This action cost a further thirty-five casualties.

As they moved towards the next objective they were again hit by machine-gun fire from the left where suppressing Havrincourt village continued to be a problem. This was dealt with by 'B' Company who concentrated four Lewis guns on it while storming it with infantry – gun and team were made prisoner. 'C' Company now moved onto the Battalion's first objective, taking another thirty prisoners. The 2/5th was now in possession of its first objective, having assisted in the taking of the outstanding objectives of the 2/6th on their way through.

'B' and 'D' Companies passed through 'C' and out into open ground – there were tank tracks though the wire there and they took their final objective with little trouble. At this point, back with 'C' Company, the York and Lancasters made contact on the left, and half an hour later contact was re-established with the 2/7th completing the encirclement of Havrincourt. 'A' Company rejoined them that evening and there they all stayed until the next day. The Battalion had carried out a near faultless attack on a heavily defended enemy position. It had put most of the training into practice – taking out defended positions with bayonet charges, grenades, machine guns or tanks as suited the moment. Casualties had been light as the enemy artillery had been unable to locate them with certainty and as they had kept up momentum.

Captain Green wrote home on 20 November:

> You will see in tonight's papers no doubt that there has been a big surprise attack in this part of France and we are in it. I feel I could tell you all about it for I am during the stunt a liaison officer for our Brigade with the Brigade on our left. We are ensconced in dugouts in our old line at the brigade headquarters.
>
> The attack has been a great thing, – it started this morning at dawn and before noon we had the information that the cavalry had been warned and had actually got beyond the line. From this distance it is a most interesting battle. Never before have I seen how a battle was worked and how all the various bits of the Army were all pulled together to work for one common object.
>
> How our own Battalion has come off I don't know; but we know that they have reached their objective and practically up to time too. As their objectives are two or three miles away they haven't done badly - have they?[6]

This mood continued into the next day:

> The battle is going on grandly. The Division has captured guns galore and my Brigade has got some. I think it quite likely that my D Company and old B Company have come in for a share of the loot. The Brigade has gone ahead to follow the fighting troops. Our casualties yesterday were comparatively slight and everyone is cheered at the prospect of what great results might come of this. Watch the papers and rejoice with the rest of us.[7]

On 20 November the Battalion lost seventeen men – either killed outright or dying of wounds. They were Thomas Harris, William Mulholland, Alfred Wilson, George W Brown, Thomas Brown, Percy Coomer, Albert Dale, Percy Fry, William Goodliff, William Green,

Edward Jewitt, Harold Marshall, Joseph Megson, Walter Mugg, David Shaw, Harry Slater and Edward Winkley. As the action was successful and the ground on which they fell was held, most of these soldiers have graves either in Grand Ravine, on the line of the advance, or at Hermies Hill where some casualties from Havrincourt Wood cemetery were re-located after the war. A further four men, John Welby, Bernard White, Charles Iles and Thomas Woolsoncroft died of their wounds the next day.

Going a little too far – Beyond Havrincourt and the fight at Bourlon Wood

On 21 November at 11:00 a.m. the Battalion had completed its walk up to a field on the south-west side of Graincourt. There were only two small roads leading through Graincourt and several brigades were trying to get through them so there was a long delay. The 2/5th sat in this field until 5:00 p.m. and then moved again in the twilight through the village to two sunken roads leading north-west out toward the Bapaume – Cambrai road. These are on a reverse slope from the German positions on the other side of the road. 'A' Company and Battalion HQ were on the southernmost of the two roads, 'C' and 'D' companies on the north-ernmost and 'B' Company plugged the gap between the two, giving them a solid defensive position should a counter-attack arrive. On the other side of the ridge just such a counter-attack was starting to form. The enemy recovered magnificently from the first shock and reinforce-ments began to flood into the Cambrai sector. Their attacks came from Bourlon Wood, Bourlon Village and from the so far untouched areas of the Hindenburg line on the eastern side of the Canal Du Nord. These attacks surged up the ridge on the other side of the Cambrai – Bapaume road and established positions near the crest. The 185th Brigade was tasked with pushing them off this ridge – the 2/6th and 2/8th would once again be in the lead.

On 22 November, 'A' Company went into action with the 2/6th and suffered heavily.

For the CO of the 2/6th, Colonel Hoare, the day was very frustrating. Having moved into position in the dark and without guides, he found himself at dawn in a salient of one trench about 800 yards long [see map]. It is easy to see how this happened, the Hindenburg Support Line runs north – south at this point. Colonel Hoare wanted to set up an east – west line and he dropped off 'D' Company in the first such trench and the rest of the Battalion went on. However there was not another east – west trench suitable and so the Battalion ended up in an L shaped position. He had himself gone out 500 yards to find any other units and

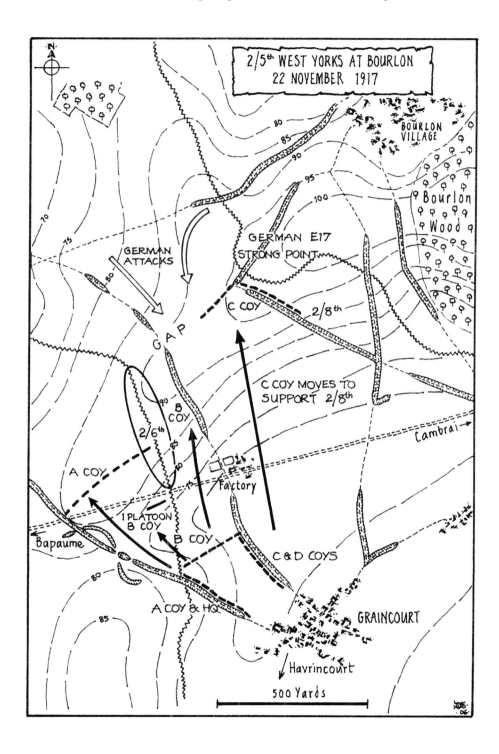

2/5th West Yorks
at Bourlon. A
panorama of the
22 November
battlefield.
Dr M Beggs

Block on
Cambrai–Bapaume Road

2/6th in a
salient

B Company

failed, as had his patrols. He had expected to find the 36th Division on
his left, holding the ground over to the canal; they were not there. Off
to his right he expected to find the 2/8th holding the valley and the high
ground to his right. They were not there either. He also found himself
overlooked by three or four large spoil heaps and, as the light improved,
the enemy took a great interest in him. He fought with both sides of the
trench manned. 'A' Company of the 2/5th, depleted from the fighting
before Havrincourt, was moved into an east – west line linking 'D'
Company 2/6th with the road. There was a convenient curving communication trench here. 'A' Company did succeed in blocking the road
and was moving up the trench when the whole of the 2/6th position
collapsed and everyone retreated to the Cambrai – Bapaume road.
Colonel Hoare in his after action report commented:

> I wish to place on record my appreciation of the great assis-
> tance rendered to me by the company of the 2/5th West Yorks
> Regiment placed at my disposal for operations. 2/Lt Davidson,
> who was commanding the Company, moved forward with the
> greatest promptitude and did splendid work until he was
> wounded. It was through no fault of his that my left flank
> was unsecured.[8]

There is no record in the Army List of a Second Lieutenant
Davidson in the 2/5th, however the list of wounded in the Divisional

History identifies him as R M Davidson whose records have not survived.

As the situation of the 2/6th became critical, Colonel Waddy sent up another platoon, of B Company, to assist them, forming up just south of the road where the 2/6th would emerge from the trench line. Although this position is visible from about 200 yards north of the 2/5th HQ this element of B Company disappeared into a maze of trenches and gas haze and communication was lost with them. He sent out a patrol, an officer and two men, to locate them. The officer was killed and the two men went missing. As the 2/5th lost only one officer on the 22nd (Norman George Airey who was one of the Battalion's newer officers having only arrived in August 1917) it is assumed that he led this patrol. There is no record that 'B' Company linked up with the 2/6th; most likely it became jammed in the retreating men at the road.

Of the two men who went missing, the fate of one is known. Bugler Kirk, who had corresponded with the *Harrogate Herald*, went with Norman Airey that day.

> Private Harry Kirk, of the 2/5th West Yorks, son of Edward Kirk, 1 Cheltenham Road, is missing, though up to the present no official notification of the fact has come. He has only been back from leave six weeks, after septic poisoning. He has not been heard of for a month. Mrs Kirk has received a letter from

his chum relating the circumstances. Kirk was with the writer of the letter through all the battle, and took everything which came in good heart and spirit. The time came along when volunteers were wanted, and Kirk, along with another chum and an officer, volunteered. The officer has been officially announced killed; but there is no news of his chum. If you boys know anything, I hope you will write to Mrs Kirk or to me. There is nothing definite to show them that he has been killed, and it may be that he is a prisoner. I hope the latter is found to be the case. Before Kirk went into battle he gave his chum a brief note to be sent to his mother in case he should fall. I have seen this letter, for it has been forwarded home. I can assure you it is a letter of a man, and a hero who is in the fullest sense a credit to his race.[9]

A few weeks later Mr Breare was able to report that Private Kirk was safe.

Private Henry Kirk, West Yorks, son of Mr and Mrs Edward Kirk, 1 Cheltenham Road, Harrogate, whom you will remember was missing, and I enquired about the other week, I am pleased to say, is a prisoner, at Munster, Westf., Camp II.[10]

'C' and 'D' Companies were to support the 2/8th. Their job was to establish a line on the crest of the ridge running from half way to Bourlon Wood to the flank of the 2/6th. There does not appear to have been much in the way of existing trenches on this position and it was over-looked by a German strongpoint at E17 Central. Colonel James of the 2/8th was leading the defence of this sector and he established his head-quarters in the remains of a factory on the Bapaume – Cambrai road. From this position he could see most of the ridgeline his troops were trying to hold. He was in charge of his own four companies, 'C' and 'D' of the 2/5th and he acquired another two of the York and Lancs. He set about forming them into a line but had difficulties in getting everything into place.

'C' Company was in position quite quickly and faced a series of attacks with parties coming in from the north-west, machine-gun fire and strafing by aircraft. Although artillery SOS messages were sent up, no barrage ensued so all attacks were beaten off with rifle and Lewis gun fire, and the customary hail of rifle grenades at which the 2/5th now was so proficient. Although forced out of their positions on at least one occasion they counter-attacked and took all the ground back. The real problem was off to their left, in the shallow depressions between themselves and the 2/6th.

Here Colonel James discovered a gap between the 2/6th West Yorks and his position of about 1,000 yards. Into this he tried to put 'D' Company of 2/5th West Yorks and positioned a further company of the 2/5th West Yorks (assumed to be 'B' less the one platoon, off with the 2/6th, as this is the only one left) behind to cover any further gaps. However for some reason 'D' Company did not move into this position and was still in the sunken road outside Graincourt forty minutes later. Whether it did ever move up, or became lost in the chaos down by the road is not clear but it never arrived to fill the gap and it was only a counter-attack from the left by the 36th Division that took the pressure off this sector. Colonel James does not mention names in his report but he does say of the performance of 'C' Company: 'Special mention must be made of the gallant way in which C Company 2/5th West Yorkshire Regiment, held their ground. They never yielded a yard, though hard pressed.'[11]

On 23 November all companies of the 2/5th were withdrawn from the line and returned to Leschelles. The nature of the fight is captured in the citations for the officers decorated for the action on 20 – 23 November. As the action took place over three days it is not possible to say exactly which officers were in which fight; however the citations give an idea of the type of fighting the Battalion engaged in. Second Lieutenants Tewson and Veal were each awarded the MC. Second Lieutenant Tewson's citation reads:

> For conspicuous gallantry and devotion to duty. When his men came under very severe machine-gun fire, he dashed in front, and so encouraged them by his fearless example that they drove the enemy back and captured the objective. When the fire became so heavy that a gap was caused on his flank, he ran along the front of the line, rallied the men and formed a defensive flank, thus saving a critical situation.

Second Lieutenant Veal also distinguished himself; his citation reads:

> For conspicuous gallantry and devotion to duty. When the left flank of his battalion was exposed he collected a small party of men and under very heavy fire charged a body of the enemy who were attempting to take advantage of the gap and drove them back with heavy casualties. He held them at bay until a

defensive flank was thrown out and by his prompt action undoubtedly saved the situation.

The war diary describes the mood at the end of the engagement: 'everybody tired but in high spirits at the success that attended the operation.' The newspapers were also reaching the front and by the 24th, Arthur Green was able to comment on the coverage in England:

> We have seen the account in the *Times* of the 22nd and it is not worked up too much. Many an old score has been wiped out and for the first time they were able to get at the Boche with bullet and bayonet. We feel soldiers now and not merely cannon fodder. Tanks had a field day and got prisoners in the hundreds and knocked out the enemy by swarms.[12]

Despite the hard fighting on 22 November the casualties were again light. The Battalion lost twelve men – Edward Acton, Tom Barff, Arthur Bycroft, James Campbell, Fred Cox, Edward Evans, Ernest Gilyard, Arthur Matley, Charles Scarth, Stanley Simpson, Arthur Wilkinson and Gilbert Wilson. This may well have been due to the nature of the fighting. The Germans had to leave their prepared positions and come out into the open to counter-attack while the Yorkshire men remained in cover. According to a number of witnesses, soldiers passing General Braithwaite on their way back from the battle shouted to him: 'This wipes out Bullecourt sir!'

Bourlon – the wood on the hill
The Battalion would have seen, during its fight on the Bapaume – Cambrai road, the sinister form of Bourlon Wood, an isolated ridge overlooking the whole plain and studded with machine-gun posts. It represented the last major obstacle preventing an advance on Cambrai and the Division now set about taking it. Originally this was to be a continuation of the attack but the men were so exhausted by the original Cambrai fighting that an immediate assault was not possible. Sadly, this also gave the enemy time to flood new units into the area and strengthen their defences.

The 26 November started in confusion for the 2/5th as responsibility for the Battalion shifted to 187th Brigade, then to 186th and then back to 187th before they could move. Finally they were ordered into position on the south side of Bourlon Wood [see map] and moved there at 8 p.m. – without any reconnaissance. When they got into position about 10 p.m. they found there were no trenches. Enemy artillery was

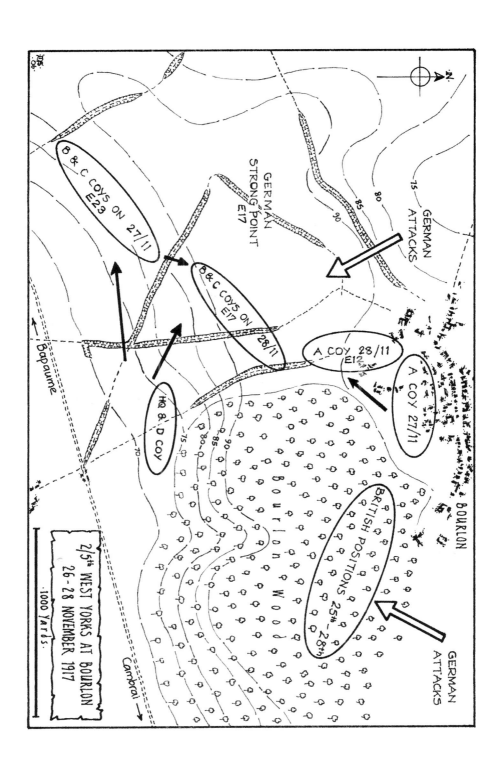

B & C COYS ON E23 27/11

GERMAN STRONG POINT E17

GERMAN ATTACKS

B & C COYS ON E17 28/11

A COY 28/11 E12

A COY 27/11

Bapaume

HQ & D COY

BOURLON

British Positions 25th – 28th

Bourlon Wood

GERMAN ATTACKS

Cambrai

2/5ᵗʰ WEST YORKS AT BOURLON
26 – 28 NOVEMBER 1917

1000 Yards.

Bourlon Wood seen from the
German strongpoint. 2/5th positions
on 27 November 1917.
Dr M Beggs

Bourlon Village and A Company

searching their area so they got HQ into a dugout at the south-west
corner of the wood and the men dug in around it. The front line was
somewhere up on the crest, the enemy had been pushed almost off the
crest and back into Bourlon village but it was dark, the wood was tangled
and full of troops and the situation very confused. The adjutant, Hedley
Heaton, was sent forward to find either 187th Brigade HQ or another
unit with orders from that Brigade but could find only a Guards unit
who were equally perplexed – and the attack they were supporting was
due to go off at 6:20 a.m. the next day.

On 27 November at 7:30 a.m., Colonel Waddy discovered that the
2/5th York and Lancasters were a few hundred yards up the Sunken
Road. Asked for support, he moved 'A' Company up onto their left at
9:30 and they took up a position on the forward slope (at E12b). This
company was to form a block between Bourlon village and the rest of
the position – there was heavy fighting in the village at this point with
tanks and several thousand men engaged in house to house fighting – it
was unclear whether a German attack would suddenly emerge from the
confusion. At 10:00 a.m. the 2/5th KOYLI informed him that the
enemy was moving around their left flank – this would appear again to
be the strongpoint at E17 central which had yet to be cleared. Colonel
Waddy sent 'B' and 'C' Companies up to form a defensive flank. The
2/5th now had only one company left in reserve. A CO's conference was
held between Colonel Waddy and the OCs 2/5th Y&L and 2/5th
KOYLI, and it was decided to call on a further supporting battalions as
they has been told 'the high ground must be held at all costs'. While this
message was being passed a unit of the 40th retired through the 2/5th

Bourlon Wood

HQ and D Company

B & C Company Positions

position. This was the first actual information about what was going on at the front. It seemed that they (the 40th) had been relieved and that the front line, far from crumbling was strongly held. When the 2/8th West Yorks answered the call for help they found themselves trying to get into trenches already crammed with troops and were forced to dig in further down the slope at E17b central. The two battalions formed a defensive perimeter for the night.

The 2/5th held this position all the next day, then 'B' and 'C' Companies moved off without relief as their positions were now covered elsewhere. An officer of the 15th London Regiment arrived with orders to relieve the other companies. The Battalion reassembled itself and moved off through a cloud of gas on the Cambrai – Bapaume road into the Hindenburg support line. This was a fairly unsatisfactory ending to an otherwise successful engagement; had Bourlon been successfully stormed the breakthrough would have been complete and the road to Cambrai opened. As it was, most of the ground was recaptured by German counter-attacks. However, the 2/5th had now proved itself in a set piece battle and in a series of company level actions. It had also for the first time fought in the open without artillery support.

As Captain Green commented: 'We have become rather distinguished and taken our place in the crack Divisions.'[13]

During the period of fighting at Bourlon, the Battalion lost Second Lieutenants Gibson and Hutchinson. Second Lieutenant L F Walker was wounded, as was Lieutenant G B Foster and fifty-two other ranks became casualties.

Thomas Ernest Gibson, who was unmarried, was 23 years old and from Leeds. His body was never found. He had been commissioned in April 1917 and had been with the Battalion since June.

For Lieutenant Hutchinson the situation is confused. William Hutchinson who was part of the 2/5th but was on attachment to the 2/8th Battalion was lost on 22 November. The C/O of the 2/8th Colonel James reported his death. He was from Harrogate, aged 22.

> Second Lieutenant W Hutchinson, eldest son of Mr & Mrs Hutchinson, 12 Grange Avenue, Harrogate, was killed in action on November 22nd, near Bourlon Wood, whilst gallantly leading his men. He was the grandson of Mrs Hutchinson, of Sheriff Hutton, and Mrs Mills, Thornton-le-Clay, and only 22 years of age. Second Lieutenant Hutchinson joined the West Yorks in September, 1914. With the Beechwood Boys he went to France 15th April, 1915, and was gassed in July. He came back to Blighty with trench feet in November, 1915, and for a time was at the Military Hospital, Southall. Returning to France June, 1916, he was wounded at Thiepval at the taking of the Schwaben Redoubt in September 1916. He came home for a commission in December, 1916, trained at Bristol University, and returned to France on 20th July, 1917. He was apprenticed to Mr Harker, grocer, King's Road, before enlisting.[14]

The details of his death emerged shortly afterwards:

> Mr Hutchinson, of 12 Grange Avenue, Harrogate, has had a telegram from the Records Office, York, confirming the death of his son, the late Second Lieutenant W Hutchinson. His lieutenant writes : 'Dear Mr Hutchinson, Your letter to hand this morning. Now that the battalion is out of line and at rest I find it easier to write to you and tell you all I know in connection with the death of your son. It was between 7 and 8am when you son was in the act of sending up an SOS signal rocket, when the enemy were counter-attacking us heavily near Bourlon village, that he was hit in the head by a bullet from a machine gun. He died instantaneously and could not possibly have suffered any pain. His men, together with another platoon in my company, without a doubt saved the situation that morning; and it was without a doubt due to his example and leadership that helped them to do so well. They would do

anything for him, and he is a great loss to us all. Please convey our most heartfelt sympathies to your family.[15]

In the war diary of the 2/5th a Second Lieutenant Hutchinson is recorded as dying on 27 November. Second Lieutenant George Russell Hutchinson of the 2/8th West Yorks is the only Hutchinson to die on this day. George Hutchinson was from Scarborough, had enlisted in 1914 and went to France in July 1915. He had been commissioned into 7th Battalion West Yorks in August 1917 and attached to 2/5th though it is unclear when he arrived.

Second Lieutenant Leslie Walker was formerly a private in 7th Battalion Gordon Highlanders and was wounded with shrapnel in his right knee. He was evacuated to England on 30 November and remained in hospital until April 1918.

No details have survived for Lieutenant G B Foster.

A further twelve other ranks died or were killed – Albert Brayshay, Ingram Elsdon, Francis Ando, Alfred Barnett, George Coultish, George Hawkins, Hugh Hinton, Wilson Jackson, Ernest Bell, Thomas Gallagher, Joseph Gibson and Samuel Jones. Over the next two months, six of the more seriously wounded succumbed to their injuries – Joseph Dunham, Walter Andrews, George Chambers, John Mazieko, Thomas Edmondson and Ernest Gains.

After several days of effort it became clear that Bourlon could not be taken with the troops available and that without its capture the road to Cambrai remained shut. The Army fell back to the ridge between Havrincourt and Flesquieres and dug in there to pass the winter.

Chapter 7
Success at Bucquoy

The Patrol War 1918

The Battalion passed a peaceful Christmas in 1917, well out of danger. Captain Green wrote home:

> We have left the comfortable districts where we had fires and electricity, a 12 mile march brought us to a rambling old village way behind the guns similar to the billet we had on first arrival last year and as cold 20 – 30 degrees of frost. Planning Christmas fun – we have turkeys galore, eggs and sausages and everything that's nice and barrels of beer for the men.[1]

This period of relaxation lasted into the New Year. On 14 January Captain Green's letter showed a picture of the Battalion at rest:

> Now, although we are on fairly new ground we are in the lap of luxury, instead of going on parade we trekked to see The Pelicans – our divisional Pierrot troupe, there is also the cinema show nightly two hour exhibition of pretty good pictures, you may book a seat in advance. There are two shows belonging to a neighbouring division and only a few minutes away, Tommy can see a show for 2½d, at a neighbouring town 3 miles away there are several celebrated troupes and bands, using large buildings and theatres in town, boxes and plush seats.

While the records for the early months of 1918 stress how quiet a period it was, this is a rather misleading picture. Although the Battalion did not fight in any major action, that was the norm for most battalions generally. In fact the 2/5th was engaged in an active patrolling and raiding war on whatever sector it occupied. January 1918 saw them in the Oppy sector, north-east of Arras. Even by the standards of the Western Front this area is flat and featureless. The ground had been heavily fought over in the spring of 1917 but the lines had only moved a few hundred yards. The positions were organized as a series of posts which provided all round defence, loosely linked by lightly held trenches; further back there were lines of continuous trenches. The Battalion went into a routine of time spent in the front line, in support and in reserve. From 17 to 20 January they were in the front line, then spent 21st to 24th in reserve. From 25 January to 3 February they were in support, returning to the camp in Roclincourt for rest and working parties from 3 to 6 February. On 7 February they went back into the front line.

The weather in January was very wet and many of the trenches were impassable. The Battalion front was formed by four posts – Oppy, Wood, Beatty and Bird. Each was held by one company, normally 'A' in Oppy, 'B' in Wood, 'C' in Bird and 'D' in Beatty [see map]. Once in position each company would begin the business of gathering information on enemy activity and suppressing enemy movements in their sector.

On the night of 18/19 January, Second Lieutenant Weston of 'A' Company went out to check on no man's land. He went out at 7:30 p.m. with five men for a general tour of the area in front of Oppy Post [see map] and to examine the track through no man's land. They found nothing and enemy activity was limited to three flares while they were out. They were back by 11:00 p.m. all safe. The Battalion was shelled that night leading to the deaths of Alfred Coldwell and Frank Roper.

On the next night it was time for a new man to show his paces. Second Lieutenant Donkersley had reported to the Battalion with a new draft of officers including Second Lieutenants De Ville, De Lacey, R Bailey and R B Walker. Reynold Donkersley was no novice and soon set about making his mark. On this first night he went out from Bird Post heading for the German strongpoint, Canteen Post, with six men. About forty yards away from it they saw three enemy leave the post and go up the track towards the south corner of Oppy Wood. The patrol took cover in a shell hole and waited to see what would happen next. They saw three distinct parties of enemy troops going into the post and concluded a relief was in progress. There were further posts to the south and Second Lieutenant Donkersley watched it all, noting that these posts were strongly manned, and returned to the lines at 10:00 p.m.

Canteen Post was a worry – too strong and too close. The Battalion

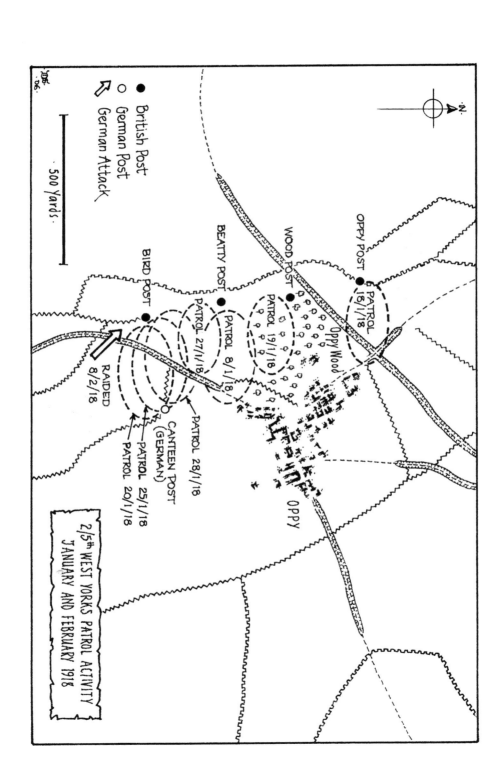

2/5th WEST YORKS PATROL ACTIVITY
JANUARY AND FEBRUARY 1918

British Post ●
German Post ○
German Attack ⇨

500 Yards

OPPY POST

PATROL 16/1/18

WOOD POST

Oppy Wood

BEATTY POST

PATROL 19/1/18

PATROL 8/1/18

PATROL 27/1/18

BIRD POST

RAIDED 8/2/18

PATROL 28/1/18

CANTEEN POST (GERMAN)

PATROL 25/1/18

PATROL 20/1/18

OPPY

Oppy Wood and the area of Canteen Post.
Photo courtesy of the Imperial War Museum, London, IWM Panorama 558.

rotated into support for a few days but they were back in the line on 25 January. Second Lieutenant Donkersley went back to have another look at Canteen Post, taking Second Lieutenant Simpson with him and six men. He came out of Bird Post ('C' Company), took up a position fifty yards from Canteen Post and observed the patrols moving south of Oppy Wood. The moonlight was very bright that night and they were seen returning and fired on by a machine-gun post.

On the night of the 27/28 January it was decided to stir thing up a little. After Second Lieutenant Donkersley and his band of five men had observed patrols and working parties all around Canteen Post, a brief artillery barrage on the sunken road made the enemy take cover and allowed him to get into position to launch eight rifle grenades into Canteen Post and move quickly back to the British lines.

On the night of 28/29 January he went back again, this time they were fired on as they left Bird Post but still carried out observation on Canteen Post for a few hours. All were back safe by 9:30 p.m.

Writing from a spell in reserve, Arthur Green commented:

> No doubt we are the cream of the Division, in four days in the line we were the first to get prisoners and we were the last to go up the line. C Coy had a Bosche give himself up but we had to scrap for ours. The Bosche came over on a prisoner snatching expedition and all but got one man, another of our lads came along with a revolver result one dead Bosche the

other three fled. We got good identification from the one left
behind, the man who got him I hope will get the MM.[2]

After a spell in reserve, the Battalion's concern with Canteen Post
continued. On 8 February, Lieutenant Geoffrey Skirrow, 'C' Company
commander at the time – went out to Canteen Post with a group,
possibly as a preliminary to a raid. They found disused dugouts in the
sunken road to the north-west and that the road was patrolled. Though
fired on they were unable to see where from. They returned without
casualties.

The enemy had obviously tired of the attention they were getting and
mounted a raid. At 4:30 a.m. on 8 February a sudden barrage of 77-mm
shells hit the front line and a party of twenty men entered Wood Post,
which was held by 'D' Company at the time. Colonel Waddy reported:

> After a sharp fight during which all the garrison of the post
> was either killed or wounded the raiders were driven off but
> succeeded in taking one sergeant and one private with them.
> Apparently the two men captured offered much resistance as
> later one of the captured men was found outside our wire
> dead. He had been shot, stabbed and his head battered in.
> The Lewis gun in number 4 post which was temporarily on
> the flank of its original post enfiladed the enemy and killed 2.
> The total casualties on our side were 2 killed, 7 wounded and
> 1 missing.[3]

The dead were John Griffiths and James Patterson; of the seven
wounded Ernest Sanderson and John Guest died of their injuries. It is
possible that this action was also the origin of the deaths of David
Richardson and Harry Kettlewell who passed on in the following weeks.
George Evenson died of natural causes around this time and was buried
in Aubigny-en-Artois, north-west of Arras.

From the German point of view the raid may have been regarded as
a success – they got a prisoner and identified the Battalion. However
they took at least two killed – the Battalion got the bodies, and stretchers
were seen leaving the German positions so a few more were put out of
action.

The Battalion defence scheme was clear on what to do in these situ-
ations. In Wood Post were one platoon and three Lewis guns. There
was another platoon in close support and a third back in Earl Trench
with a further Lewis gun. Orders clearly stated that the front line was to
be held at all costs and certainly the lead platoon lost an entire section

before help arrived. The Lewis guns along the line would open up to prevent any further attack while the support platoon – which was responsible for local counter-attacks and reinforcement – arrived. Their arrival seems to have persuaded the Germans to depart leaving their dead. As this was on the last night of the Battalion's occupation of this sector, there was no opportunity for revenge.

Arthur Green, 'D' Company at the time, reported laconically: 'Three extra days in the trenches, raided by Bosche knocked out a number, one or two of ours badly injured and one a prisoner.'[4]

The Kaiser's Battle – the 2/5th helps to turn back the final German offensive

The general view is that the German offensive of March 1918 was a final attempt to bring the war to an end before the Americans could bring their resources to bear on the battlefield. It certainly had a massive effect on the fairly stationary warfare that had followed the Cambrai engagement.

From the middle of February the Battalion had been in quiet sectors of the line for a few days, or had been in intensive training. The standard training programme started with individual skills – musketry and fitness. It moved onto specialist training – bombing and Lewis gun work having particular attention paid to them. There were inter company patrol competitions, shooting competitions and, of course, drill. In addition to these, there was training for the whole Battalion in defence, which would prove useful shortly.

The 2/5th was in reserve near Willerval, (near Arras) when the offensive opened. Though not in the front line they did get some of the bombardment and lost three men, Arthur Worrall, William Henshaw and Albert Howes. The main enemy thrust at this time was further south and the Brigade moved towards it at speed. On 23 March they were at Ecurie Wood Camp, on the 24th they moved to Agny and on to Bucquoy and then on the 25th out beyond it to a line between Achiet Le Petit and Logeast Wood. This was a very exposed position and as they were in the rear of the village their left flank was rather open, so they were pulled back to the eastern edge of the village of Bucquoy itself by 8:00 a.m. on 26 March.

Arthur Green recalled the move up:

> We heard about the attack and knew a bit about it but everything was very calm and serene. In time we were relieved and got to a nice comfy camp behind the lines and stayed the night there. Next morning we trekked just a nice mild trek to be a

little more central for anything which might happen. The place we got to and at which we were going to put up for the night was being shelled and most of our billets went up in the air before night so we camped in the open and saved our skins.

The next morning we roused early at about 04:00 and got on the move in half an hour. We looked forward to the day and it was a move into the blue, we dressed up in our best – nice puttees, spurs etc.

By noon we reached our destination and then as events were moving it dawned on us that we might soon be seeing the advancing Bosche. In a very short time we got our equipment in fighting order, got our ammunition and rations and advanced to cover the guns and the retiring tired troops all within ten hours of reveille. So far we went over familiar ground from 1917 areas and finally settled in a suitable ditch or trench. I'm not quite sure where it was . . . . Before dawn we got orders to withdraw a couple of miles; which we did. Then we got into position in front of a village.[5]

Holding the line at Bucquoy

The final position taken up by the Battalion was almost ideal for defence [see map]. Between the edge of the village and the north – south road was a series of fields and scrub woods about 200 yards wide; this gave plenty of room to dig in. On the other side of the road was a slight rise in the ground which allowed a field of fire of about 250 yards from their positions but blocked direct observation of their trenches from enemy observers at any distance. They set up with three companies in line and one in support behind the southernmost which again used the ground well – the swell in the ground was less at this end and a slight rise along the road meant that the support company could engage over the heads of the front company, if required, and had a slightly longer field of fire. The bulk of the position was hidden from observation and thus from direct shellfire.

The Battalion dug in behind the track way, giving themselves good cover from the front, and put the HQ back in the edge of the village where it had good observation of the whole position. HQ contained Colonel Waddy, Lieutenants Stuart, B M Riley (Intelligence) and Sawyer (Transport officer), Captain Riley (the QM) and Captain Pringle (the MO) and Second Lieutenants Kermode (Bombing officer) and Avis (acting adjutant). Hedley Heaton was away. For a period from January until May 1918 he was adjutant of the East Kent

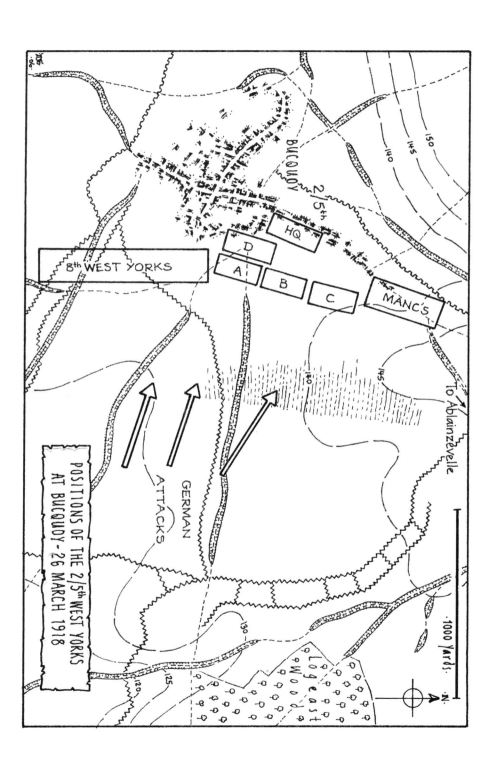

BUCQUOY

150
145
140

2/5th

HQ

8th WEST YORKS

D

A

B

C

MANC'S

To Ablainzevelle

140

145

GERMAN ATTACKS

POSITIONS OF THE 2/5th WEST YORKS AT BUCQUOY – 26 MARCH 1918

130

120

125

Logeast Wood

1000 Yards.

N.

Positions of 2/5th at Bucquoy today, taken from the crest 200 yards in front of the position from which 2/Lt Kermode sniped at the advancing Germans.
Dr M Beggs

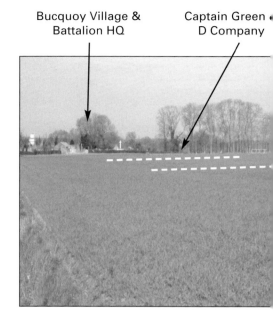

Bucquoy Village & Battalion HQ

Captain Green D Company

Bucquoy in trees

D Coy

A Coy

B Coy

The positions at Bucquoy taken in 1916. The arrow for Bucquoy is in the centres of the 2/5th's positions. The Germans attacked right to left.
Photograph courtesy of Imperial War Museum, London, IWM Panorama 304

Lt. Wilson &
A Company

Captain Anderson &
B Company

Captain Skirrow &
C Company

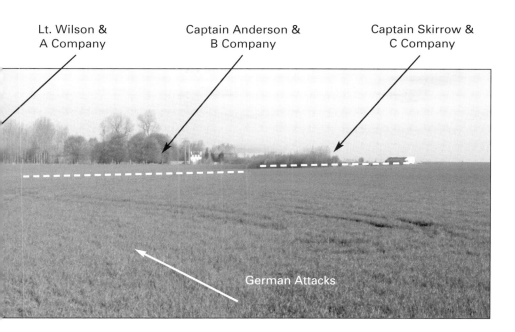

German Attacks

Line of ridge

Ablainzevelle

Coy

German Attacks

Yeomanry (or Mounted Rifles) in Ireland. It is not recorded why.

'A' Company was on the right commanded by Lieutenant E Wilson supported by Second Lieutenants Gould, Pinkerton and De Ville. 'B' Company was in the centre commanded by Captain J M Anderson with Second Lieutenants Willey, De Lacey and McLintock. 'C' Company under Lieutenant Skirrow was on the left with Second Lieutenants Schindler, Foster and Fisher leading the platoons and 'D' under Captain Green behind 'A' in support with Second Lieutenants Wade, Simpson and Bailey.

There was an abundance of wire. The companies set up their machine-gun posts with care and acquired eight machine guns and crews from a unit of the 40th Division that had become detached and was found in their area. Lieutenant Wilson of 'A' Company on the far right put a post with two Lewis guns and one of the machine guns forward of its line in a position to sweep the front of the Battalion position. It would also have a better view of any attack from the direction of the road from Achiet Le Petit.

The Battalion was in touch with 8th West Yorks to the south and sent patrols out to find the Manchesters to the north and bring them into alignment. Around this time appeared a machine-gun officer of the 42nd Division who was without orders. His four guns were added to the support company, 'D', and set up to provide a barrage. The 62nd Divisional MG Company brought two more guns, which were placed with Captain Anderson and 'B' Company, one firing down the valley towards Achiet and one northward along the wire in front of the posi-tion. As the Battalion would have had about thirty-six Lewis guns as a matter of course, plus the eighteen machine guns it had acquired, it now had massive firepower.

As the Battalion was largely defending a reverse slope the view for the 'C' and 'B' Companies was rather obscure and it would have been hard to get advance warning of an attack. Second Lieutenant Kermode had a solution to this. It appears that he took up a position on the far ridge so that he could see beyond the crest and amused himself with sniping until the enemy got too close and then returned to the lines warning of the attack.

He was decorated (a bar to his MC) for his actions in the battle, both for going out under heavy fire to link in the Battalion on the right but also in going forward to provide early warning of the attack – and to encourage his men.

> He earlier crawled out to a position in front of the lines
> and after shooting five of the enemy brought back valuable

information as to their position. He showed fine courage and energy.[6]

The first attack came in at 5:30 a.m. There would be four more attacks that day. John Anderson's 'B' Company was hit hard and two of its guns put out of action but two more were brought up from the support company and the position was held. Shelling was intense between the attacks but it would appear that the enemy believed the Battalion to be on the edge of the village rather than on the track as most of the shells fell there – disrupting communications and breaking telephone wires but not impeding the defence. Battalion HQ, located in the edge of the village must have been a very unpleasant spot.

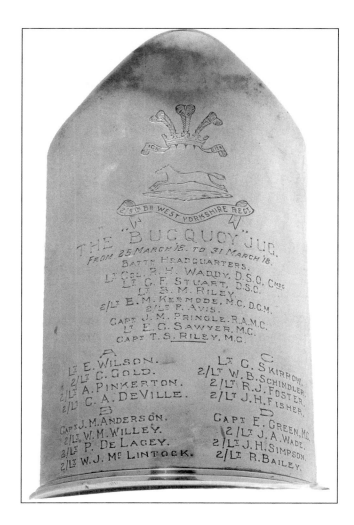

The Bucquoy Jug
– a shell case
inscribed with the
names of all the
officers who
fought in the
action.
Colonel J Waddy

Once the attacks started the enemy artillery had to hold off due to their uncertainly about where the 2/5th actually was and the danger of hitting their own men – probably shelling the village to impede re-inforcements. As far as Captain Green was concerned this allowed him to focus on the business of the infantry battle. Between attacks they sheltered from the barrage and waited for the next round:

> We got into a position in front of a village and dug like fun for 2 hours before the first lot of Bosche came up. Then we had a really good time. A real solid hard fight with rifles and machine guns and no infernal artillery or bombs. Most interesting – we knocked out scores of Bosche and he desisted but during the afternoon he got his guns up and absolutely went mad and blew up and down and from side to side and after each dose he attacked. We held on and beat him back time and time again and that night handed over the line to our successors while we stayed behind to support where we got the shelling and none of the sport.[7]

The Battalion pulled out on the night of 26 March leaving 'C' Company in position, and its place was taken by 2/7th West Yorks. The 2/5th went into support near Rettemoy Farm and stood to throughout the 27th in case they were needed as reinforcements. The weather broke on the 28th and the trenches filled with water but the Brigade was now rotated into reserve at Rettemoy Farm. By 31 March the Battalion was 500 yards behind the line in Biez wood and the defence of Bucquoy was over.

This was a significant battle for the Battalion. At Havrincourt it had shown itself to be capable of a deliberate and rehearsed attack. This was very different. The men had been on the move for some days, they had not had time to be properly fed and the ground they were defending was largely unfamiliar – although any survivors from 1917 would know Achiet Le Petit fairly well. They managed to prepare and conduct a good defence at short notice and use their initiative in acquiring an additional arsenal of machine guns. This largely forgotten engagement was probably the best piece of work the Battalion ever did. They commemorated it by inscribing a shell case, the 'Bucquoy Jug' with the names and appointments of the officers who fought.

It was not without cost. The Battalion had some thirty casualties on 26 March, thirteen of whom were killed outright and another two men killed on the 28th. Over the next two weeks eight more men would die of their wounds. However compared with the casualties of other units in the retreat, this was a light bill and the Battalion had good cause to be pleased with its performance. Sadly many of the orders for this action were verbal and there was little time for record keeping so it is very difficult to identify the actions of individual officers or soldiers during the battle.

The following men lost their lives during this period; Stanley Bowland died of wounds a few days before the battle. On the 26th, Percy Blakey, Charles Brotherton, Arthur Cammidge, Jonas Gledhill, Edward Hackers, Joseph Hawke, Edwards Holmes, William Ironmonger, John Jarvis, Walter Makin, Fred Sadler, Frank Thompson and William Youll were killed. From 27 March until 1 April, William Lucas died and then Harry Sedgewick, George Ball, William Stott, John Driscoll, James Steele, Rupert Walker and Ralph Sykes.

Jonas Gledhill was from Bradford and may have been one of the men transferred in when the 2/6th was disbanded.

> Another edition to the local casualty list is announced, Pte J Gledhill (West Yorks.) of 27 Ashfield Road, Harrogate, having been killed by a shell bursting on his dugout on March 26th. He leaves a wife and two children, and his parents reside in Bradford. He joined up in 1914, and went to the Front a year last January and was wounded on November 20th 1917. He returned to France eight weeks ago. His officer says: 'He died doing his duty like a British soldier and a man. It will comfort you to know that he was well liked and respected by his officers and men of his company, being always cheerful in doing his duty.' His Company QMS says: I can assure you that a better man could not be found. He was very willing to do everything that was asked of him. They were all killed by one shell that burst amongst them. You have my sympathy and I can assure you the same from all who knew Joe. [8]

Private Stott was a Harrogate man:

> Mr. and Mrs. S. Stott, 3 Regent Terrace, Harrogate, have lost another son in the war, Gunner Wm. Stott (West Yorks.) being killed in action on March 28th. The official notice includes the sympathy of their Majesties the King and Queen. Gunner Stott joined up about a year ago, and went to France last November. He was employed by Mr. W. Bonsall, Rose Ville Nurseries, before enlisting. Drum-Major George Procter, writing to the deceased's sister says: - 'It grieves me very much to have to tell you that your dear brother was killed by a shell, along with his

chum named Ball on Thursday March 28th. They were buried side by side in the old British Cemetery at Benvillers by six of my buglers, who sounded the 'Last Post' after the burial service read by two clergymen.' Procter adds that the Company Sergt.-Major is very much grieved and says Willie was a good lad and an expert machine gunner, in which capacity he was acting when he was killed. If it is any consolation to you may rest assured of the fact that he suffered no pain, also that he died a hero, being one of the men of this Division which was the first to stop the advance of the Boche – not only stop him, but hold him up for six days until relieved.

Please convey my deepest sympathy to your family, and accept same yourself. May God grant you strength to bear this great burden.[9]

Back to normal, digging and patrolling

With very little rest the Battalion resumed its basic activity of holding the line, dominating no man's land and making life miserable for the Germans. After a short period of reorganization General Braithwaite conducted an inspection and was pleased with what he found. Throughout April the Battalion was engaged in holding the line near Essart or in improving the reserve and support lines. Their greatest danger was shellfire and during April, eighteen men lost their lives. Wilfred Lamb and Thomas Smith died of their wounds in early April and Frederick Dorrell was killed in action on 9 April. On 12 April, four men were killed outright and another twenty wounded, when a party was hit by a barrage on the rear trench system; Frederick Barker, Ernest Day, Frederick Hillyard, Arthur Ryde, John Astley, Charles Davy, Lawrence Hoyle, and Harry Mark were killed or died of wounds. Three more men died of their wounds over the next week, Samuel Crossland, John Smith and Nathan Longfellow.

The casualties of April reflect the day to day war of attrition. The Battalion was neither patrolling nor in the front line but the constant harassing shelling took a life every couple of days. On 19 April William Bumstead was killed while working on the support line; on the night of the 20/21 April Ernest Russell died of his wounds and the next day Merle Sharratt was caught in a trench mortar bombardment and killed. Even the relief by the 13th KRRC was carried out under shellfire, costing the life of Robert Herring.

Early to mid May was spent at Louvencourt, largely resting and training but with some digging parties out. In this lull, recognitions began to arrive for the work at Bucquoy. On 2 May Second Lieutenant

Simpson received the French Croix De Guerre, most likely for his patrolling work up to Bucquoy where he was generally Second Lieutenant Kermode's companion in no man's land. On 11 May, Corporal J H White of 'A' Company received his MM. Then on 13 May, Lance Corporal Bradley of 'B' Company and Lance Corporal Ewbank of 'D' Company received bars to their MMs while Sergeant Symonds (D), Private W Haigh (B), Private R Cope (A), Private G Rushworth (A), Sergeant Irving (B), Private C E Bryant (D), and Lance Corporal C W Lamb (C, attached Transport section) were all awarded the Military Medal.

On 17 May the Battalion re-entered the lines near Bucquoy for a period of intense patrolling and relieved the 6th Bedfords in the right sub sector at Biez Wood. On arrival they began working on the trenches and on the night of the 18/19 came under machine-gun fire, which caught Frederick Bott as he worked, and killed him.

Reynold Donkersley was patrolling in Biez Wood sector on 20 May, though the record does not give his orders. By this stage the patrol actions in any new area follow a sequence – a few short patrols to get the feel of the ground followed by reconnaissance patrols to locate strong points and obtain identification, then some probing attacks and some bombing to see the reaction. This was followed by a raid toward the end of their time on that stint. On that day Second Lieutenant Donkersley was beginning the sequence and in June 1918 he was awarded the Military Cross for these patrols. The citation reads:

> For conspicuous gallantry and devotion to duty when in command of a fighting patrol sent out to obtain an identification. Two hostile sentries were found to be on the alert. He disposed of one himself but the other escaped. A large enemy party then rushed forward to reinforce the post and hand to hand combat ensued in which he was wounded. He held to his ground and persisted in his endeavours to obtain an identification until forced by superior numbers to retire, which he succeeded in doing after having inflicted heavy casualties on the enemy. By his fine tenacity of purpose and cool leadership he set a fine example to his men.[10]

Between 19 and 23 May the Battalion was shelled every day. In these conditions, it was only a matter of time before a dugout or post was hit. On 21 May this happened and took the lives of Frederick Gunn, John Mills, Willie Wade and Albert Wakeling. This barrage also wounded Second Lieutenant Donkersley, making no man's land temporarily a safer place for the Germans. On 23 May the shelling was again costly as John Dawson, Charlie Swallow and John Bedford were all killed and the following day Fred Bray, Joseph Harrison and John Milner died.

By 24 May the Battalion's patience had run out and Second Lieutenant Kermode entered no man's land to redress the balance. Second Lieutenant Kermode was bombing officer at the time. He was one of the 2/5th's most talented patrol commanders, fluent in German and thus well suited to listening patrols. He now had something more aggressive in mind. The war diary only records that this raid, for which he was awarded the DSO, took place south-west of Bucquoy, in the Biez Wood sector. There is an account from one of the participants. Sergeant Bowman's memories were recorded in an interview in *White Rose* in 1972:

> 2/Lt Kermode had asked to carry out this raid and selected just a few men to accompany him. He stationed Sgt Bowman as the observer for the raid. The party tunnelled into an old communication trench, crawled up to the German post, hurled in a few grenades knocking out the sentries and rushed into the post. The rest of the Germans were in the dugout, but with their arms stacked against the parapet of the trench above. Kermode's party threw the German arms away over the trench top and he went down with a pistol and drove them out and came back with 14 prisoners and the machine guns which we have in our museum.[11]

Second Lieutenant Kermode's parents donated a silver model of the machine gun to the Battalion officers' mess. It is preserved today by the Prince of Wales's Own Regiment of Yorkshire in the TA Centre at Fulford Road barracks. His citation reads:

> For conspicuous gallantry and devotion to duty in carrying out several daring reconnaissances under heavy fire. On one occasion he led his party forward with the greatest courage and gained a hostile outpost capturing many prisoners and a machine gun. Before withdrawing he entirely destroyed the position by placing boxes of enemy bombs in the entrance and igniting them. His courage and fine leadership inspired his men with the utmost confidence and enabled his operations to be entirely successful.[12]

On 25 May Simon Raftery was killed in action. On 29 May Edgar Binns and Ernest Midgely were killed, possibly in an aircraft attack. Despite these losses, May had been successful. June saw the Battalion engaged in heavy patrolling near Fonquevilliers. On 2 June while attending to the wire Thomas Baker was killed in action and the MO's batman went missing but, as Baker was the only man killed that day, he was either made prisoner or later located. On 4 June 'A' Company's listening post was bombed, killing Norman Ratcliffe and wounding one other man. The next day a trench mortar bombardment caught Dennis Gleadall, mortally wounding him. During the rest of June Andrew Riddiough, Wilfred Long and Reginald Hall died of wounds and Harry Jeavons and Alfred Foster were killed in action.

On 11 June Second Lieutenant Kermode MC and Bar, DCM was awarded the DSO for the May raid and Second Lieutenant Donkersley was awarded the MC. On 21 June 4 officers, Lieutenant Sawney MC, Second Lieutenant Bardsely, Second Lieutenant J Hall MC and Lieutenant Stuart Smith, and 147 ORs arrived from the 2/7th. A few days later – in the midst of the Battalion's flu epidemic, came awards of the Meritorious Service Medal to 240010 CSM L Pickard, 266804 Sergeant A Wilson and 200788 Corporal C Molyneux. Colonel Waddy received his DSO for the Bucquoy battle.

Green records the awards to Kermode with enthusiasm:

> One of the subalterns – Kermode – has lately got a bar to his MC for jolly good work and got a DSO and a fortnight's leave for one of the finest raids ever done, and all this with an auto-graphed letter by Sir Julian Byng. He now carries his DSO, MC and Bar and DCM and is worth every one of them.[13]

July also promised to be quiet. There was plenty of time for re-organization and for training. Training on the company level attack took up a significant chunk of time. The Battalion was brought up to its full complement of thirty-six Lewis guns and the gunners were trained intensively.

There was also time for the Battalion Sports competition (won by 'B' Company) and for the Brigade Sports competition. The 3 mile race was won by Second Lieutenant Weston with the Battalion taking 2nd, 3rd, 6th and 7th places as well. Overall the 2/5th won the Brigade sports, taking over half the prize money and was clearly in high fettle. The Officers' Mule Race however was not without risk, Second Lieutenant H Wilcock fell from his mule and injured his back.

The names of the officers involved in the Sports day were recorded with their Companies. At this point - Captain Skirrow was leading 'A' Company, Lieutenant Dickes, who had also stood in as adjutant at times had 'B' Company, Captain Grigson led 'C' Company and Captain Sharpe had 'D' Company. In 'A' Company was Second Lieutenant Wright, in 'B' Company, Second Lieutenant Wilcock. Second Lieutenant Donkersley was in 'C' Company and Second Lieutenant Simpson in 'D' Company. The CSM of 'D' Company was Laycock, and CSM Pickard looked after 'C' Company. This was the organization of the Battalion as it made its way to its last engagement.

Returning wounded meant that a draft of 4 officers and 72 men had to be posted away to get the strength down to 40 officers and 920 men, Second Lieutenants J H Fisher, Nicholson, Thackery and Bailey went to base.

This was the last great flourishing of the 2/5th; they had demonstrated that they had perfected the art of patrolling. In whatever sector it was, the officers would lead out reconnaissance and fighting patrols with regularity and meet with success. They had fought both offensive and defensive battles with great success. They were well led, their morale was high, their losses had been light and they were better prepared for battle than they had ever been.

Now they were ready for their last battle.

Chapter 8
The Advance to Victory

62nd Division moved to support the French Fifth Army
The March offensive in the south had been very successful for the Germans. A large salient had been created on the Marne, south-west of Reims, pushed out as far as Chateau Thierry. The French wanted to cut this off. The March offensive had forced the allies to cooperate more closely and British Divisions were now being moved to support French attacks in parts of the country that they had not seen before. For the Marne battle, British Divisions were promised of which two were the 51st and 62nd. The 51st was formerly the 1st Highland Division and was also a Territorial based formation. It had been in France since May 1915 and had also had a fairly poor start – the HD of Highland Division had once been said to stand for 'Harper's Duds' after the Divisional Commander. However their fighting reputation was enviable by 1918, being highly respected for their aggression. The cloud that had hung over the 62nd was now also far in the past; it was seen as a Division that could be relied upon in the attack.

On the eve of the move south the 2/5th was in good shape. It had professional soldiers in the key command positions and many of the company officers had been promoted from the ranks after distinguishing themselves in combat. There was a strong representation of experienced patrol officers and the training had focused on the sort of aggressive and fluid action they would now go into. They were heavily armed, with extra Lewis guns having been issued, and intensive specialist training had made them perfectly familiar with their equipment. They had taken few casualties, getting off lightly at Havrincourt and at Bucquoy, morale was high and it was with some confidence that they approached their next engagement.

The Division entrained at Doullens over the course of two days from 14 July. The move south took longer than expected. Though there had

been considerable preparation the movement of 18,000 men with
6,000 horses and 1,000 wagons remains at any time a problem. It
would take the Division five hours to march past any one spot and it
occupied fifteen miles of road with each brigade taking 5,000 yards.
The 2/5th marched from billets in Authieule to Doullens, they
detrained at Arcis Sur Aube, and were bussed to Juvigny. They were
ordered to move to Plivot but discovered that it was too small to
accommodate them all and ended up in bivouacs at Bisseul. On 18 July
they were cleaning up and trying to dry off their equipment after a rain-
storm. They also had some time off for swimming. Sadly, however,
Guy Atkinson and Albert Beer of the transport line drowned there. On
19 July, when Horace Rhodes died of his wounds at Vertus and was
buried in the local cemetery, the 2/5th reached St Imoges. Here the
field ambulance was setting up – and from there the officers went
forward to reconnoitre the route up to Pourcy. The briefing for officers
was at 7:30 p.m. on 19 July in St Imoges; the attack was set for
8:00 a.m. the next day

Arthur Green was pleased with his new surroundings:

> We are now living in the open in very charming country, by far
> the finest I have ever seen, grapes figure largely, corn is ripe
> and the vegetation superb. The great battle goes well and we
> can hear the barrages, we are all happy as sand boys and the
> French villagers are full of confidence.[1]

The 2/5th moves up to the attack

The Battalion was to form up in front of Pourcy but there is no easy
route there from St Imoges. The 185th Brigade officers looked at the
good, but longer, route via Nanteuil and the shorter forest route via
Courtagnon. The road from Nanteuil was rejected, possibly because it
would have exposed them to observation from Marfaux, so the men
wended their way along the forest tracks. They set off at 10:00 p.m.,
having been ready to move since 5:30 that morning and it took until
dawn on the 20th for them to arrive at Pourcy. There are no surviving
descriptions of the move up from the Battalion however officers of the
8th West Yorks and the Devons reported a nightmare journey of ever
narrowing roads and track ways with local guides who had no idea of
the destination, language problems, units becoming mixed up and the
Lewis gun teams having to abandon their carts and spares when the
track ways became impassable. It is likely the 2/5th arrived at Pourcy in
similar disorder.

Just in front of Pourcy is a deep gully, with a small stream running

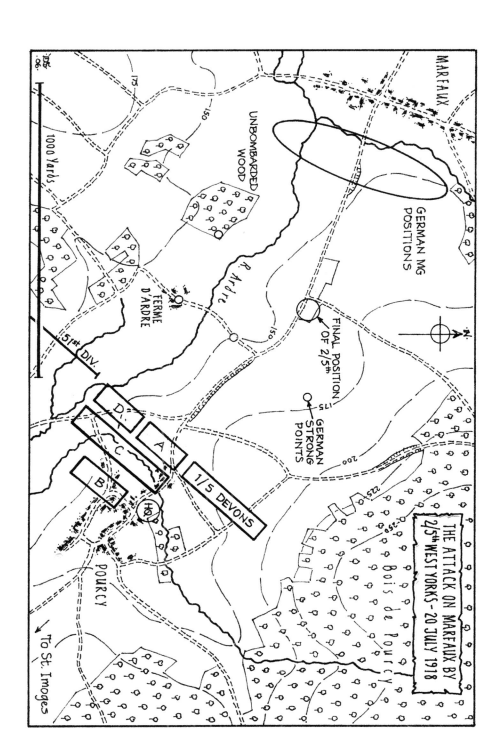

THE ATTACK ON MARFAUX BY
2/5th WEST YORKS - 20 JULY 1918

MARFAUX

GERMAN MG
POSITIONS

UNBOMBARDED
WOOD

R. Ardre

FINAL POSITION
OF 2/5th

GERMAN
STRONG
POINTS

FERME
D'ARDRE

51st DIV.

1000 Yards

D.

C

A

B

HQ.

1/5 DEVONS

POURCY

To St. Imoges

Bois de Pourcy

N.

175
150
150
150
175
200
225
250

90
105

Looking from the start line toward Marfaux.

The Ardre Valley from Pourcy to Marfaux.

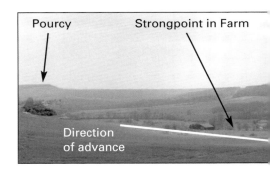

south-west. The Battalion formed up there in the dead ground. To the left was the river Ardre – described as a 'small stream' at the time – high summer having depleted it. The 2/5th was the left flank of the Division – the next unit was part of the 51st Division. There is no record of whether the 2/5th was in touch with them on the left; it seems likely, given the next set of events, that they did not advance side by side. Their boundary to the right was the Pourcy-Mafaux road, the 8th West Yorks would advance on their right on the higher ground, with the 1/5th Devonshires in support behind them both.

There were some immediate causes for concern in the intended conduct of the attack. There was no time to reconnoitre the ground. Most of the officers were seeing the terrain for the first time along with their men as they started forward. This was compounded by a shortage of maps; where these were available they were badly out of date to the

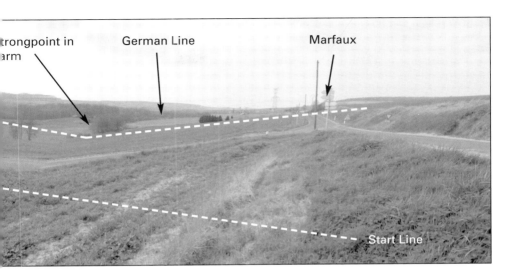

point that copses existed on the ground that were not shown on the maps. The Battalion was not supported by the 62nd Division's own artillery – the barrage was laid by French and Italian guns. While the individual quality of these gunners may have been high, the basics of communicating with them were untried. As there was such uncertainty about where exactly the friendly troops were, they laid the barrage 1,000 yards ahead of the believed positions. It would appear that the guns firing were also of light calibre, one officer refers to them as 77-mm, which are unlikely to be able to break open well entrenched positions, in the event that they did hit them. German morale appears to have been good; if British High Command believed the Germans were about to lose the war, this belief was not shared by the defenders of Marfaux. German positions were well prepared and had not been located by photo reconnaissance or by patrols. Rather than a long line of wired trenches their defence was based on a depth of individual machine-gun posts well dug in and camouflaged. Numerous accounts of this phase of the war praise the professionalism and courage of the German machine-gun units. They were now to be attacked by troops who had been under arms all day and walked all night with disorientated officers unsupported by tanks, aircraft or effective artillery.

The Attack

The gap between the river and the road is narrow; the Battalion advanced on a front of a few hundred yards. Colonel Waddy put 'A' Company on the right parallel to the road and 'D' on the left with its flank on the river. 'C' was in support and 'B' behind that in reserve. As planned, at 8:00 a.m. they moved off towards Marfaux. The ground still had corn on it, which provided some cover from observation, but as they crested the first rise it became clear that the barrage had not been effective. The village itself, the rises before the village and the woods on the left all contained active machine-gun posts.

Captain Grigson and 'A' Company were on the right, by the road. Shielded by the rolling ground for the first few hundred yards they passed a small crest and were then exposed on a forward slope to the gunners at Marfaux and enfiladed from the left by the gunners in a wood over the river. They got to a series of shell holes about half way to Marfaux and took cover on the right of the road but were no longer an effective fighting unit by the time they got there. At some time around 10:00 a.m. Second Lieutenant C Gould of 'A' Company got a message back to Lieutenant B M Riley (Intelligence Officer) who sent back to Battalion HQ:

> 2/Lt Gould (A Company) reports that only about 20 men A Company left, wants instructions. Dukes appear to have passed him on the left, and Hants on the right. He is not in touch with any others of the 2/5th W. Yorks.[2]

'D' Company was on the left, on flat land down by the river where there was least protection offered by the ground. Here they were closest to the wood, which was on the Divisional boundary and had been entirely missed by the artillery and was not under attack by the 51st Division. The Battalion set about taking out the machine-gun posts with a combination of Lewis gun and rifle grenades but it diverted them from their line of attack and broke up the leading companies.

Lieutenant Bardsley was commanding one of the forward platoons. He won the MC for his attempts to deal with the machine-gun positions:

He worked forward with one man and opened enfilading fire with a Lewis Gun on an enemy machine gun which he put out of action with casualties to the team. The platoon that had been checked was then able to advance. He was wounded in performing this gallant action.[3]

Despite these local successes, the situation in 'D' Company had also become critical. Second Lieutenant Waugh was hit and made his way back to Battalion HQ; his company only had one officer left at this point and the men had suffered heavily. They were holding on to what they had got. Second Lieutenant R B Walker commanding 'D' Company had only six West Yorks men left by 11:00 a.m. He sent a message back by runner:

> Am occupying 2 shell holes SE of Chamuzy, only 6 men of ours left and 8 men and 1 officer of the Devons, in touch with Hants on the right (150 yards) and but nobody on the left. What am I to do? At present holding and consolidating.

He described himself as being south-east of Chamuzy, rather than Marfaux which may have been the confusion of battle or may be that he had no map. By 12:30 p.m. he had found a few more men and was mixed up with the Hampshires as they had come forward and been hit by the same machine-gun barrage. A further message came back:

> Have sent 3 messages for reinforcements as I have only 16 OR (10 West Yorks, 6 Devons) and 1 Devons officer, am holding 3 shell holes 900 yards right of Chaumuzy and in rear am consolidating. MG fire very heavy from ridges on all sides am in touch with Hants on right and left in very small numbers. What am I to do as it is impossible for me to go forward owing to small numbers?

The last message from 'D' Company, sent around the same time reads:

> 2 officers wounded and 1 cannot be found. I am slightly wounded in the foot myself.
> Snipers on all sides.[4]

Second Lieutenant J H Simpson, an experienced patrol commander, was already wounded at this point as was Lieutenant Sawney. The missing officer is likely to have been Lieutenant Schindler, who was probably already dead.

'C' Company in support came forward to assist 'A' and 'D' Companies, crossing the same deadly open ground. Second Lieutenant Gwynn of 'C' Company was soon the only officer left in his company. He returned to Battalion HQ in person, despite the shellfire, to report that he was now in touch with the 51st Division. The 5th Hampshires – who were to pass through his position – were also held up and he had formed a line with the remnants of the Battalion, which now mustered about thirty men per company. It would appear that the surviving men of 'C' Company had been pushed right, perhaps moving up under cover of the knoll in the centre of the battlefield to escape from the enfilading fire and ending up on top of the survivors of 'A' Company by the road. The estimated casualties at this point were already 400 men and Second Lieutenant Donkersley was dead.

The embattled forward companies called upon their reserves and Lieutenant Dickes led 'B' Company into action and was soon in trouble; Second Lieutenant McLintock, reported back:

> Lt Dickes and 2/Lt De Lacey became casualties shortly after we attacked. I am occupying a shell hole with 16 men. We have no stretcher bearers and . . . [illegible] is badly wounded and unable to walk – can you send assistance?[5]

But assistance was not to come. The rolling nature of the ground meant that reinforcements from the reserve company were also exposed to fire and it was reduced to less than thirty men. Also the relay posts designed to bring information back had been wiped out. Back at Battalion HQ in Pourcy it became clear to Colonel Waddy that his Battalion was being destroyed and that the attack was stalled. He wrote to the commandant of the French 86th Regiment for help:

> The attack is being held up in front of Marfaux – we have suffered heavy casualties and the enemy is reported to be collecting in the valley between Marfaux and the Bois the Pourcy.[6]

The 7th Argyles finally attacked the wood on the boundary but it was too late for the 2/5th. 'A' and 'D' Companies of the 2/4th Duke of Wellington's had come up on the left and the 2/4th Hampshires on the right but no one was going forward. They were all under heavy shell-fire. Most of all the Battalion needed a protective barrage but there seems to have been no clear way to organize this. At around 11:45 a.m. the Division had moved its reserve Brigade around to the right to exploit the success of the 187th Brigade further north and so come at Marfaux from the flank and rear. No further reinforcements came into the frontal attack and the units there were told to hold on.

Battalion HQ was not idle. A number of officers who were not commanding companies moved forward to help. Lieutenant Bernard Riley, the intelligence officer was on attachment from the 1/6th Battalion West Yorks. He was a pre-war territorial, who had seen service in France in 1915 and 1916. Many of the messages that did get back to Battalion had reached Lieutenant Riley's forward position; he had set himself up so that he could oversee the battle and was able to watch the units on the flanks as well as his own Battalion. He won the MC that morning:

> He went forward repeatedly under heavy artillery and machine gun fire to obtain information and later on he volunteered to go out under fire from machine guns and snipers to reconnoitre the front which he did with great success, bringing back complete information to his commanding officer.[7]

As the officers in the field were killed off, Acting Captain J C Airey, one of the most long standing and experienced officers in the Battalion, moved forward. It would appear he reached the front line and took command of what he could find. His MC citation states:

> For conspicuous gallantry and initiative. He made a reconnaissance under heavy machine-gun fire to the front of our position, bringing back valuable information and keeping in touch with allied troops on our flank. It was largely due to his courage and clear appreciation of the situation that the positions captured were so quickly consolidated.[8]

Captain Reginald White was also in harm's way. His role in the Battalion is not recorded but he was shot through the chin and jaw by a round from a machine gun which puts him close to the action. At dusk, Second Lieutenant Gwynn proceeded to the outpost line and collected the odd groups holding shell holes and organized the defence. He produced a hand drawn map, which shows that the Battalion was concentrated on the Pourcy – Marfaux road having advanced about 700 yards. They were now down to sixty men in total. His MC citation for this action reads:

Under a heavy bombardment he collected and reorganized the remnants of various temporary posts, and getting in touch with units on both flanks he established a good defensive position. His coolness under heavy artillery and machine gun fire was worthy of great praise.[9]

The Battalion was to be relieved on the night of the 20th, however the message did not reach them so the remaining sixty men hung on. They were finally withdrawn on 22 July. The final position of the 2/5th is 750 yards south-east of Marfaux – which raises speculation about whether the officers reporting a similar position near Chamuzy simply did not know which village was in front of them. This position is also the site of the Commonwealth War Graves cemetery and may therefore have been the largest concentration of bodies.

In all eighty-five men died outright on 20 July, over twice the loss suffered at Bullecourt. The toll among the officers was high. Captain Grigson, Second Lieutenant De Ville and Second Lieutenant Donkersley were killed. Wounded were Captain R F White, Lieutenants Dickes and Waugh, Second Lieutenants De Lacey, Sawney, Bardsley,

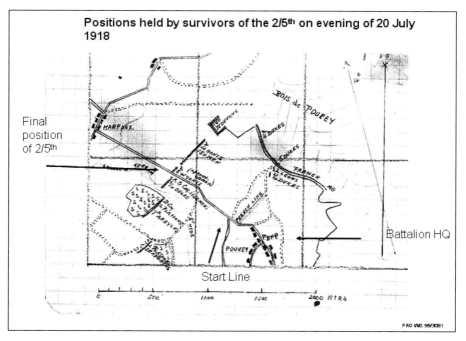

Map of the positions held by survivors of the 2/5th on evening of 20 July 1918. *National Archives WO95/3079*

The resting place of most of the 2/5th's casualties in Marfaux.

Simpson and Walker. Second Lieutenant Schindler was missing at the end of the day and was later found dead.

Kenneth Grigson MC was on attachment from the 7th Devons and had been with the Battalion since before it came to France. An undergraduate at Durham University and a member of the OTC when the war broke out, he enlisted as a private soldier in October 1914, was a sergeant by February 1915 and was commissioned in March 1915. His MC was gazetted on 3 June 1918 but it is not known for which action. He lies in Marfaux Cemetery.

William Barron Schindler was born in Bradford and attended Belle Vue School, next to the barracks of the 6th Battalion. The son of a naturalized British subject originally from Switzerland, he had enlisted as a private soldier on 19 September 1914 in 1/6th West Yorks. He had been wounded in July 1915 by shrapnel in the head and he was sent home in July 1916 with gunshot wounds to his right thigh, taken on the first day of the Somme. He was commissioned on 26 June 1917, posted to the 2/5th and is buried in Marfaux Cemetery.

Reynold Donkersley, of whom little more is known than he was from Almonbury in Huddersfield – his records having been lost – is also buried among his men in Marfaux.

Charles Arthur De Ville was from Loughbrough and was married. At the time of his death his son Wilfred Arthur De Ville was 17 months old.

The bodies of soldiers lost on that day were mostly recovered. They lie in Marfaux cemetery, not far from where they fell.

Leonard Allison
Albert Banks
Arthur Barnett
Tom Bentley
John Bromfield
Robert Brown
Joseph Busfield
James Coggan
Arthur Doyle
Cyril Eldridge
Harold Freeman
Ernest Grimbleby
Harry Hoare
Ernest Jones
Thomas Lidster
Henry Lyons
Sidney Moran
James O'Melia
Henry Pattinson
John Plant
Herbert Pratt
William Rowland
Sidney Simpson
Robert Stanger
Harold Taylor
James Thacker
Percy Tunnicliffe
Robert Waldby
Robert Young

William Appleby
Ernest Barker
Harry Beaumont
William Bird
George Brown
George Burgess
Frank Caldecoat
John Deacon
Ernest Drew
George Elvidge
James Gartland
Leonard Harris
George Hubbard
Percy Keightley
Horace Littlewood
Arthur Martin
Frederick Mosey
William Parnaby
Ernest Pearce
Daniel Poole
Ernest Pycock
Lewis Seymour
Cyril Slater
Allan Swift
John Taylor
Herbert Thornton
Fred Upshaw
Tom Welton

George Ashworth
Henry Barker
William Bell
Bernald Bisby
John Brown
John Burman
Arthur Coates
Fred Doughty
William Ducket
Samuel Ford
Alfred Greenwood
Geoffrey Hewson
Francis Hutchinson
William Laycock
Joseph Lynch
Robert Merrick
Harry Neville
George Parsons
Harry Pickard
Ernest Poutney
Edward Randall
William Shaw
Thomas Stephenson
James Swinscoe
Thomas Taylor
Albert Thorpe
Allen Vernon
Frank Wilson

Very little is known of most of these men. Some were long standing members of the Battalion – Harry Lyons who was killed by shellfire on the 20th, had been awarded the Military Medal in June. He was in 'A' Company whose officers were largely wiped out, and one of his comrades wrote to his parents:

> He was loved by everyone in the Company, from the Captain (who I am sorry to say was also killed) to the youngest recruits. Rest assured that those of us who are left will never forget him, for no one will be missed more than Harry.[10]

Harry Lyons MM.
Don Jackson

Harry's brother was a prisoner at the time and he had two other brothers serving with the forces.

Some were newer to the Battalion. Signaller A W Swift of 'D' Company had arrived with the draft from the disbanded 2/7th less than a month before the battle. He had originally joined the 15th West Yorks – Leeds Pals – in September 1914 and had been wounded in the summer of 1917 and sent to Harrogate to recover. He used the quiet time in July well, painting a number of watercolours and learning French. The photograph of his grave gives some idea of the appearance of the Marfaux cemetery just after the war.

For Captain Reginald White, this was his second wounding. He was a solicitor from Whitby and had enlisted early in the war, gone to France with the 1/5th and been hit by shrapnel in both thighs in September 1916. He came to the 2/5th in late 1917.

Second Lieutenant Raymond Walker was back in England by 24 July 1918 with a gunshot wound to his left foot. He had been a sergeant with the 2/8th and was recommended for a commission in April 1917. When wounded he was 32 years old. He recuperated with the 3/5th and then returned to the front in the 9th West Yorks – now commanded by Colonel Waddy. On 4 November 1918 he was captured but released on the 11th.

Second Lieutenant John Wade's life may have been saved by an acci-

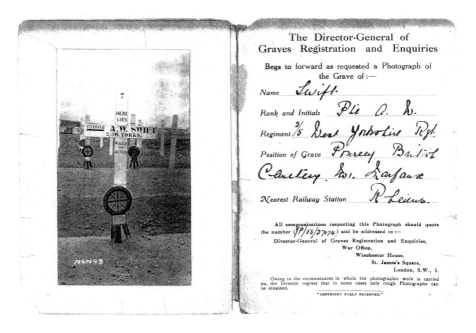

The Director-General of
Graves Registration and Enquiries

Begs to forward as requested a Photograph of
the Grave of :—

Name   *Swift.*

Rank and Initials   *Pte A. W.*

Regiment *2/5 Dent Yorkshire Rgt.*

Position of Grave   *Pourcy British*

Cemetery No. I. Lasaux

Nearest Railway Station   *R Leeus.*

All communications respecting this Photograph should quote
the number (P/55/2774) and be addressed to :—
Director-General of Graves Registration and Enquiries,
War Office,
Winchester House,
St. James's Square,
London, S.W., 1.
Owing to the circumstances in which the photographic work is carried
on, the Director regrets that in some cases only rough Photographs can
be obtained.
"COPYRIGHT FULLY RESERVED."

Signaller Swift, D Company 2/5th West Yorks.
Robert Carrington

dent for he was unable to take part in the attack on Marfaux due to an injury of his hand. Wartime discipline being strict on 'accidental and self inflicted wounds' Colonel Waddy had to report on the incident. It took place on 13 July 1918 and was examined sometime after the battle, however gathering evidence was difficult:

> All witnesses of the case are casualties in recent operations but from verbal information received at the time it would appear that Wade cut his hand opening a bottle.[11]

Poor communication and poor preparation

The reasons why this attack went so badly wrong are clear. The British Army at the time had created a formula for success based on the close cooperation of tanks, artillery and infantry; tanks were needed to take on strong points, a close barrage was needed to protect the infantry from the machine guns until they were right on top of them and to provide counter-battery fire to suppress the enemy barrage. From the infantry point of view they learned over and over that unless they advanced in line with other units they were going to get into trouble. Some of these problems could be worked out on the day using trench mortars and machine guns to provide local barrages but if any major element of this mix was not present there would be huge casualties and likely failure.

In this case there were additional elements – the lack of preparation for the attack. Even if it was not possible to rehearse attacks in the way they were used to on the Somme, the lack of time for reconnaissance meant that the officers were unable to manage the battle in the way they had at Havrincourt or Bucquoy. For this Battalion in particular this was a tragedy. There were any number of officers who could have led patrols to locate the machine-gun posts. The front they were advancing on was a few hundred yards wide, a delay of one night would have pinpointed the opposition and allowed for either a decent barrage or dedicated parties to destroy them.

The number of the officers actually taking part is also significant. Standing orders at the time stated that only two out of four company commanders were to go into battle:

> Only 20 Officers per battalion are to be taken into the line. Seconds in Command and 2 Company Commanders per battalion will be left at their Battalion wagon line.[12]

In the reports from companies no mention is made of Captain Sharpe who a week previously had commanded 'D' Company, nor of Captain Skirrow who had 'A' Company, nor were they among the wounded. Captain Sharpe was a highly experienced officer both as a combat soldier and as an administrator. He was a company secretary before the war and was 25 years old when he joined the 13th Worcesters in August 1914 and stayed until he was commissioned in January 1915. He then had a series of staff postings until active service with 1 Royal Inniskillings at Gallipoli. He was wounded in July 1915, and in October 1915. In July 1916 he went to 2/5th and requested to stay with them when they went overseas as he felt he had had a significant role in training them. He was acting adjutant and captain in 2/5th from February 1918. After the war he stayed on with TF and resigned due to work commitments in 1921 in Worcester.

It is likely that these officers were left in the wagon lines while their juniors fought their companies. Higher Command may have had some insight into what was about to take place and would not lose all its experienced leaders in a day. Although experienced officers were in the line they became casualties so quickly that the others were left without leadership. Against such professional opposition, once the key officers were incapacitated the Battalion was unable to manoeuvre. Against heavily camouflaged and dug in machine guns, the Lewis guns and rifle grenades of the infantry had little chance. Without tank and air support and unable to call down accurate artillery fire there was little to do but stay in shell holes and wait for relief.

No narrative of operations by Colonel Waddy has survived for this period. Lieutenant Colonel Bastow of the 1/5th Devons however appended to his narrative a set of eleven points for consideration. Given that this was in the last few months of the war it is hard to read these quite gently phrased observations to Brigade in anything other than a critical tone:

> The following points appeared to me as worth remembering in any future operations of a similar nature.
>
> 1.   The absolute necessity of giving battalion commanders time to reconnoitre the terrain thoroughly before they issue their orders for the attack.
> 2.   The grave danger in trying to capture strong points in a valley before making good the heights on either side.
> 3.   The necessity of the closest liaison between the infantry and artillery and especially so when the artillery is that of another nation.
> 4.   The great value of tanks in attacking through fields of standing corn where staunch machine guns could lie up in shell holes and wipe out a platoon without being discovered.
> 5.   The necessity of holding woods subjected to severe hostile gun fire with a large number of small posts well scattered about, an automated rifle in each post.
> 6.   In woods fighting the great value of 'abattis' wire to shepherd the attackers to ground covered by M. G. fire.
> 7.   The dangers in using known paths and tracks in woods was most noticeable. They were all continuingly struck by enemy gun fire.
> 8.   Apparently it is almost impossible to capture a wood without the support of a large volume of gun fire.
> 9.   The value of small M.G. or Lewis Gun posts placed in corn fields in advance of the main M.G. or strong point.
> 10.   The great difficulty of intercommunications between units and Brigade.
> 11.   The difficulty of fixing on a Battalion HQ beforehand in open warfare was most noticeable.[13]

The conclusion from this analysis is that the Germans had conducted a well planned defence and the Brigade had thrown away most chances of success before it set out from St Imoges.

Arthur Green took the long view of their activities or perhaps he may also not have known the full picture when he wrote home on 23 July:

> I have just returned from the greatest battle our Division has ever fought, for 4 days it has raged and other people are still carrying on. Bear in mind it is not the Bosche that are attacking but we and we are doing it to some tune and prisoners come in galore. I can't tell you where we are of course but we are taking part in the great battle, probably the decisive battle of the war. What happened at Chateau Thierry, I don't know but on our part we are going at it hammer and tongs and the number of prisoners we are fetching in is a good mark.
>
> I have been rather lucky for I have been with the brigade during the whole of the show as a liaison officer with a neighbouring Division, a most interesting but not very dangerous job.

This paragraph concludes with perhaps the most chilling remark in the hundreds of pages of Arthur Green's letters. The man who had corresponded so movingly with John Winterburn's widow finishes his description of the engagement at Marfaux with a perfunctory:

> In the battalion I have lost many friends but that has to be.[14]

He then goes on to describe the weather and the pleasant fields they have been marching through.

The final act
The battle was not over. The German artillery had a pretty good idea of where the troops would be preparing for the next assault. Between 21 and 23 July a further ten men died of wounds or were killed by shell-fire. Second Lieutenant B M Riley was wounded, hit in the right arm and shoulder; he took a fever and was evacuated to England on 30 July, the shaky signature on his transfer forms attests to the damage. Leonard Scott, Charles Mason, Thomas Bradley, William Brogden, Ernest Fox, Frederick Newitt, William Whiting, David Johnson, Loftus Layfield and Harry Gaunt all died.

Loftus Layfield was from Pateley Bridge, David Johnson from

Scotton and was a veteran of Bullecourt. The time when the deaths of soldiers were marked by the printing of exchanges of letters and messages from comrades and officers had passed; a fairly standard few lines with a couple of personal remarks was the most a soldier would get by the summer of 1918:

> A telegram was received on Thursday morning by Mrs. Layfield, Church Street, Pateley Bridge, stating that her husband, Pte. Loftus Layfield, had been seriously wounded, and later in the day another wire was received conveying news of his death. Pte. Layfield was very well known throughout Nidderdale. He was a draper in business in Church Street, the business now being carried on by his wife. His death will be very much regretted by all who knew him, and deep sympathy will be felt for his widow and little girl.[15]

> Mrs. David Johnson, of Manor Farm, Scotton, received intimation from the War Office on Friday morning that her husband, Pte. David Johnson (West Yorks.), eldest son of Mr. and Mrs. B. Johnson, had died from wounds on July 23rd. Pte. Johnson went out at the same time as the late 'Bob' Preston and 'Jack' Joy, two Harrogate lads, in September 1916, having joined up in June of that year. He was slightly wounded at the time Bob Preston was killed, and assisted in laying his old comrade to rest. He was wounded again on May 3rd 1917, and came home that time returning to the Front on July 26th 1917.[16]

On 24 July the 2/5th pulled back to a valley behind Pourcy to reorganize; this seems to have thrown the enemy artillery off for a while so that there were no deaths on the 24th – the narrow valley seems to have protected them. However they were found on the 25th. As the Companies relieved the 3/86th Regiment (French) in front of Pourcy, the baggage and wagon lines were located and shelled killing two men out right and wounded three more – one mortally. As men continued to die of wounds from the previous engagement, the death toll that day was Frederick Brown, Fred Annakin, Henry Halliday and Charles Wilding.

Fred Annakin got his few lines:

> Official intimation has been received of the death of Pte. F Annakin (West Yorks.) of Knaresborough, who was killed in action in France on July 25th. He was the second son of Mr. and Mrs. F. Annakin, York Place, and was one of four brothers

serving, one of whom is a prisoner of war in Germany.[17]

On 25 July the Battalion reorganized into composite companies with 'B' Company made up of the remnants of 'B' and 'D', and 'A' Company made up of 'A' and 'C'. The next day, while in position in Pourcy, 5 or 6 officers and 246 other ranks arrived – Second Lieutenants Barrett, Cole, Jennings, Reed and Banks and, for some reason, Second Lieutenant Jennings is recorded again. Proper reorganization was impossible in this position. The Battalion was at full strength before arriving at Marfaux, during the week it had lost a little over 100 men killed. There are no casualty reports but if the usual ratio is applied, there were probably another 300 wounded, something like half the total Battalion, or two thirds of its fighting strength. Alfred Davis was killed in action that day.

On 27 July Second Lieutenant Kermode was mortally wounded by shellfire in Pourcy. He was evacuated back through the dressing station at St Imoges, where he is buried. Edgar M Kermode was originally in the 1/6th Battalion West Yorks. He enlisted on 25 August 1914 and went to France on 15 April 1915. He reached Lance Sergeant No. 2190

The resting place of 2/Lt Kermode at St Imoges.

and was commissioned into 5th West Yorks on 27 March 1917. He died of his wounds in 2/1st West Riding Field Ambulance. His father wrote requesting particulars of his death and whether any one had recorded any last message but there is no record of any reply.

Walter Atkinson expired from his wounds on the same day.

On 28 July the assault on the Mont De Bligny started. This was carried out famously by the 8th Battalion West Yorks and it was for this action that the unit was awarded the Croix De Guerre – one of the very few times that this honour was given to an entire British battalion. The attack went off well and the 2/5th was only marginally involved, with 'A' Company requested to move forward and act as a defensive flank for the 5th Devons. The Battalion then provided two companies to the 8th Battalion and two to the Devons to assist in consolidating the position. One of these platoons occupied the wood on the reverse slope of the hill able to cover out to the east and west of the position. Number 16 Platoon was sent forwards to support 'Naylor's Post' held by Lieutenant H R Burrows of the 8th West Yorks. He recalled in his diary the situation in the small hut immediately in front of 16 Platoon's position:

> There is nothing so harrowing as an ear splitting nerve racking bursting of trench mortar shells, such as began in the early afternoon. The little stone hut began to shake as shell after shell burst round it. We sought shelter on what we considered was the safe side of the building, for as a T.M. shell comes down vertically this, after all, was only moral protection. Then to our discomfort and astonishment French or Italian 77's directed battery fire against our unfortunate residence, and four shells burst at the very entrance. We sought shelter at the other side of the building. This was all very well until both the Trench Mortars and the 77's set to work at the same time. We returned to find our dinners covered with portions of the hut, though most of the structure still remained intact.[18]

William Edwards was killed in this action.

On 29 July it was found that the enemy still occupied a strip of old French trenches on the left of the Mont De Bligny. How this came about was also recorded by Lieutenant Burrows:

> During the morning GSO2 paid a visit to the stone hut bringing along with him a sensible map. On it were shown two small woods of identical shape and both on the same side of

the hill. We argued long over the position of one of these woods but I had to admit it in the end that our flank should have gone as far as the second wood. Of course our maps had not shown the wood or the trees in the wood. We had secured an old line of trenches on the far side of the Montange and we had been content. However he presented us with his map and this we guarded with zealous care. Later in the day a company of 2/5th West Yorkshires under Captain Green MC attacked and captured the second small wood – about 150 yards away. [19]

Orders were received at 6:30 a.m. for this attack to go in at 7:45 a.m. 'D' Company carried it out. This strip of trench is in dead ground to the summit of the Mont, from it the forward slopes of the Mont can be fired on and thus observation of the valley and on to Sarcy can be prevented. This had happened to Lieutenant Burrows as snipers crawled up into the wood. It would appear there were artillery observers there as well, for the accuracy of the fire laid down on 8th West Yorks was very good. The first objective for the attack was the trench itself and the second was a position 150 yards beyond it where a good observation of Sarcy could be obtained. It was not clear whether there was a trench system or any physical feature that marked the second objective. The war diary reads:

> First Objective was captured but two platoons who went for the second objective have not been heard of since, from the very little evidence obtained from a wounded man these platoons appear to have lost direction and been captured. . . . 2/Lt Cole killed, about 6 men wounded, 2/Lt Jennings and 45 other ranks missing and 20 men slightly gassed by enemy barrage which was very heavy.

Captain Green was back in command of 'D' Company for the attack. He wrote a note for Battalion HQ at 10:45 a.m:

> Have got 1st Objective OK and hold in great strength with additional help of 8th West Yorks who are holding part.
> 2nd Objective very obscure. Have completely lost touch at present with Jennings and his 2 platoons who were to take it. I think they have gone too far to the left and got down the steep bank i.e. west of the M of the Montange De Reims. I have been to our proper 2nd objective and encountered some Bosche so he is not there. Am trying to get second objective with men left.

The final attack by Capt Green in which 2/Lts Cole and Jennings were killed, looking south from Naylor's post.

Casualties light except for Jennings and his missing men who will I expect turn up soon. Cole killed – reported so.[20]

When Green wrote home he described himself as having been on one occasion surrounded by Boche and forced to run very quickly indeed. It would seem likely that this was during his attempts to locate Jennings and his platoon.

However Jennings and his men did not turn up and the casualty list was much longer than expected. Cole and Jennings had not had time to be properly posted to the 2/5th, they had only arrived a matter of days before and are buried under headstones from their original regiments. Many of the missing from that day were buried in the same cemetery at Chambrecy, about 100 yards from the bottom of the steep slope Green described. It seems that these platoons slid off down this slope and were caught in the valley below where they would have been very exposed. The remnants of 'D' Company were relieved next day and the Battalion reunited at Chamuzy. On 31 July they were back where they started at St Imoges.

William Thomas Cole may have recognized some of the men around him when he arrived in Pourcy. He had joined the West Yorks at Colliergate Drill Hall in York in June 1915 then aged 18 years 8 months. The attesting officer was Lieutenant Hedley Heaton. He became 201409 Sergeant Cole and went to France in March 1917. He was wounded in May 1917 and rejoined the Battalion in August, in 'A'

Stone Hut / First objective – Strip Wood / Jenning's route / Direction of attack

Company. He was sent home for a commission in December 1917 and obtained it in May 1918 with the 4th Battalion Yorkshire Regiment. He was unmarried and his effects were left to his mother in Ripon.

William Jennings remained missing until 10 December 1918. Word was received then that his pay book was returned in September to the Central Office for Effects. His name was on a list sent via the Red Cross from Germany. In September 1919 his mother received a further letter:

> Secretary of the War Office presents his compliments to Mrs F Jennings and begs to inform her that certain effects belonging to the late 2/Lt W. Jennings Yorkshire Regiment have been returned to this country by the German Government through diplomatic channels including 126 francs which were credited to the estate.[21]

Jennings had died on 1 August 1918 and was buried in the military cemetery at Guyencourt. He left 125 francs, 1 cigarette case with 1.45 cents, 1 penny, 1 book, 3 tobacco pipes, 2 knives with whistles, 1 bracelet and some letters. He had joined the Yorkshire Regiment aged 19 in September 1914 and had gone to France in August 1915. He had returned to the UK for his commission in October 1917. He got off the boat at Boulogne on 8 July and went to the holding camp at Etaples for two weeks and then set out for the 2/5th Battalion on the 24th spending two days on the journey. William Jennings was with the

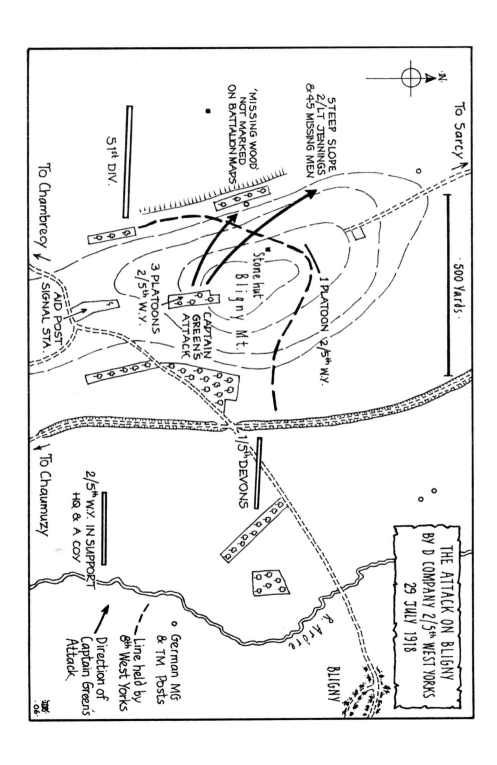

THE ATTACK ON BLIGNY
BY D COMPANY 2/5th WEST YORKS
29 JULY 1918

Battalion less than a week and was taking part in his first engagement as an officer.

The final action of the 2/5th cost the lives of a further twenty-two men; Ernest Irvine, Joe Sykes, Thomas Whincup, Arthur Williamson, Walter Whetstone, George Allinson, Robert Barker, Clifford Campbell, Ernest Chadwick, Alfred Dent, Norman Feather, Edwin Harvey, John Johnson, Walter Magson, Harold Snell, Walter Spivey, Joseph Teasdale, Gilbert Tyler, Ebenezer Watson, Fred Robertshaw, Herbert Sharp and Ernest Butler.

Thomas Whincup barely gets a mention.

> Private T. Whincup (West Yorks.) of Fisher Gardens, Knaresborough has died of wounds in France.[22]

The final verdict

From a strategic point of view, the 'Champagne Show' as Captain Green referred to it was a considerable success.

> It has been an eventful three weeks just one point will show you how up and down it has been. Only once during all that time and then only from 9 to 2am have we had billets. All the other nights we have either slept in trains, in buses under the trees or in cellars of deserted houses or else as often happened spent the night moving. The men naturally have been pretty hard at it, apart altogether from the hard fighting for the only protection in the front is underground. Consequently every move meant hacking out sufficient earth either off the flat or out of a bank if you are lucky to have one facing the right way and when you move two or even three times a night as sometimes happens it is hard work and probably you may attack next morning.
>
> Our results are great and I am not divulging secrets when I say we have taken a not inconsiderable part in flattening that great German salient between Soissons and Rheims. The French were very pleased with us and everyone is hugely satisfied. We have remade the good name we got at Cambrai and Bucquoy and have added fresh laurels to the West Riding troops.[23]

General Braithwaite wrote to his men. His tone of admiration, pride and enthusiasm is in contrast to many of the rather stilted and formal notes of congratulation that one finds elsewhere:

The Operations which commenced on the 29th July were brought to a successful termination at midnight on the 30th July. During the whole of this period the 62nd Division has had continuous fighting, manoeuvring and marching in new and hitherto unseen country of a character entirely different from anything in which it has operated before.

The Division made a great name for itself at the Battle of Cambrai. It enhanced that reputation at Bucquoy where it withstood the attacks of some of the best German troops, up to that time flushed with success. It has, in this great battle, set the seal on its already established reputation as a fighting force of the first quality . . . .

It is with intense pride that once again after a great victory I have the honour to sign myself as Commander of the 62nd West Riding Division.[24]

This note was matched by one from the French General Bertholot, which was translated and distributed throughout the Division.

Marfaux, Chamuzy, Montagne De Bligny – all these famous names will be written in gold in the annals of your regiments. Your French comrades will always remember with emotion your splendid gallantry and your perfect fellowship in the fight.[25]

Chapter 9
Marching Off

The 2/5th in August 1918

1918 was the worst year of the war for casualties. The killed and wounded inflicted by the March offensive and the return to war in the open were colossal, outstripping the losses of the Somme in 1916 and Third Ypres in 1917. High Command once again faced the reality that many battalions were so far below strength that they would be unable to carry out significant attacks or hold even half the length of line expected.

Faced with the need to bring units up to effective strength, the army would normally look to recruits coming from the depots. However ordinary recruiting had long dropped off, replaced by conscription. The vast majority of men eligible to enlist had done so and unless the age restriction was changed the pool of recruits was about half a million men in the UK who would come of age each year. Putting more pressure on the colonies or extending conscription to Ireland had their own problems and did not provide troops immediately. Once again brigades were reorganized to bring battalions up to strength.

In numerical terms the 2/5th did not appear too badly off after Marfaux. It had some 763 ORs and 27 officers. However the numbers disguised the true state of affairs. Taking out line of communication and support staff, the Battalion was unable to field more than two full strength companies. Also of these men, 250 were drafts that had arrived in the middle of the battle and were disorganized, untrained in working in their new teams and unfamiliar with their leaders.

In officers the damage was greater yet. While the full order of battle was not recorded, it is clear that some long standing and experienced officers were dead. Among the dead were officers who had been with the Battalion since training in England in 1916, such as Captain Grigson and Second Lieutenant Kermode, the most decorated officer in the Battalion. Most of the company officers who had direct responsibility for the day to day leadership and care of the men had become casualties. Some officers had been killed before even getting onto the official strength. The effect on morale can only be guessed at but it cannot have been lost on the men that they had just participated in a badly planned and executed engagement. After Bullecourt where there were fewer casualties it took six months for the Battalion to regain its form. The Army did not have the leisure to let that take place in the summer of 1918 – the 2/5th would have to be broken up and used to reinforce other battalions.

News of the decision reached the officers on 9 August 1918. Hedley Heaton, once again adjutant, wrote in the war diary:

> 62nd Division Letter A/303/67 of 8/8/18 received. This letter confirms the rumour that this battalion is to be disbanded owing to lack of reinforcements – the news is a terrible blow to us all, the esprit de corps of the battalion was at a very high standard. At 2:15 the CO paraded the battalion and told them the sad news.

Arthur Green wrote home:

> The worst thing ever is about to take place, our battalion is to be broken up and to be distributed among the other Yorkshire battalions in the Division. The fact is there are so many men on munitions work in Yorkshire that reinforcements are difficult to keep up and they have to do with one battalion less. We are all sick but there is nothing to do but see it through.[1]

The reason they were given, lack of recruits, was not an incredible justification given the general situation and the difficulties of recruiting in Yorkshire where many men had munitions or mining jobs, which were reserved occupations.

The final parade

The Battalion was at Vauchelles at the time of the disbandment, the men were living in and around the chateau. Immediately behind the chateau is a large flat field easily large enough for several Battalions with room to spare for a parade ground. The final parade was set for 12 August with the Brigade drawn up on three sides of a square as they had been for the marching off of the other disbanded units – for some of the men in the 2/5th this was the second or third time they had done this. The war diary records:

> Inspection outside Brigade Headquarters by GOC Division, the men turned out splendidly and were a great credit to the Battalion. The GOC expressed his regret that they were to be broken up but emphasized the fact that this Battalion was one of the smartest and best fighting battalions in the whole Division. Getting the men ready to move off tomorrow.

The first task was to allocate the ORs, and a set of drafts was created based on the immediate needs of other battalions in the division. The men were allocated as follows:

To 8th West Yorks Regiment	203
To 5th West Riding Regiment	20
To 2/5th West Riding Regiment	118
To 5th KOYLI	40
To 2/4th KOYLI	175
To 2/4th Yorks and Lancaster's	201
To Base WO Class 1	1
RQM Sgt	1
CQMS	4
Total	763

On 13 August the Battalion was broken up and the men marched off to their new homes leaving behind the officers and their servants, the QM staff, transport staff and the orderly room staff.

The disposition of officers was finalized by 15 August:

To Base:	Lt Colonel Waddy, DSO
	Major KES Stewart MC
	Captain Heaton
	Captain Green MC
	Lt Sharpe
To 1/5th Devon Regiment	Lt (A/Captain) J M Anderson,
	Captain and QM T Riley MC
	Lt Airey (10th Royal Scots attached)

Vauchelles Chateau. *Author's Collection*

To 2/4th KOYLI,	Lt (Acting Captain) G Skirrow
To 2/4th Hampshires	Lt T Catterall
	2/Lt C Gould
To 5th KOYLI	Lt S Smith
	Second Lieutenant R S Foster
To 8th West Yorks	Lt G F Stuart DSO
	2/Lt H R Wright
	2/Lt H E Wilcock DCM
	2/Lt J A Wade
	2/Lt H V Tewson MC
	2/Lt W M Willey
	2/Lt J Hall
	2/Lt N K Barrett
	2/Lt S Cork
	2/Lt W G S Read
	2/Lt H Banks
	2/Lt E C Sawyer MC
	Captain A H Lucas
	Lt C Friend

Second Lieutenant W J McLintock was sick in England and so was not posted. The acting RSM and remaining warrant officers including RQMS Richmond were to proceed to base.

Arthur Green describes this melancholy period:

> I am writing almost a series per day of letters to bereaved families. The men have gone to other units and now the officers are gradually dribbling away, me and Heaton to base. It's rather a painful period, final dinners to officers, pathetic and reminiscent speeches, every night rather boring.[2]

That left Battalion HQ. Hedley Heaton kept the Battalion organization going until he closed the war diary on 15 August 1918 with the words:

> The Battalion is to officially cease to function from 9:00am on 18/8/18.

While the war was over for the 2/5th as a unit, it was not so for the individual members of the Battalion. As the soldiers were scattered across regiments and battalions it is hard to follow their fortunes. However there were still the Battalion's wounded in hospitals across England and France. On 2 September Ernest Ainsley, aged 19, died near his home in North Ormsby, Middlesborough and on 17 September, George Watkins died in one of the hospitals at Rouen. The last to die was Frederick Whiston on 8 November 1918 who was buried in the local cemetery at Wetley Rocks.

The last soldier to die in action was Bertram Bailey who was killed on 1 November 1918. It is not known which unit he was serving with at the time and his body was never recovered.

Final Accounting.

The Battalion went to France with over 1,000 men. During the time it was there the war diary records 1,254 casualties of which 388 were deaths. In total the Battalion recorded drafts of 976 men. The chance of becoming a casualty while serving as a private solder was about 63 per cent and about 33 per cent of those men died. Researching the lives of the ORs remains difficult as individuals are rarely identified. Looking at the Regimental numbers of the casualties it is clear that by the end of the war there were many drafts from other units. The places of origin have also changed. Where the casualties of Bullecourt are heavily concentrated in Yorkshire and Lincolnshire, the casualties of Marfaux are more distributed. Although 63 per cent are still from Yorkshire there are soldiers from Scotland, Tyneside, the Midlands and London and the unit had lost much of its local, territorial character by then. In particular replacements were allocated from depots on the basis of availability – the individual Territorial soldier's control over his place of service had long gone. Some 37 per cent of the men have no known grave.

About thirty-five officers went to France, of whom eighteen were killed and twenty-six wounded. There were thirty-one replacements or returning wounded. The overall chances of becoming a casualty for the officers were the same as for the men, however once leave, sickness and convalescent time were taken out, the chances of being injured for company and platoon officers were very high indeed. Of the officers who went to Harrogate in early 1915 only five were with the Battalion at the end of July 1918; Dr Pringle, Hedley Heaton, Arthur Green, T M Riley and Geoffrey Skirrow. Of these Dr Pringle as MO, Captain Heaton as the adjutant and Captain Riley as the QM had not had immediate combat roles. Arthur Green did not have a combat role at Cambrai or Marfaux but fought at Bullecourt, Bucquoy and the Mont de Bligny. Geoffrey Skirrow fought at Bullecourt and Bucquoy but missed the Battle of Cambrai through illness and Marfaux by being 'left out of battle'; he would be in action again near Bapaume in August 1918. These were the only company officers who survived the war with the Battalion from start to disbandment.

Those who died of wounds or were killed at Bucquoy, Havrincourt or Marfaux generally have recorded resting places, as they died either in casualty clearing stations or on battlefields that were held by the Division and their bodies could be recovered. Of those who died at Bullecourt, few were recovered and their names are together on the Memorial to the Missing at Arras. On night patrols the men went to extraordinary efforts to bring back their wounded, as the rescues of Hanley Hutchinson and Angus Girling show. However for the men killed on patrols, their bodies were rarely recovered and their names are on the memorials nearest to their last action. The proportion of officers whose bodies have never been identified is slightly higher at 44 per cent.

In terms of decorations, twenty-seven of the Battalion officers were recognized in some way from a Mention in Dispatches to MCs and DSOs. Among the ORs seventy-eight men were decorated, some on multiple occasions.

Oblivion

After the war the 5th Battalion (once again a peacetime Territorial battalion of the West Yorks) had a lively Old Comrades' Association, which continued to meet until the 1970s, and its dinners and trips are

The 5th Battalion war memorial in Colliergate drill hall.
Colonel C W Crossland

recorded in the Regimental magazines. However, they met for themselves and while their names are recorded, their memories have largely
passed away with them. The Drill Hall at Colliergate in York commemorated all the dead of the 1/5th and 2/5th Battalions with a large
memorial, lists of names written on wooden panels. The Drill Hall
closed many years ago and is now a hardware and furnishing shop.

Colonel Bottomley survived the war to die aged 58, at Hesterhaven,
Aston-on-Clun in 1929. After leaving the 2/5th he worked with Ministry
of National Services which administered arbitration cases related to
conscription. At some point he was mentioned in the Secretary of
State's list for valuable services in connection with the war, perhaps in
tacit acknowledgement of how much he contributed against the odds in
the early years of the Battalion.

Colonel Josselyn, after distinguished service in Russia where he
commanded a brigade in the Dvina River Expedition, returned to
England. He saw another World War through to victory and died in
October 1945. He was buried at Fairlight church near Hastings in Sussex.

Colonel Waddy went on to command 9th West Yorks after the
disbandment. After the war he returned to regular soldiering and
commanded the 2nd Battalion Somerset Light Infantry. He retired in
1937 with thirty-one years of service. He was recalled to command a
training unit in 1939. He died on 16 April 1952 at the age of 66.

Hedley Heaton returned to the 1/5th and was soon commanding a
company. In October 1918 he won the MC:

> For conspicuous gallantry at Avesnes-le- Sec, from the 11th to
> 16th October 1918, when his courage, coolness and initiative
> were a fine asset to his company, which was in the frontline
> throughout the attack, and performed excellent service.
> Despite heavy shelling of the advanced posts, machine-gun
> fire, and an extraordinary amount of shell-gas, he, by his
> personal example and devotion to duty maintained a splendid
> spirit amongst his men.

After the war he returned to banking. He and Margaret had three children and he died in the Isle of Wight in 1956.

A W L Smith's records show little after he was wounded and he did
not return to the Battalion. However he must have returned to the front
as he was awarded the Croix de Guerre, possible for the famous action
of the 8th Battalion West Yorks at Bligny in July 1918. It has not been
possible to confirm this.

Of Arthur Green little is known. His wife was called Alice and in 1925 they visited the Heaton family. Arthur was known to Hedley's children as 'Uncle Susie'. He lived for a time in Larne, Northern Ireland and had at least one son. David Green deposited his letters in the Liddle Collection in Leeds. It has proved impossible to trace him.

Edgar Kermode became the most commemorated of the officers. Second Lieutenant Kermode has the most striking personal memorial of any soldier of the 2/5th; the entire east window of St Peter's Church in Shipley is dedicated to him. It was given by his father who was a member of this church for twenty-six years. A gift was also made to the officers' mess of the 5th Battalion in his memory – a silver model of a machine gun, still in the possession of the Regiment with the inscription:

Presented to the officers of the 5th Battalion West Yorkshire
Regiment PWO
By Mr & Mrs W M B Kermode of Shipley
In Memory of 2/Lt Edgar Marsden Kermode
DSO, MC and Bar, DCM
Killed in action Ecueil, Marne 26 July 1918
Whilst serving with the 2/5th Battalion West Yorkshire Regiment
Faithful Unto Death

Kermode's machine gun.
3rd Battalion Prince of Wales's Own Regiment of Yorkshire

Saying Goodbye

On Wednesday 7 June 1922 a party of 150 veterans set out from all parts of the country for Havrincourt to take part in the unveiling of the memorial to the 62nd Division. It stands at the end of the sunken road in which the 2/5th reorganized during the early stages of the attack. Many of the men wore their khaki, and the train as far as Arras was filled with the songs of the early war years. As they approached the old front line the mood quietened:

> After leaving St Pol behind, the signs of the war began to appear and those of the party who were visiting the war zone for the first time were deeply impressed by the partly filled in shell holes which pock marked the ground, the crumbling trenches which seared the countryside and the gaping gun pits which no longer contained their deadly weapons.

The memorial was unveiled next day by General Berthelot in front of a large number of dignitaries including Colonel Viscount Hampden, late commander of the 185th Brigade. The speeches echoed the General's order of the day at the time, praising the endurance and courage of the Division. The newspapers reprinted Sir Douglas Haig's dispatch:

> The 62nd West Riding Division stormed Havrincourt where parties of the enemy held out for a time and operating northwards from Havrincourt made important progress. Having carried the Hindenburg reserve line north of that village it rapidly continued the attack and captured Graincourt. This attack constitutes a brilliant achievement in which the troops concerned completed an advance of four and half miles from their original front, over running two German defence system and gaining the possession of three villages.[3]

The newspaper does not record the names of the soldiers of the 2/5th who returned for the ceremony. However after the unveiling, wreaths were placed by relatives of the fallen, whose names also are not recorded.

In 2005 the monument had been refurbished, cracks in the stonework, possible resulting from subsidence in the German dugout that lies thirty feet below it, had been repaired and worn stones replaced. The trees have grown up again and the Chateau and village have been entirely rebuilt; however low patches of scrub in the corners of fields mark the position of bunkers and wire pickets and shells still appear at each ploughing.

Epilogue

At this point the 2/5th Battalion passed out of recorded history and into a long silence. In the writing of the Official History many senior officers were contacted to check the narrative of battles – among them Colonel Josselyn – but there is no record of his ever replying. Many of the men who led the Battalion were from other regiments and did not record their service in a second line Territorial battalion. West Yorkshire officers who might have chosen to do so lie in France and had no opportunity.

In discussion with many of the relatives of officers most commented that their fathers and grandfathers had said and written nothing and at least one senior officer is remembered as becoming abrupt and angry if questioned. There was a pamphlet published in the 1930s about both the 1/5th and the 2/5th which gave a bald narrative in a few pages, largely derived from the Regimental History. In the 1980s Captain J M Anderson, who served with the Devonshires when the Battalion was broken up, was interviewed. The interviewer focused largely on experiences in Cologne after the war. Captain Anderson refused to be drawn on his battle experience, limiting his comments to having spent time in no man's land 'keeping an eye on the Germans'. Despite his MC, his patrols and his leadership of a company at Bucquoy he claimed 'never to have done anything dangerous'. This is belied by the citation for his MC in the *London Gazette* on 10 January 1919:

> Lt John Millar Anderson, 5th Bn., W. York. R., T.F., attd. 5th Bn., Devon. R., T.F. This officer went forward to tape out the assembly position in advance of a line, and although under heavy and continuous fire, and in spite of darkness, he successfully accomplished his task. At a later date during an attack, when the troops, owing to heavy casualties, had become dis-

organized, he made a careful reconnaissance under heavy fire to clear up the situation. His gallantry and devotion afforded a fine example to all ranks.

Following disbandment there was one more officer who would not see the end of the war. Within a few days of posting to the 2/4th KOYLI Captain Geoffrey Skirrow was making his mark. As he was the only officer transferred to this Battalion, taking 175 men with him, it is likely he was still leading a number of troops who had known him for some time. In the fight to recapture Bapaume in August 1918 he found himself leading 'D' Company in the advance on Mory. This was familiar ground – the 2/5th had lived at Ervillers within sight of Mory to the west, and had built Camp A, on the road between Mory and Favreuil to the south. Before the Battle of Bullecourt, tanks were concealed at Mory Copse and Geoffrey may have gone to examine them. He now found himself approaching a line between Mory village and Mory Copse a few hundred yards to the north. The village and the copse are connected by a sunken road which allows a covered approach to the hedge at the boundary of the wood. The war diary relates:

> Capt G. Skirrow, in command of D Company in support, noticed that the enemy were working round the left flank and were in possession of Mory Copse. Taking two platoons with him he rushed for the copse, attacking the crew of a machine gun with his revolver he accounted for them all and in getting in touch with the Guards who were now coming in from the north, drove the enemy out and cleared the copse. A considerable number of prisoners were collected.[4]

During the next day's advance 'D' Company was held up trying to retake the ground between Mory and Vaux Vraulcourt. Somewhere on this featureless French plain Geoffrey Skirrow was killed by shellfire. His body was evacuated to the aid post at Abbey Farm in Mory and he was buried in the small cemetery on the other side of the road. In the same cemetery lie two other members of the Battalion, James Judge and Albert Rawlings, who had died in April 1917. In a letter to the family, published in the *Harrow School Memorial Book*, his commanding officer, Colonel Chaytor, described his last days:

> On August the 25th 1918 his leadership and example were mainly instrumental in driving back an enemy counter attack at a critical moment, and all the officers and men who saw him

during that period state that his conduct was absolutely magnificent then, as well as later on when he had to consolidate the ground under very heavy shell fire. He did not seem to know what fear was and his men were absolutely devoted to him. He is a great loss to us.[5]

Geoffrey Skirrow was commissioned into the 5th (Reserve) Battalion West Yorkshire Regiment in February 1915. He and the other officers took the Battalion on a journey from an under trained and under equipped group of amateurs to a professionally led fighting Battalion; a proud part of one of the best Divisions in the British Army and a superb example of the capabilities of the Territorials.

Notes

Chapter 1

1.   Territorial and Reserve Forces Act 1907
2.   ibid.
3.   Tempest, *History of the 6th Battalion West Yorkshire Regiment* Volume I,
4.   Beckett & Simpson, *Nation in Arms*
5.   Musketry Regulations 1909, Appendix 4 Table B
6.   Laurie Magnus, *West Riding Territorials in the Great War*
7.   Tempest, op. cit.
8.   A. J. Smithers, *The Fighting Nation*
9.   ibid.
10. Kitchener's letter to County Associations, National Archives W032/11341
11. Ray Westlake, *The Territorial Force 1914*
12. A.G. Wilson, *Peter – A Life Remembered*
13. *Yorkshire Gazette*: 29/9/14
14. A E Green: Liddle Collection 12/9/14
15. A E Green: Liddle Collection 15/10/14

Chapter 2

1.   *Yorkshire Herald*: 25/9/1914
2.   A E Green: Liddle Collection 4/10/14
3.   Laurie Magnus, op. cit.
4.   E C Gregory, *History of the 6th Battalion West Yorkshire Regiment* Volume II
5.   A E Green: Liddle Collection 12/9/14
6.   A J Peacock, *York in the Great War*
7.   AE Green: Liddle Collection 22/11/14
8.   A E Green: Liddle Collection 29/11/14
9.   A E Green: Liddle Collection 15/11/14
10. A E Green: Liddle Collection 28/2/15
11. A E Green: Liddle Collection 14/2/15

12.   A E Green: Liddle Collection 11/4/15
13.   A E Green: Liddle Collection 23/5/15
14.   E.C. Gregory, op. cit.
15.   A E Green: Liddle Collection 8/8/15
16.   A E Green: Liddle Collection 13/6/15
17.   A E Green: Liddle Collection 7/11/15
18.   *Harrogate Herald* :1/12/15
19.   National Archives: WO 374/1154
20.   E.C. Gregory, op. cit.
21.   ibid.
22.   ibid.
23.   ibid.
24.   ibid.
25.   ibid.
26.   National Archives: WO 374/7817
27.   A E Green: Liddle Collection 14/5/16
28.   National Archives Office: WO 374/7817
29.   E.C. Gregory, op. cit.
30.   A E Green: Liddle Collection 30/7/16
31.   E.C. Gregory, op. cit.

Chapter 3

1.   A E Green: Liddle Collection 9/1/17
2.   *Harrogate Herald*: 24/1/17, www.harrogatepeopleandplaces.info
3.   ibid.
4.   A E Green: Liddle Collection 27/1/17
5.   A E Green: Liddle Collection 2/2/17
6.   The Harrogate Cenotaph 21/2/17
7.   A E Green: Liddle Collection 16/2/17
8.   National Archives: WO95/3068
9.   *Harrogate Herald*: 16/3/17 www.harrogatepeopleandplaces.info
10.   Recollections of George Radford as told to David Lockwood York 1984
11.   *Harrogate Herald*: 7/3/1917
12.   A E Green: Liddle Collection 3/3/17
13.   A E Green: Liddle Collection 22/2/17
14.   Copied by A E Green in letter of 22/2/17
15.   *Harrogate Herald*: 3/3/1917
16.   *Yorkshire Gazette*: 27/7/18
17.   A E Green: Liddle Collection 9/3/17
18.   *Harrogate Herald*: 4/4/17, www.harrogatepeopleandplaces.info
19.   Records of Museum of Royal Welch Fusiliers
20.   National Archives: De Falbe to Falls 3/7/37, CAB45/116
21.   War diary 2/5th Battalion 12/4/17

Chapter 4

1. *Harrogate Herald*: 9/5/17,www.harrogatepeopleandplaces.info
2. *Harrogate Herald*: 2/5/17, www.harrogatepeopleandplaces.info
3. *Harrogate Herald*: 9/5/17,www.harrogatepeopleandplaces.info
4. National Archives, 2/5th War Diaries WO 95/3081 – 185 Brigade Orders Appendix 17
5. ibid. and Appendix 24
6. Letter from Mrs Josselyn to Captain Green, September 1917, Liddle Collection
7. National Archives: WO95/3082 2/6th War Diaries, April 1917 Appendix 2
8. Letter from Pelham Pearson: Prince of Wales's Own Regimental Museum
9. National Archives: WO95/3079, July, Appendix 1, 1/6/17
10. National Archives: WO95/3080 May Appendix 6H to the Brigade War Diary
11. National Archives: WO95/3079 May Appendix 6G
12. ibid.
13. National Archives: WO95/3079 May, Appendix 6I
14. Everard Wyrall *History of 62nd Division*
15. Jonathon Walker: *Blood Tub*, page 186
16. E.C. Gregory, op.cit.
17. A E Green: Liddle Collection, May 1917
18. Airey to Green, Liddle Collection
19. National Archives: CAB 45/116 File H
20. *Harrogate Herald*: 2/5/17, www.harrogatepeopleandplaces.info
21. *Harrogate Herald*: 17/10/17, www.harrogatepeopleandplaces.info
20. *Harrogate Herald*: 9/5/17, www.harrogatepeopleandplaces.info
22. A E Green: Liddle Collection 1/5/17
23. A E Green: Liddle Collection 6/5/17
24. *Harrogate Advertiser*: 16/3/18
25. *Harrogate Advertiser*: 30/6/17
26. *Harrogate Herald*: 12/12/17, www.harrogatepeopleandplaces.info
27. *Harrogate Advertiser*: 16/3/18
28. *Harrogate Herald*: 4/7/17, www.harrogatepeopleandplaces.info
29. *Harrogate Herald*: 29/1/19, www.harrogatepeopleandplaces.info
30. Margaret Heaton to Captain Green 6/6/17
31. Corporal Hall to the Prisoners' Welfare Association. Prince of Wales's Own, Regimental Museum York 11/1/19
32. *Yorkshire Evening Post*:10/5/17
33. National Archives: WO 374/75447
34. National Archives: WO 374/13709
35. Letters of Pelham Pearson, Prince of Wales's Own, Regimental Museum
36. *Harrogate Herald*: 23/5/17
37. *Harrogate Herald*: 20/5/17

38.   *Harrogate Herald*: 4/7/17
39.   A E Green: Liddle Collection 16/9/17

Chapter 5
1.   National Archives:WO95/3081 16/5/17
2.   A E Green: Liddle Collection 5/6/17 Airey to Green
3.   *Harrogate Herald*:20/6/17
4.   Ca Ira, 1936, Prince of Wales's Own Regimental Museum York
5.   A E Green: Liddle Collection, Clubb to Green 28/5/17
6.   A G Wilson: op. cit. entry for 28/7/17
7.   ibid.
8.   National Archives:WO 95/3079 August 1917 Infantry Brigade Intelligence Summary
9.   Tony Ashworth, *Trench Warfare 1914 – 1918 The Live and Let Live System*
10.   National Archives: W095/3081 Lt Birbeck 12/9/17
11.   A E Green: Liddle Collection 27/5/17
12.   Smith to Green, Liddle Collection 17/6/17
13.   Billie to Green Liddle Collection 28/5/17
14.   National Archives: WO95/3079 Daily Intelligence Summaries August 1917
15.   *Harrogate Herald*: 12/9/17
16.   Colonel J Waddy, unpublished memoirs

Chapter 6
1.   AE Green: Liddle Collection 5/11/17
2.   *Harrogate Herald*: 21/11/17 www.harrogatepeopleandplaces.info.info
3.   AE Green: Liddle Collection 5/11/17
4.   National Archives: WO95/3081 185th Infantry Brigade Offensive Instruction Number 7
5.   National Archives: WO95 /3081 War Diary for November App 11
6.   AE Green: Liddle Collection 20/11/17
7.   AE Green: Liddle Collection 21/11/17
8.   National Archives: war diaries of 2/6th Battalion West Yorks November 1917 Appendix 10
9.   *Harrogate Herald*: 19/12/17 www.harrogatepeopleandplaces.info.info
10.   *Harrogate Herald*: 16/1/18 www.harrogatepeopleandplaces.info.info
11.   National Archives: war diaries of 2/8th Battalion West Yorks November 1917 – Narrative of Operations
12.   AE Green: Liddle Collection 24/11/17
13.   AE Green: Liddle Collection 24/11/17
14.   *Harrogate Herald*: 5/12/17 www.harrogatepeopleandplaces.info.info
15.   *Harrogate Herald*: 19/12/17 www.harrogatepeopleandplaces.info.info

Chapter 7

1.   AE Green: Liddle Collection 21/12/172.
2.   AE Green: Liddle Collection 28/1/18
3.   National Archives WO95/3079 War Diaries of 2/5th January 1918
4.   AE Green: Liddle Collection 12/2/18
5.   AE Green: Liddle Collection 1/4/18
6.   Lieutenant Colonel A M Cooper OBE: White Rose 1960 Volume II
7.   AE Green: Liddle Collection 1/4/18
8.   *Harrogate Advertiser* 27/4/1918
9.   ibid.
10. Lieutenant Colonel A M Cooper OBE: White Rose 1960 Volume II
11. ibid.
12. Supplement to *London Gazette* 16 September 1918
13. AE Green: Liddle Collection 14/6/18

Chapter 8

1.   A E Green: Liddle Colection 17/7/18
2.   National Archives WO95/3081 July 1918 Appendix 29
3.   Supplement to *London Gazette* 7/11/18
4.   National Archives WO95/3081 July 1918 Appendix 29
5.   National Archives WO95/3081 July 1918 Appendix 29
6.   National Archives WO95/3081 July 1918 Appendix 30 – 31
7.   Supplement to *London Gazette* 7/11/18
8.   ibid.
9.   ibid.
10. *Yorkshire Herald* 26/8/18
11. National Archives WO374/70789
12. National Archives WO95/3081, July 1918 Appendix 23
13. National Archives WO95/3083 July 1918 Appendix B4
14. A E Green: Liddle Collection 23/7/18
15. *Harrogate Advertiser* 27/7/18
16. *Harrogate Advertiser* 24/8/18
17. *Harrogate Advertiser* 17/8/18
18. National Archives WO 95/3083 July 1918
19. ibid.
20. National Archives WO95/3081 July 1918 Appendix 55
21. National Archives WO374/37433
22. *Harrogate Advertiser* 5/10/1918
23. A E Green Liddle: Collection before 6/8/18
24. National Archives WO95/3081 July 1918 Appendix 61
25. ibid.

Chapter 9

1. A E Green: Liddle Collection 10/8/18
2. AE Green: Liddle Collection 16/8/18
3. *Leeds Mercury* 7/6/22
4. War Diary 2/4th KOYLI
5. *Harrow School Memorial Book*

Appendix 1
Other Ranks Roll of Honour 2/5th Battalion West Yorkshire Regiment 1914 – 1918

Abbott, Harold, b. York, e. Harrogate, Yorks., r. Harrogate, 200557, Private, KIA, 03/05/17, commemorated on the Arras Memorial to the Missing, obituary in *Harrogate Advertiser* 16/3/1918.

Acton, Edward Joseph, b. Holborn, Middlesex, e. Stratford, London, 52000, Private, KIA, 22/11/17, commemorated on the Cambrai Memorial, Louverval.

Ainsley, Ernest, e. Leeds, 268298, Private, DOW, Home, 02/09/18, aged 19, buried at Middlesborough (North Ormsby) Cemetery.

Allinson, George Henry, b. Newton-on-Ouse, Yorks., e. Harrogate, Yorks, 49369, Private, KIA, 31 /07/18, aged 25, buried at Chambrecy British Cemetery, obituary *Harrogate Herald* 29/1/1919.

Allison, Leonard William, b. North Kensington, London, e. Shepherd's Bush, 51952, Private, KIA, 20/07/18, formerly 229501, R.O.D., Royal Engineers, buried at Marfaux British Cemetery.

Ando, Francis Benjamin, b. Plumstead, Kent, e. Woolwich, 20934, Private, KIA, 27/11/17, aged 26, formerly 235292, R.F.A., commemorated on the Cambrai Memorial Louverval.

Andrews, Walter, b. Lesingham, Lincs, e. Sleaford, Lincs, 201874, Private, Died, 03/12/17, buried at Tournai Communal Cemetery Allied Extension.

Angus, Joseph, b. Ruskiton, Lincs, e. Lincoln, r. Bardney, Lincs, 202110, Private, KIA, 03/05/17, buried at H.A.C. Cemetery, Ecoust-St Mein.

Annakin, Fred, b. York, e. Harrogate, Yorks, r. Knaresborough, Yorks, 201752, Private, KIA, 25/07/18, buried at St Imoges Churchyard, near Marfaux, obituary *Harrogate Herald* 17/8/18.

Apedaile, John Edwin, b. Acomb, York, e. York, r. York, 201972, Private, KIA, 29/09/17, buried at Favreuil British Cemetery.

Appleby, William, b. Hull, e. Hull, Yorks, 52220, Private, KIA, 20/07/18, aged 19, buried at Marfaux British Cemetery.

Arden, Sylvanus, e. York, r. York, 200916, Sergeant, KIA, 01/09/17, commemorated on the Arras Memorial to the Missing, obituary *Yorkshire Gazette* 29/9/17.

Ashworth, George Albert, b. Birkenshaw, Yorks, e. Bradford, Yorks, 21/911, Private, KIA, 20/07/18, aged 26, commemorated on the Soissons Memorial.

Astley, John, b. Birmingham, e. Birmingham, 54886, Private, KIA, 12/04/18, aged 22, commemorated on the Pozieres Memorial.

Atkin, John, b. Molton Marsh, Lincs, e. Boston, Lincs, 201904, Private, KIA, 10/04/17, aged 30, commemorated on the Arras Memorial to the Missing.

Atkinson, Guy, b. York, e. York, 201964, Private, Died, 18/07/18, aged 21, commemorated on the Soissons Memorial.

Atkinson, Walter, e. Leeds, r. Leeds, 266962, Lance Corporal, DOW, 27/07/18, aged 20, buried at Terlincthun British Cemetery, Wimille.

Ayscough, Arthur, b. Grimsby, Lincs, e. Grimsby, 202020, Private, KIA, 18/02/17, commemorated on the Thiepval Memorial.

Bacon, Charles Edward, e. Harrogate, r. Hawes, Yorks, 2935, Private, Died, 26/01/17, aged 38, buried at Ste Marie, Le Havre.

Bailey, Bertram, b. Leicester, e. Leicester, 27319, Private, KIA, 01/11/18, Formerly 24471, Leicestershire Regiment, commemorated on the Memorial to the Missing at Vis-en-Artois.

Baines, Archie, b. Pateley Bridge, Yorks, e. York, 201671, Lance Corporal, KIA, 03/05/17, commemorated on the Arras Memorial to the Missing, Obituary *Harrogate Advertiser* 6/4/18.

Baker, Thomas, e. Harrogate, Yorks, r. Harrogate, 201119, Private, KIA, 02/06/18, aged 31, commemorated on the Pozieres Memorial.

Ball, George, b. Hednesford, Staffs, e. Hednesford, 42022, Private, KIA, 28/03/18, aged 28, buried at Bienvillers Military Cemetery.

Banks, Albert, b. Thirsk, Yorks, e. Yorks, 41304, Private, KIA, 20/07/18, buried at Marfaux British Cemetery.

Banks, John Wilfred, b. Ripon, Yorks, e. Ripon, 200318, Private, KIA, 18/02/17, commemorated on the Thiepval Memorial, obituary in *Ripon Observer* 15/3/17.

Barff, Tom, b. Leeds, e. Leeds, 34031, Private, KIA, 22/11/17, commemorated on the Cambrai Memorial, Louverval.

Barker, Ernest, e. Leeds, r. Leeds, 266059, Private, KIA, 20/07/18, aged 22, buried at Marfaux British Cemetery.

Barker, Frederick Charles, b. Leeds, e. Leeds, 37455, Private, DOW,

12/04/18, aged 20, buried at Gezaincourt Communal Cemetery Extension.

Barker, Henry Arthur, b. Halifax, Yorks, e. Harrogate, Yorks, r. Knaresborough, Yorks, 200041, Private, KIA, 20/07/18, aged 26, buried at Marfaux British Cemetery.

Barker, Robert, b. Goole, Yorks, e. Pontefract, Yorks, 55605, Private, KIA, 31/07/18, aged 19, buried at Chambrecy British Cemetery.

Barnett, Alfred, b. Plaistow, Essex, e. East Ham, 20935, Private, KIA, 27/11/17, formerly 235225, R.F.A., commemorated on the Cambrai Memorial, Louverval.

Barnett, Arthur, b. Bucknall, Staffs, e. Hanley, Staffs, 57224, Private, KIA, 20/07/18, buried at Marfaux British Cemetery.

Baul, Ernest, b. Harrogate, Yorks, e. Harrogate, 202050, Private, KIA, 03/05/17, commemorated on the Arras Memorial to the Missing.

Beaumont, Harry, b. Meltham, Yorks, e. Huddersfield, Yorks, 21/756, Private, KIA, 20/07/18, commemorated on the Soissons Memorial.

Bedford, John William, b. St. Mary's, Kent, e. Hull, Yorks, r. Hull, 52233, Private, KIA, 23/05/18, buried at Bienvillers Military Cemetery.

Beer, Albert, b. Chard, Somerset, e. Selby, Yorks, r. Chard, 200129, Private, Died, 18/07/18, aged 23, commemorated on the Soissons Memorial.

Bell, Ernest Reid, e. Dundee, r. Newport, Fife, 20441, Private, DOW, 28/11/17,

Formerly 1382, 2/1st Highland Divisional Transport (TF), aged 21, buried at Rocquigny-Equancourt Road British Cemetery, Manancourt.

Bell, Robert Stanley, e. Selby, Yorks, 2783, Corporal, KIA, 18/02/17, commemorated on the Thiepval Memorial.

Bell, William, b. St. Margaret's, Durham, e. Durham, 52224, Lance Corporal, KIA, 20/07/18, buried at Marfaux British Cemetery.

Benson, Charles Edward, b. Darley, Yorks, e. Harrogate, Yorks, 4198, Private, Died, 01/03/17, buried at Mont Huon Military Cemetery, Le Treport.

Bentley, Tom, b. Leeds, e. Leeds, 49476, Private, KIA, 20/07/18, buried at Marfaux British Cemetery.

Betson, Frank, b. Retford, e. Lincoln, r. Retford, 201909, Private, DOW, 05/05/17, aged 41, buried at East Retford Cemetery.

Binns, Edgar, b. Bradford, Yorks, e. Bradford, 202273, Private, KIA, 29/05/18, commemorated on the Pozieres Memorial.

Binns, Thomas Henry, b. Huddersfield, Yorks, e. Selby, Yorks, 201732, Private, KIA, 01/03/17, commemorated on the Thiepval Memorial.

Bird, William Arthur, b. Barnsley, Yorks, e. Barnsley, 270121, Lance Corporal, KIA, 20/07/18, aged 33, buried at Marfaux British Cemetery.

Bisby, Bernald, b. Ackworth, Yorks, e. Dewsbury, Yorks, 57221, Private, KIA, 20/07/18, buried at Chambrecy British Cemetery.

Blakey, Ernest Arthur, b. Bratoft, Burgh, Lincs, e. Spilsby, Lincs, 202117, Private, DOW, 10/05/17, buried at Ervillers Military Cemetery.

Blakey, Percy, b. Moortown, Yorks, e. Tadcaster, Yorks, r. Tadcaster, 36733, Private, KIA, 26/03/18, aged 26, commemorated on the Arras Memorial to the Missing.

Boothroyd, Joseph, b. Barley, Yorks, e. Bradford, Yorks, 26146, Private, DOW, 13/09/17, aged 29, buried at Favreuil British Cemetery. Obituary in *Bradford Weekly Telegraph* 28/9/17

Bott, Frederick, b. Ilkley, Yorks, e. Ilkley, 203682, Private, KIA, 18/05/18, aged 36, buried at Bienvillers Military Cemetery.

Bowland, Stanley John, b. Norton, Malton, Yorks, e. Malton, 23500, Private, DOW, 23/03/18, aged 29, buried at Aubigny Communal Cemetery Extension.

Bowlby, Stephenson, e. York r. York 200984 Private, died 10/04/17 aged 26, buried at Bishopthorpe (St Andrew) Churchyard.

Bradley, Thomas William, b. Castleford, Yorks, e. Leeds, r. Leeds, 305527, Lance Corporal, DOW, 22/07/18, aged 23, buried at Sezanne Communal Cemetery.

Bratley, Martin, b. Wragby, Lincs, e. Lincoln, r. Wragby, 202006, Private, KIA, 03/05/17, commemorated on the Arras Memorial to the Missing.

Bray, Fred, e. Huddersfield, Yorks, r. Huddersfield, 241964, Private, KIA, 24/05/18, buried at Gommecourt British Cemetery No.2, Hebuterne.

Brayshay, Albert Edward, b. Leeds, e. Leeds, 306847, Private, DOW, 24/11/17, buried at St Sever Cemetery Extension Rouen.

Brogden, William, b. Newcastle-on-Tyne, e. Newcastle-on-Tyne, 57503, Private, DOW, 22/07/18, buried at Sezanne Communal Cemetery.

Bromfield, John, e. Louth, Lincs, r. Louth, 201906, Private, KIA, 20/07/18, M.M., buried at Marfaux British Cemetery.

Brotherton, Charles, b. York, e. York, 201532, Private, KIA, 26/03/18, aged 26, commemorated on the Arras Memorial to the Missing.

Brown, Bertie, e. Knaresborough, Yorks, r. Knaresborough, 2845, Lance Corporal, DOW, 17/02/17, buried in Varennes Military Cemetery. Obituary in the *Harrogate Herald* 28/2/17.

Brown, Frederick William, b. Staxton, Yorks, e. Scarborough, Yorks, r. Seamer, Yorks, 52226, Private, DOW, 25/07/18, aged 19, buried at St Sever Cemetery Extension Rouen.

Brown, George, b. Bradford, Yorks, e. Leeds, 17/337, Private, KIA, 20/07/18, commemorated on the Soissons Memorial.

Brown, George Richard, e. Ripon, Yorks, r. Norby, Thirsk, Yorks, 200963, Sergeant. KIA, 03/05/17, commemorated on the Arras Memorial to the Missing.

Brown, George William, b. Spennymoor, Durham, e. Ferryhill, Durham, 52223 Private, KIA, 20/11/17, aged 19, buried at St Sever Cemetery Extension Rouen.

Brown, John, b. Edinburgh, e. Edinburgh, 56911, Private, KIA, 20/07/18, Formerly

22541, 6th Res. Cavalry Regt., buried at Marfaux British Cemetery.

Brown, Robert Fee, b. Blaydon, Durham, e. Blaydon, r. Winlaton, Durham, 54604, Private, KIA, 20/07/18, buried at Marfaux British Cemetery.

Brown, Thomas William Edward, b. Sunderland, Durham, e. Sunderland, 52232, Private, KIA, 20/11 /17, aged 19, commemorated on the Cambrai Memorial, Louverval.

Brown, William, b. York, e. York, 201728, Private, KIA, 03/05/17, commemorated on the Arras Memorial to the Missing, obituary in *Yorkshire Gazette* 30/3/18.

Bumstead, William Patterson, b. Elland, Yorks, e. Elland, 42011, Private, KIA, 19/04/18, aged 24, buried at Bienvillers Military Cemetery.

Burgess, George Arthur, b. Leeds, e. Leeds, 21/649, Private, KIA, 20/07/18, buried at Marfaux British Cemetery.

Burman, John, b. Brigg, Lincs, e. Brigg, 202113, Private, KIA, 20/07/18, aged 22, buried at Marfaux British Cemetery.

Busfield, Joseph, e. Bradford, r. Windhill, Shipley, 241866, Private, KIA, 20/07/18, M.M., aged 21, commemorated on the Soissons Memorial.

Butler, Ernest Charles, b. Colne, Lincs, e. Chesterfield, 58803, Private, DOW, 06/09/18, buried at St Sever Cemetery Extension Rouen.

Bycroft, Arthur, b. York, e. York, 200752, Private, KIA, 22/11/17, aged 25, buried at Grand Ravine British Cemetery, Havrincourt, obituary in *Yorkshire Gazette* 10/12/18.

Caldecoat, Frank Ernest, b. Cambridge, e. Huntingdon, Cambs, 51959, Private, KIA, 20/07/18, formerly 217947, R.O.D., Royal Engineers, buried at Marfaux British Cemetery.

Cammidge, Arthur, e. York, r. York, 201192, Private, KIA, 26/03/18, aged 20, commemorated on the Arras Memorial to the Missing.

Cammidge, Arthur, b. York, e. York, 201825, Private, KIA, 18/02/17, aged 37, commemorated on the Thiepval Memorial.

Campbell, Clifford, b. Mirfield, Yorks, e. Halifax, Yorks, r. Luddenden, Yorks, 53888, Private, KIA, 31/07/18, aged 18, buried at Chambrecy British Cemetery.

Campbell, James, b. Bradford, Yorks, e. Bradford, 201794, Private, KIA, 22/11 /17, commemorated on the Cambrai Memorial, Louverval. Notice in *Bradford Weekly Telegraph* 1/2/18

Carey, Edward, b. York, e. York, 201384, Private, Died, 12/05/17 buried at Flesquieres Hill British Cemetery.

Cawthorne, William, b. Tank, St. Clements, Norfolk, e. Holbeach, Lincs, r. Sutton Bridge, Lincs, 4567, Private, KIA, 08/02/17, buried at Courcelles-Au-Bois Communal Cemetery Extension.

Chadwick, Ernest, b. Guiseley, Yorks, e. Keighley, Yorks, 32523, Private, KIA, 31/07/18, aged 31, commemorated on the Soissons Memorial.

Chadwick, Percy, e. York, r. Holbeck, Leeds, 3605, Private, KIA, 16/02/17, buried at Ten Tree Alley Cemetery, Puisieux.

Challoner, Maurice Blyton, b. York, e. York, 201986, Private, KIA, 03/05/17, aged 20, buried in Croisilles Railway Cemetery.

Chambers, George William, b. Wainfleet, Lincs, e. Wainfleet, 202016, Private, DOW, 07/12/17, aged 27, buried at St Sever Cemetery Extension Rouen.

Chapman, Walter, b. York, e. York, 1557, Lance Corporal, KIA, 16/02/17, aged 19, buried at Ten Tree Alley Cemetery, Puisieux, obituary *Yorkshire Herald* 13/4/17.

Clark, George Henry, b. York, e. York, 201059, Sergeant, DOW, 03/05/17, aged 47, buried at Achiet-Le-Grand Communal Cemetery Extension, obituary *Yorkshire Herald* 16/5/17.

Clark, Samuel, b. Snaith, Yorks, e. Harrogate, Yorks, 201990, Private, KIA, 03/05/17, commemorated on the Arras Memorial to the Missing.

Clayden, William, b. Goldsborough, Yorks, e. York, r. Deighton, Escrick, 201512, Private, Died, Whalley (Queen Mary's hospital) 31/12/17, Military cemetery.

Coates, Arthur, b. Bradford, Yorks, e. Bradford, 57017, Private, KIA, 20/07/18, aged 26, buried at Marfaux British Cemetery.

Coggan, James William, b. Thornbury Hill, Maltby, Yorks, e. Pontefract, Yorks, r. Medge Hall, Doncaster, 20400, Private, KIA, 20/07/18, buried at Marfaux British Cemetery.

Coldwell, Alfred, b. Barnsley, Yorks, e. Barnsley, 27560, Private, DOW, 18/01/18, formerly 24079, Yorks & Lancs Regt., buried at Roclincourt Military Cemetery.

Coomer, Percy, e. Leeds, r. Leeds, 267005, Private, KIA, 20/11/17, buried at Hermies Hill British Cemetery.

Coultish, George, b. Broomfleet, Yorks, e. Beverley, Yorks, 52246, Private, KIA, 27/11/17, commemorated on the Cambrai Memorial, Louverval.

Cox, Fred, b. Manchester, e. Huddersfield, Yorks, 42014, Private, KIA, 22/11/17, aged 24, commemorated on the Cambrai Memorial, Louverval.

Crossland, Samuel, b. Crofton, Yorks, e. Wakefield, Yorks, r. Wakefield, 57757, Private, DOW, 13/04/18, buried at Gezaincourt Communal Cemetery Extension.

Dalby, Ernest, b. York, e. Wetherby, Yorks, r. East Keswick, Yorks, 33975, Private, KIA, 13/09/17, aged 37, buried at Favreuil British Cemetery.

Dale, Albert, b. Harrogate, Yorks, e. Harrogate, 201000, Private, KIA, 20/11/17, buried at Grand Ravine British Cemetery, Havrincourt.

Davies, Richard Lewis, b. Swansea, e. Swansea, 20899, Private, Died, Home, 16/05/18, Formerly 229048, R.F.A., aged 26, buried at Swansea (Cwmgelly) Cemetery.

Davis, Alfred, b. Smethwick, Staffs, e. Lichfield, Staffs, 59136, Private, KIA, 26/07/18, aged 19, buried at Chambrecy British Cemetery.

Davy, Charles, b. Wainfleet, Lincs, e. Spilsby, Lincs, 202115, Lance
   Sergeant, KIA, 12/04/18, buried at Gommecourt British Cemetery No.2,
   Hebuterne.

Dawson, John Henry, e. Bradford, Yorks, r. Bradford, 240625, Acting
   Sergeant, KIA, 23/05/18, M.M., aged 27, buried at Bienvillers Military
   Cemetery, Obituary in *Bradford Weekly Telegraph* 14/6/18

Day, Ernest, b. Dewsbury, Yorks, e. Lincoln, r. New Cleethorpes, Lincs,
   202003, Acting Corporal, DOW, 12/04/18, aged 22, buried at Bienvillers
   Military Cemetery.

Deacon, John, e. Leeds, r. Headingley, Leeds, 306269, Private, KIA,
   20/07/18, aged 20, buried at Marfaux British Cemetery.

Deighton, Herbert Wilfred, b. Thorner, Yorks, e. Harrogate, Yorks, 203588,
   Private, KIA, France & Flanders, 03/05/17, commemorated on the Arras
   Memorial to the Missing.

Dent, Alfred, b. Walker, Durham, e. Newcastle-on-Tyne, 61630, Private,
   KIA, 31/07/18, aged 19, buried at Chambrecy British Cemetery.

Dixon, Albert, b. Bardney, Lincs, e. Lincoln, 201940, Private, KIA,
   03/05/17, commemorated on the Arras Memorial to the Missing.

Donaldson, John, e. Harrogate, Yorks, 3111, Private, Died, Home,
   09/07/16, aged 34, buried at Yester Parish Churchyard.

Dorrell, Frederick William, b. Oxford, e. Harrogate, Yorks, r. Oxford,
   201743, Private, KIA, 09/04/18, commemorated on the Pozieres
   Memorial.

Doughty, Fred, b. Barton-on-Humber, Lincs, e. Barton-on-Humber, 27273,
   Lance Corporal, KIA, 20/07/18, Formerly 20953, N. Staffs Regt., aged
   22, commemorated on the Soissons Memorial.

Doyle, Arthur, b. Morpeth, Northumberland, e. Leeds, r. Leeds, 17/309,
   Private, KIA, 20/07/18, buried at Marfaux British Cemetery.

Drew, Ernest, b. Liversidge, Yorks, e. Heckmondwike, Yorks, 241960,
   Sergeant, KIA, 20/07/18, buried at Marfaux British Cemetery.

Driscoll, John, b. Cardiff, e. Penarth, r. Penarth, 51934, Private, KIA,
   29/03/18, Formerly 157540, I.W.T. Royal Engineers, commemorated on
   the Arras Memorial to the Missing.

Driver, Frank, e. Harrogate, Yorks, r. Marton-Cum-Grafton, Yorks,
   201154, Private, KIA, 03/05/17, commemorated on the Arras Memorial
   to the Missing, mentioned in Brigade orders for Meritorious Service
   30/5/1917

Ducket, William, e. Leeds, r. Leeds, 41252, Private, KIA, 20/07/18, buried
   at Marfaux British Cemetery.

Dunham, Joseph Edgar, b. Somercoates, Lincs, e. Lincoln, 201929, Private,
   DOW, 02/12/17, buried at Grevillers British Cemetery.

Durdey, Thomas, b. Gringley-on-Hill, Notts, e. Lincoln, 4431, Private,
   KIA, 15/02/17, aged 27, commemorated on Thiepval Memorial.

Eastgate, George William, b. Hangaby, Lincs, e. Spilsby, Lincs, r.

Sutton-on-Sea, 201996, Corporal, KIA, 01/09/17, commemorated on the Arras Memorial to the Missing.

Eccles, Joseph William, e. York, r. York, 200806, Sergeant, DOW, 20/05/17, aged 37, buried in St Sever Extension Rouen, obituary *Yorkshire Herald* 6/6/17.

Edmondson, Thomas Claude, b. Leeds, e. Leeds, 38784, Private, DOW, 08/12/17, aged 30, buried in Mont Huon Military Cemetery, Le Treport.

Edwards, William Henry, b. Scarborough, e. Scarborough, Yorks, 52257, Private, KIA, 28/07/18, aged 20 buried in Marfaux British Cemetery.

Eldridge, Cyril, e. York, r. York, 33983, Private, KIA, 20/07/18, commemorated on the Soissons Memorial.

Ellwood, Thomas Roy, b. Bedale, Yorks, e. Harrogate, 200970, Lance Sergeant, KIA, 18/02/17, aged 21, commemorated on Thiepval Memorial.

Elsdon, Ingram Thomas, b. Dipton, Durham, e. Consett, Durham, 52256, Private, DOW, 26/11/17, aged 19, buried in Etaples Military Cemetery.

Elvidge, George Harold, b. Sheffield, e. Sheffield, 27712, Private, KIA, 20/07/18, Formerly 1887, 1/4th York & Lancs Regt, T.F., buried in Marfaux British Cemetery.

Evans, Edward, b. York, e. York, 201522, Private, KIA, 22/11/17, commemorated on the Cambrai Memorial, Louverval.

Evenson, George, b. Huddersfield, e. Huddersfield, 57525, Private, Died, 17/02/18, aged 32, buried in Aubigny Communal Cemetery Extension.

Fairclough, James Edward, e. Bradford, Yorks, r. Bradford, 4015, Private, KIA, 17/02/17, commemorated on Thiepval Memorial.

Fawcett, Fred, e. Leeds, 201709, Private, KIA, 08/04/17, aged 19, commemorated on the Arras Memorial to the Missing.

Feather, Norman, b. Bradford, e. Bradford, Yorks, 62076, Private, KIA, 31/07/18, aged 19, buried at Chambrecy British Cemetery, Obituary in *Bradford Weekly Telegraph* 20/9/18.

Flanagan, Edward, b. Dringhouses, York, e. York, 201717, Private, KIA, 03/05/17, commemorated on the Arras Memorial to the Missing.

Flanagan, Thomas, b. York, e. York, 200654, Corporal, KIA, 03/05/17, commemorated on the Arras Memorial to the Missing.

Flatt, Charles, b. Northdelph, Norfolk, e. Grimsby, r. Stepney, London, 201928, Private, KIA, 24/02/17, commemorated on Thiepval Memorial.

Ford, Samuel, b. Driffield, Yorks, e. Derby, 20461, Private, KIA, 20/07/18, Formerly 75360, A.S.C., commemorated on the Soissons Memorial.

Forth, Joseph, b. York, e. York, r. Tadcaster, 201683, Private, KIA, 12/04/17, commemorated on the Arras Memorial to the Missing.

Foster, Alfred Frederick, b. Rotherhithe, e. Rotherhithe, 51930, Private, KIA, 21/06/18, Formerly 258341, R.E., I.W.T., buried at Bienvillers Military Cemetery.

Fox, Ernest, b. Wath-on-Dearne, e. Mexborough, Yorks, 57394, Private, DOW, 22/07/18, aged 23, buried at Sezanne Communal Cemetery.

Franklin, Isaac, b. Walcott, Lincs, e. Sleaford, Lincs, 201882, Private, KIA, 03/05/17, aged 36, commemorated on the Arras Memorial to the Missing.

Freeman, Harold, b. Bradford, e. Bradford, Yorks, 268644, Private, KIA, 20/07/18, buried at Marfaux British Cemetery.

French, William, e. York, r. Ripon, 200772, Private, KIA, 03/05/17, commemorated on the Arras Memorial to the Missing.

Fry, Percy, b. South Normanton, South Derbys, e. Chesterfield, Derbys, 42048, Private, KIA, 20/11/17, aged 21, buried at Hermies Hill British Cemetery.

Gains, Ernest Frank, e. Otley, Yorks, 201266, Private, DOW, 01/01/18, aged 19, buried at St. Sever Cemetery Extension, Rouen.

Gallagher, Thomas, b. Easingwold, Yorks, e. York, 201761, Private, DOW, 28/11/17, aged 36, buried at Abbeville Communal Cemetery Extension.

Gamble, Harry, b. Knaresborough, Yorks, e. Harrogate, 4466, Private, DOW, 19/02/17, aged 20, buried at Bertrancourt Military Cemetery, obituary in *Harrogate Advertiser* 3/3/17.

Gartland, James, b. Stockton, Yorks, e. Richmond, Yorks, r. Thornaby-on-Tees, 52265, Private, KIA. 20/07/18, buried at Marfaux British Cemetery.

Gaunt, Harry, e. Dewsbury, Yorks, r. Dewsbury, 28520, Private, Died, 23/07/18, buried at Terlincthun British Cemetery, Wimille.

Gibson, Joseph, e. Skipton, Yorks, r. Morecambe, 236103, Sergeant, DOW, 28/11/17, Formerly 3627, West Riding Regt., aged 31, buried at Rocquigny-Equancourt Road British Cemetery, Manancourt.

Gilyard, Ernest William, b. Bradford, Yorks, e. Shipley, Yorks, 28688, Private, KIA, 22/11/17, aged 26, commemorated on the Cambrai Memorial, Louverval

Gleadall, Dennis, b. Tickhill, Yorks, e. Conisborough, Yorks, 270138, Private, DOW, 05/06/18, buried at Couin New British Cemetery

Gledhill, Jonas, e. Harrogate, Yorks, r. Starbeck, Yorks, 200998, Private, KIA, 26/03/18, commemorated on the Arras Memorial to the Missing.

Goodliff, William Henry, b. Stamford, Lincs, e. Stamford, 202024, Private, KIA, 20/11/17, commemorated on the Cambrai Memorial, Louverval, obituary *Harrogate Advertiser* 27/4/18.

Goundry, Oliver, e. Ripon, Yorks, 200994, Sergeant, KIA, 03/05/17, commemorated on the Arras Memorial to the Missing. Obituary *Harrogate Advertiser* 30/6/1917.

Graham, Ernest Arthur, b. Harrogate, e. Harrogate, Yorks, 201505, Private, KIA, 03/05/17, commemorated on the Arras Memorial to the Missing, obituary *Harrogate Advertiser* 16/3/18

Greaves, John Bernard, e. York, r. York, 201233, Private, KIA, 05/04/17, buried at Croisilles British Cemetery, obituary *Harrogate Herald* 25/4/1917.

Green, John, b. Martin, Lincs, e. Lincoln, r. East Barkwith, Lincs, 201919, Private, DOW, 06/05/17, buried at Hem-Lenglet Communal Cemetery.

Green, William, e. York, r. York, 201157, Lance Corporal, KIA, 20/11 /17, buried at Fifteen Ravine British Cemetery, Villers-Plouich.

Greenwood, Alfred, e. Bradford, Yorks, r. Bradford, 241362, Lance Corporal, KIA, 20/07/18, commemorated on the Soissons Memorial.

Griffiths, John, b. Birmingham, e. Walsall, Staffs, 57769, Private, KIA, 08/02/18, aged 39, buried at Orchard Dump Arleux-En-Gohelle

Grimbleby, Ernest, b. Barrowhaven, Lincs, e. Barton, Lincs, 202090, Corporal, KIA, 20/07/18, commemorated on the Soissons Memorial.

Guest, John, b. Barnsley, Yorks, e. Cleethorpes, Lincs, 57673, Private, DOW, 09/02/18, aged 26, buried at Anzin-St. Aubin British Cemetery.

Gunn, Frederick, b. Quarnford, Derbys, e. Hanley, Staffs, 58657, Private, KIA, 21/05/18, aged 19, buried at Bienvillers Military Cemetery.

Hackers, Edward Horace, b. Selby, Yorks, e. York, 57583, Private, KIA, 26/03/18, aged 26, commemorated on the Memorial to the Missing at Arras.

Hackney, John, e. Harrogate, r. Huby, Yorks, 201094, Corporal DOW, 26/05/17, aged 36, buried at Etaples Military Cemetery obituary in *Harrogate Herald* 6/6/17.

Hall, Reginald, b. Killamarsh, Derbys, e. Rotherham, Yorks, 57584, Private, DOW, 18/06/18, Formerly 43758, York & Lancs Regt., buried at Gezaincourt Communal Cemetery Extension.

Halliday, Henry, e. Selby, r. Selby, 201028, Private, KIA, 25/07/18, buried in St Imoges Churchyard.

Halliday, James, e. Selby, r. Selby, 200837, Private, KIA, 17/02/17, commemorated on the Thiepval Memorial.

Harris, Leonard Wilson, b. Boston Spa, Yorks, e. York, r. Tadcaster, York, 203587, Private, KIA, 20/07/18, buried at Marfaux British Cemetery.

Harris, Thomas, b. Newcastle-on-Tyne, e. Newcastle-on-Tyne, 30176, Private, DOW, 20/11/17, buried at Metz-En-Couture Communal Cemetery British Extension.

Harrison, Joseph, e. Lichfield, 242110, Private, KIA, 24/05/18, aged 25, buried at Gommecourt British Cemetery No.2, Hebuterne.

Harrison, William, b. Brimington, Derbys, e. Lincoln, r. Lincoln, 201868, Private, KIA, 03/05/17, aged 36, commemorated on the Memorial to the Missing at Arras.

Harvey, Edwin John Luscombe, b. Kentish Town, London, e. Kettering, r. Finedon, Northants, 53421, Private, KIA, 31/07/18, commemorated on the Soissons Memorial.

Hawke, Joseph Henry, b. Leeds, e. Leeds, 21/525, Private, KIA, 26/03/18, commemorated on the Memorial to the Missing at Arras.

Hawkins, George William, b. Lincoln, e. Lincoln, 202061, Private, KIA, 27/11/17, commemorated on the Cambrai Memorial, Louverval.

Hawkins, Henry, b. Harewood, e. Leeds, 202041, Private, DOW, 13/09/17, buried at Favreuil British Cemetery.

Henshaw, William, b. Rocester, Staffs, e. Mossley, Lancs, r. Mossley, 57772, Private, KIA, 21/03/18, buried at Roclincourt Military Cemetery.

Herring, Robert, b. West Hartlepool, e. West Hartlepool, 17434, Private, KIA, 25/04/18, buried at Gommecourt British Cemetery No.2, Hebuterne.

Hewson, Archibald, b. Knaresborough, e. Harrogate, 201982, Private, KIA, 03/05/17, commemorated on the Memorial to the Missing at Arras, obituary in *Harrogate Advertiser* 20/4/18.

Hewson, Charles Wilfred Thomas, e. York, r. York, 200805, C.S.M., KIA, 26/05/17 commemorated on the Memorial to the Missing at Arras.

Hewson, Geoffrey Halliday, b. Carlton, Miniott, e. Harrogate, 201742, Lance Sergeant, KIA, 20/07/18, aged 21, buried at Marfaux British Cemetery.

Hillyard, Frederick William George, b. Gateshead, e. Newcastle-on-Tyne, 57189, Private, DOW, 12/04/18, aged 31, buried at Bienvillers Military Cemetery.

Hinton, Hugh Raymond, e. Leeds, r. Aberford, Yorks., 267097, Rifleman, KIA, 27/11/17, commemorated on the Cambrai Memorial, Louverval.

Hoare, Harry, b. Bradford, e. Mexborough, Yorks, 61885, Private, KIA, 20/07/18, buried at Marfaux British Cemetery.

Holdsworth, John, e. York, r. Bradford, 3522, Private, KIA, 18/02/17, commemorated on the Thiepval Memorial.

Holmes, Edward, b. Birstall, e. Birstall, Yorks, 57774, Private, KIA, 26/03/18, aged 32, commemorated on the Memorial to the Missing at Arras.

Horner, Christopher, e. Knaresborough, r. Knaresborough, 201288, Private, DOW,12/05/17, buried at St Sever Extension Rouen, obituary *Harrogate Advertiser* 26/5/17.

Horner, Harry, b. Winksley, Yorks, e. Ripon, 201678, Private, KIA, 03/05/17, commemorated on the Memorial to the Missing at Arras.

Horner, James Henry Howard, b. Harrogate, e. Harrogate, 200013, C.S.M., KIA, 03/05/17, commemorated on the Memorial to the Missing at Arras.

Hornsey, Thomas Edward, b. York, e. York, 201830, Private, KIA, 26/05/17, commemorated on the Memorial to the Missing at Arras.

Hotchin, Christopher, b. Gaytenby Wold, Lincs, e. Louth, Lincs, 201920, Private, KIA, 08/04/17, commemorated on the Memorial to the Missing at Arras.

Howes, Albert, b. Otley, e. Otley, Yorks, 57775, Private, KIA, 21/03/18, buried at Roclincourt Military Cemetery.

Hoyle, Lawrence, b. Elland, Yorks, e. Barnsley, Yorks, 57531, Private, KIA, 12/04/18, buried at Gommecourt British Cemetery No.2, Hebuterne.

Hubbard, George, b. Burslem, Staffs, e. Burslem, 20866, Private, KIA, 20/07/18, Formerly 240701, R.F.A, aged 20, buried at Marfaux British Cemetery.

Hudson, John, b. Bradford, Yorks, e. Halifax, Yorks, 42108, Private, DOW, 27/05/17, buried at Achiet-Le-Grand Communal Cemetery Extension.

Hutchinson, Francis, b. Sutton-in-Ashfield, e. Mansfield, Notts, 42084, Private, KIA, 20/07/18, buried at Marfaux British Cemetery.

Iles, Charles Henry Cecil, b. York, e. York, 48601, Private, KIA, 21/11/17, commemorated on the Cambrai Memorial, Louverval.

Ironmonger, William Henry, b. Burley, Yorks, e. Leeds, 307410, Private, KIA, 26/03/18, commemorated on the Memorial to the Missing at Arras.

Irvine, Ernest, e. York, r. York, 201183, Private, KIA, 29/07/18, buried at Chambrecy British Cemetery.

Jackson, Lawrence, e. York, r. York, 201124, Private, KIA, 03/05/17, commemorated on the Memorial to the Missing at Arras.

Jackson, Wilson, e. Leeds, r. Leeds, 202588, Private, KIA, 27/11/17, commemorated on the Cambrai Memorial, Louverval.

Jarvis, John Henry, b. Ripon, e. Ripon, Yorks, 203600, Private, KIA, 26/03/18, commemorated on the Memorial to the Missing at Arras.

Jeavons, Harry, b. Dudley, Worcester, e. Smethwick, 15335, Acting Corporal, KIA, 14/06/18, buried at Bienvillers Military Cemetery.

Jewitt, Edward, e. York, 201521, Private, KIA, 20/11/17, buried at Hermies Hill British Cemetery.

Johnson, David, e. Ripon, Yorks, r. Scotton, Yorks, 40313, Private, DOW, 23/07/18, aged 28, buried at Terlincthun British Cemetery, Wimille, obituary in *Harrogate Advertiser* 24/8/18.

Johnson, John, b. Burnley, Lanes, e. Wakefield, Yorks, 60436, Private, KIA, 31/07/18, aged 19, buried at Chambrecy British Cemetery.

Jones, Ernest, b. Leeds, e. Leeds, 49565, Private, KIA, 20/07/18, commemorated on the Soissons Memorial.

Jones, Samuel Pearson, b. Bradford, Yorks, e. Bradford, 20867, Private, DOW, 29/11/17, Formerly 240647, R.F.A., buried at Grevillers British Cemetery. Obituary in *Bradford Weekly Telegraph* 7/12/18

Judd, George, b. Holbeach, Lincs, e. Lincoln, 201951, Private, KIA, 03/05/17, aged 27, commemorated on the Memorial to the Missing at Arras.

Judge, James, e. Selby, Yorks, r. Newcastle-on-Tyne, 201065, Lance Corporal, KIA, 20/04/17, aged 32, buried at Mory Abbey Military Cemetery.

Judson, Harold, b. Hovingham, Yorks, e. Otley, Yorks, 201556, Private, KIA, 03/05/17, aged 24, commemorated on the Memorial to the Missing at Arras.

Keightley, Percy, b. Luton, e. Grove Park, r. Luton, 41987, Formerly 227195, A.S.C., (M.T.) Private, KIA, 20/07/18, aged 20, buried at Marfaux British Cemetery.

Kettlewell, Harry, b. Potterton, Yorks, e. Leeds, 38540, Private, DOW, 09/03/18, buried at Etaples Military Cemetery.

Kirk, John Philip, b. Manby, Louth, Lincs, e. Louth, 202025, Private, KIA,03/05/17, aged 22, commemorated on the Memorial to the Missing at Arras.

Knowles, James Francis, b Crayke, Yorks, e. Harrogate, Yorks, 4462, Private, DOW, 05/03/17, commemorated on the Thiepval Memorial.

Lamb, Wilfred, b. Leeds, e. Harrogate, Yorks, r. Tadcaster, Yorks, 57588, Private, DOW, 04/04/18, buried at St Sever Extension Cemetery Rouen.

Laycock, William Sydney, b. Stockton, Durham, e. Stockton, r. Thornaby, 60242, Private, KIA, 20/07/18, commemorated on the Soissons Memorial.

Layfield, Loftas, b. Pateley Bridge, Yorks, e. Pateley Bridge, 49256, Private, DOW, 23/07/18, aged 39, buried at St Sever Extension Cemetery Rouen, obituary *Harrogate Advertiser* 27/7/1918.

Lazenby, William, e.York, r. York, 201846, Private, KIA, 03/05/17, commemorated on the Memorial to the Missing at Arras.

Learoyd, Francis, b. Staveley, Yorks, e. Harrogate, Yorks, 3039, Private, DOW, 26/02/17, buried at Doullens Communal Cemetery Extension No.1, obituary in *Harrogate Herald* 3/3/17.

Lidster, Thomas Mercer, b. South Shields, e. South Shields, r. North Shields, 57884, Private, KIA, 20/07/18, aged 33, buried at Marfaux British Cemetery.

Lister, Hubert, e. York, r. Nesfield, Ilkley, 7873, Private, KIA, 15/02/17, aged 19, commemorated on the Thiepval Memorial.

Littlewood, Horace, b. Stairfoot, Yorks, e. Barnsley, Yorks, 53682, Private, KIA, 20/07/18, aged 18, buried at Marfaux British Cemetery.

Long, Wilfred Arthur, e. Harrogate, Yorks, 200954, Sergeant, DOW, 14/06/18, aged 20, buried at Gezaincourt Communal Cemetery Extension.

Longfellow, Nathan, b. Boston Spa, York, e. Leeds, 201780, Private, DOW, 16/04/18, buried at Gezaincourt Communal Cemetery Extension.

Longford, Ernest, b. Spalding, Lincs, e. Spalding, 4245, Private, KIA, 08/02/17, aged 29, buried at Courcelles au Bois Extension Cemetery.

Lucas, William John, e. Lichfield, 203987, Private, Died, 27/03/18, aged 21, buried at Humbercamps Communal Cemetery Extension.

Lynch, Joseph Leo, b. Preston, Lancs, e. Preston, 58964, Private, KIA, 20/07/18, aged 19, buried at Marfaux British Cemetery.

Lyons, Henry, b. York, e. York, 201566, Sergeant, KIA, 20/07/18, M.M., aged 26, buried at Marfaux British Cemetery, obituary *Yorkshire Herald* 26/8/18.

Mackintosh, Walter, b. Harrogate, Yorks, e. Harrogate, 201528, Private, KIA, 03/05/17, commemorated on the Memorial to the Missing at Arras, obituary in *Harrogate Herald* 30/6/17.

Magson, Walter, b. Hull, Yorks, e. Beverley, Yorks, 42618, Private, KIA, 31/07/18, buried at Chambrecy British Cemetery.

Makin, Walter, b. Leeds, e. Leeds, 39918, Private, KIA, 26/03/18, aged 37, commemorated on the Memorial to the Missing at Arras.

Mark, Harry, b. York, e. York, 57283, Private, KIA, 12/04/18, buried at Gommecourt British Cemetery No.2, Hebuterne, obituary in *Yorkshire Gazette* 11/5/18.

Marshall, Harold, b. Armley, Leeds, e. Pudsey, Yorks, 307126, Lance Corporal, KIA, 20/11/17, buried in Fifteen Ravine British Cemetery, Villers-Plouich.

Marshall, Thomas, e. Selby, Yorks, r. Selby, 201187, Private, KIA, 03/05/17, aged 28, commemorated on the Memorial to the Missing at Arras.

Martin, Arthur Reginald, b. Wolverhampton, e. Wolverhampton, 52307, Private, KIA, 20/07/18, commemorated on the Soissons Memorial.

Mason, Charles Ernest, b. Rotherham, e. Rotherham, Yorks, 53688, Private, Died, 21/07/18, aged 18, buried at Gezaincourt Communal Cemetery Extension.

Mason, John, b. Harrogate, e. Harrogate, Yorks, 201785, Private, DOW, 19/05/17, aged 38, buried in Etaples Military Cemetery, obituary in *Harrogate Herald* 23/5/17.

Matley, Arthur, b. Birkenshaw, Yorks, e. Bradford, Yorks, 201711, Lance Corporal, KIA, 22/11/17, commemorated on the Cambrai Memorial, Louverval.

Mazeiko, John, b. Poland, e. Leeds, 39035, Private, DOW, 07/12/17, buried at St Sever Extension Cemetery Rouen.

Medley, Arthur, b. Manchester, e. York, r. York, 200586, Private, KIA, 03/05/17, commemorated on the Memorial to the Missing at Arras.

Megson, Joseph, b. Ossett, Yorks, e. Pontefract, Yorks, 42006, aged 40, Lance Corporal, KIA, 20/11/17, buried at Grand Ravine British Cemetery, Havrincourt.

Merrick, Robert, b. Stockton, Durham, e. Leeds, 21/644, Private, KIA, 20/07/18, commemorated on the Soissons Memorial.

Merriman, William, b. Yorks, e. Yorks, 201862, Private, Died, 07/07/17, aged 38, buried at York Cemetery, Yorkshire.

Metcalf, Edgar, b. Grewelthorpe, Yorks, e. Ripon, Yorks, r. Azerley, Ripon, 3996, Private, DOW, 02/02/17, aged 21, buried at Varennes Military Cemetery.

Midgely, Ernest, b. Todmorden, Yorks, e. Halifax, Yorks, r. Todmorden, 202508, Private, KIA, 29/05/18, commemorated on the Pozieres Memorial.

Miller, Arthur, e. York, r. York, 201346, Private, KIA, 03/05/17, aged 18, commemorated on the Memorial to the Missing at Arras, obituary in *Yorkshire Gazette* 16/3/18.

Mills, John, b. Morley, Yorks, e. Dewsbury, Yorks, 53691, Private, KIA, 21/05/18, aged 18, buried at Bienvillers Military Cemetery.

Milner, Henry, b. York, e. York, 201827, Private, KIA, 26/05/17, aged 30, commemorated on the Memorial to the Missing at Arras.

Milner, John William, b. York, e. York, 201723, Private, KIA, 24/05/18, aged 36, buried in Gommecourt British Cemetery No.2, Hebuterne.

Moran, Sidney, b. Walsall, Staffs, e. Walsall, 47090, Private, KIA, 20/07/18, aged 30, buried at Marfaux British Cemetery.

Mosey, Frederick, b. Halifax, Yorks, e. Halifax, 55037, Private, KIA, 20/07/18, aged 33, buried at Marfaux British Cemetery.

Moss, Alfred, e. York, r. Harrogate, Yorks, 201220, Lance Corporal, KIA, 17/02/17, aged 21, commemorated on the Thiepval Memorial.

Mugg, Walter Samuel, b. Aston, Birmingham, e. Birmingham, 20477, Private, KIA, 20/11/17, Formerly T/292151, ASC., buried in Ribecourt Road Cemetery, Trescault.

Mulholland, William Andrew, b. Belfast, e. Leeds, 201796, Lance Corporal, DOW, 20/11/17, buried in Rocquigny-Equancourt Road British Cemetery, Manancourt.

Mullins, John George, b. Wortley, Leeds, e. Leeds, 201705, Private, KIA, 17/02/17, commemorated on the Thiepval Memorial.

Neville, Harry, b. Morton, Lincs, e. Gainsborough, Lincs, r. Gainsborough, 202088, Sergeant, KIA, 20/07/18, buried at Marfaux British Cemetery.

Newitt, Frederick, b. Walsall, Staffs, e. Pontefract, Yorks, 39732, Private, DOW, 22/07/18, Formerly T/37212, A.S.C., buried in Sezanne Communal Cemetery.

Nicholson, Joseph, e. York, 201057, Corporal, DOW, 05/09/17, aged 34, buried in Fulford Cemetery, York.

Ogone, Peter, b. Poland, e Leeds, 39034, Private, DOW, 23/05/17, buried in Leeds Roman Catholic Cemetery.

O'Melia, James William, b. Holmfirth, Yorks, e. Halifax, Yorks, r. Mossley, 203160, Private, KIA,, 20/07/18, formerly 10802, West Riding Regt, buried at Marfaux British Cemetery.

Owston, Frank, e. Harrogate, Yorks, r. Rillington, Yorks, 2731, Private, DOW, 25/02/17, aged 25, commemorated on the Thiepval Memorial, obituary in *Harrogate Advertiser* 10/3/17.

Parnaby, William, b. Boston Spa, Yorks, e. Harrogate, Yorks, r. Boston Spa, 57886, Private, KIA, 20/07/18, aged 19, buried at Marfaux British Cemetery.

Parsons, George, b. Ringwood, Hants, e. Southampton, 20482, Private, KIA, 20/07/18, Formerly T/4/058773, A.S.C., aged 36, buried at Marfaux British Cemetery.

Patterson, James Robert, b. Gateshead, Durham, e. Gateshead, 57161, Private, KIA, 08/02/18, aged19, buried in Roclincourt Military Cemetery.

Pattinson, Henry, e. York, 200362, Private, KIA, 20/07/18, buried at Marfaux British Cemetery.

Pearce, Ernest William, b. Islington, e. Bedford, r. Kentish Town, 59775, Private, KIA, 20/07/18, buried at Marfaux British Cemetery.

Pearson, Pelham, b. Preston, Lancs, e. York, 201722, Private, KIA, 03/05/17, aged 23, commemorated on the Memorial to the Missing at Arras.

Pickard, Harry, b. Leeds, e. Leeds, 28891, Private, KIA, 20/07/18, buried at Marfaux British Cemetery.

Plant, John Percy, b. Burslem, Staffs, e. Hanley, r. Tunstall, 59509, Private, KIA, 20/07/18, aged 19, buried at Marfaux British Cemetery.

Pocklington, Thomas, b. Hull, Yorks, e. Lincoln, r. Saxilby Mills, Lincs, 4432, Private, KIA, 15/02/17, commemorated on the Thiepval Memorial.

Poole, Daniel, b Birmingham, e. Birmingham, 14588, Private, KIA, 20/07/18, buried at Marfaux British Cemetery.

Poutney, Ernest, b. Liversedge, Yorks, e. Liversedge, 57603, Private, KIA, 20/07/18, aged 21, buried at Marfaux British Cemetery.

Pratt, Herbert Henry, e. Leeds, 41411, Private, KIA, 20/07/18, aged 29, commemorated on the Soissons Memorial.

Prest, Robert, e. Harrogate, Yorks, r. Kirby, Malzeard, Ripon, Yorks, 201062, Private, KIA, 03/05/17, commemorated on the Memorial to the Missing at Arras.

Pycock, Ernest, b. Wainfleet Bank, Lincs, e. Wainfleet, 201883, Acting Corporal KIA, 20/07/18, aged 21, buried at Marfaux British Cemetery.

Radband, Percy John, e. York, r. Acomb, York, 2877, Private, KIA, 18/02/17, commemorated on the Thiepval Memorial.

Raftery, Simon, b. York, e. York, 40841, Private, KIA, 25/05/18, commemorated on the Pozieres Memorial

Randall, Edward, b. Nottingham, e. Nottingham, 58703, Private, KIA, 20/07/18, buried at Marfaux British Cemetery.

Ratcliffe, Norman, b. Luddenfoot, Yorks, e. Halifax, Yorks, 21/986, Private, KIA, 04/06/18, aged 28, buried at Bienvillers Military Cemetery.

Rawlings, Samuel James, e. Knaresborough, Yorks, r. Starbeck, Yorks, 200978, Private, KIA, 20/04/17, aged 30, buried at Mory Abbey Military Cemetery, Mory.

Reason, Harold, b. Leeds, e. Harrogate, Yorks, r. Horsforth, Yorks, 201730, Lance Corporal, KIA, 03/05/17, commemorated on the Memorial to the Missing at Arras.

Reaston, William, b. Skipwith, Yorks, e. Selby, Yorks, 201769, Private, KIA, 03/05/17, commemorated on the Memorial to the Missing at Arras.

Reddish, William, b. Snaith, Yorks, e. York, 201666, Private, KIA, 03/05/17, commemorated on the Memorial to the Missing at Arras.

Redshaw, James, e. Leeds, r. Leeds, 201693, Private, KIA, 03/05/17, aged 21, commemorated on the Memorial to the Missing at Arras.

Reed, Ernest Albert, b. Harrogate, e. Harrogate, Yorks, 201788, Private, DOW, 03/05/17, buried at Achiet-Le-Grand Communal Cemetery Extension.

Rhodes, Horace, b. Penistone, Yorks, e. Pontefract, Yorks, r. Clayton West, Nr. Barnsley, Yorks, 205454, Private, DOW,19/07/18, aged 20, buried in Vertus Communal Cemetery.

Richardson, David Remmer, b. Sunderland, e. Sunderland, 20830, Private, DOW, 15/03/18, buried at Roclincourt Military Cemetery.

Richmond, Fred, e. Harrogate, r. Plumpton Square, Nr. Knaresborough, Yorks, 201301, Corporal, KIA, 03/05/17, commemorated on the Memorial to the Missing at Arras.

Riddiough, Andrew Pickering, b. Barnsley, Yorks, e. Barnsley, 205446, Private, DOW, 12/06/18, buried at St. Sever Cemetery Extension, Rouen.

Robertshaw, Fred, b. Bradford, Yorks, e. Bradford, 202466, Private, DOW, 01/08/18, buried at St. Sever Cemetery Extension, Rouen.

Roper, Frank, b. St. Mary's, Sheffield, e. Sheffield, 22115, Private, KIA, 18/01/18, aged 20, buried at Roclincourt Military Cemetery.

Roughton, John, b. Friskney, Lincs, e. Lincoln, r. Friskney, 4541, Private, Died, Home, 04/07/16, aged 20, buried in Friskney Cemetery.

Rowland, William Henry, b. Brompton, Yorks, e. Richmond, Yorks, r. Borrowby, Thirsk, Yorks, 60282, Private, KIA, 20/07/18, buried at Marfaux British Cemetery.

Rush, Lawrence Edward, e. York, 201475, Private, KIA, 03/05/17, commemorated on the Memorial to the Missing at Arras, obituary in *Yorkshire Gazette* 23/3/18

Russell, Ernest, e. Bradford, Yorks, r. Bradford, 242987, Lance Corporal, DOW, 21/04/18, M.M., aged 30, buried at Bois Guillaume Communal Cemetery Extension. Obituary in *Bradford Weekly Telegraph* 3/5/18

Ryde, Arthur, e. York, 200739, Private, DOW, 12/04/18, aged 25, buried at Gommecourt British Cemetery No.2, Hebuterne.

Sadler, Fred, e. Knaresborough, Yorks, 200928, A/C.S.M., KIA, 26/03/18, buried at Bienvillers Military Cemetery.

Sanderson, Ernest, b. Chesterfield, e. Chesterfield, 57794, Private, DOW, 08/02/18, buried at Maroeuil British Cemetery.

Scarth, Charles, b. Pudsey, Yorks, e. Pudsey, 202138, Private, KIA, 22/11/17, aged 20, buried in Grand Ravine British Cemetery, Havrincourt.

Scott, Leonard, b. Leeds, e. Leeds, 265545, Private, DOW, 21/07/18, aged 23, buried at Sezanne Communal Cemetery.

Sedgwick, Harry, b. Halifax, Yorks, e. Halifax, 20711, Corporal, DOW, 28/03/18, Formerly 82, Yorks M.B., Field Ambulance, aged 22, buried at Cauchie Communal Cemetery.

Seymour, James William, e. Spilsby, Lincs, 201897, Private, KIA, 03/05/17, aged 38, commemorated on the Memorial to the Missing at Arras.

Seymour, Lewis, b. Netherton, Yorks, e. Huddersfield, Yorks, 57558, Private, KIA, 20/07/18, aged 33, buried at Marfaux British Cemetery.

Sharp, Herbert, b. New Leake, Boston, Lincs, e. Lincoln, r. Stickney, Boston, Lincs, 201917, Lance Corporal, DOW, 12/08/18, buried in St. Sever Cemetery Extension, Rouen.

Sharratt, Merle, b. Linthwaite, Yorks, e. Huddersfield, Yorks, 242347, Private, KIA, 22/04/18, aged 35, buried at Bienvillers Military Cemetery.

Shaw, David, b. Huddersfield, Yorks, e. Leeds, 202034, Private, KIA, 20/11/17, aged 31, buried at Hermies Hill British Cemetery

Shaw, William, b. Helton, Durham, e. Chester-Le-Street, Durham, 60494, Private, KIA, 20/07/18, aged 19, commemorated on the Soissons Memorial.

Shepherd, Charles, b. York, e. York, 200224, Private, KIA, 10/04/17, buried at Croisilles British Cemetery.

Shepherd, William Frederick, b. York, e. York, 201535, Private, Died, 03/04/17, buried at Varennes Military Cemetery.

Simmonite, William, b. Park, Sheffield, e. Sheffield, 201276, Private, KIA, 03/05/17, aged 27, commemorated on the Memorial to the Missing at Arras.

Simpson, Sidney, b. Scarborough, Yorks, e. Scarborough, 3/10379, Private, KIA, 20/07/18, buried at Marfaux British Cemetery.

Simpson, Stanley, b. York, e. York, 200202 Acting Corporal, KIA, 22/11/17, aged 21, commemorated on the Cambrai Memorial, Louverval

Skelton, Percy, e. Harrogate, Yorks, r. Harrogate, 3327, Private, DOW, 02/02/17, buried at Varennes Military Cemetery, obituary *Harrogate Herald* 21/2/17.

Slater, Cyril, b. Leeds, e. Leeds, 37740, Private, KIA, 20/07/18, buried at Marfaux British Cemetery.

Slater, Harry, b. Roecliffe, Yorks, e. Kirby Hill, Yorks, r. Borobridge Yorks, 202045, Private, KIA, 20/11/17, aged 37, buried at Sains-Les-Marquion British Cemetery.

Smith, John, b. Kirkmichael, Ayrshire, e. Middlesbrough, 57198, Private, DOW, 13/04/18, aged 33, buried at Gezaincourt Communal Cemetery Extension.

Smith, Leonard, b. Harrogate, e. Harrogate, 242282, Private, KIA, 03/05/17, aged 21, commemorated on the Memorial to the Missing at Arras.

Smith, Mark, b. Leeds, e. Leeds, 202147, Private, KIA, 03/05/17, aged 19, commemorated on the Memorial to the Missing at Arras.

Smith, Thomas King, b. Scarborough, Yorks, e. Hull, Yorks, 267817, Private, DOW, 10/04/18, buried at Etaples Military Cemetery.

Smith, Walter, e. York, r. Harchills, Leeds, 201463, Lance Corporal, KIA, 03/05/17, commemorated on the Memorial to the Missing at Arras.

Snell, Harold, b. Leeds, e. Leeds, 202674, Private, KIA, 31/07/18, buried at Chambrecy British Cemetery

Spencer, Harry, e. Selby, Yorks, r. Leicester, 201203, Lance Corporal, KIA, 26/05/17, aged 27, commemorated on the Memorial to the Missing at Arras.

Spivey, Walter, b. Huddersfield, Yorks, e. Halifax, Yorks, 63851, Private, KIA, 31/07/18, commemorated on the Soissons Memorial.

Stabler, Robert Hildreth, b. York, r. Norton, Malton, Yorks, 201914, Corporal, KIA, 17/02/17, commemorated on the Memorial to the Missing at Arras.

Stanger, Robert Henry, b. Keighley, Yorks, e. Halifax, Yorks, r. Greetland, Halifax, 52340, Private, KIA, 20/07/18, aged 19, buried at Marfaux British Cemetery.

Steele, James, b. Holtby, Yorks, e. Leeds, r. Sherburn-in-Elmet, Yorks, 49270, Private, KIA, 29/03/18, commemorated on the Memorial to the Missing at Arras

Stephenson, Thomas Edward, e. York, 201199, Lance Corporal, KIA, 20/07/18, aged 22, buried at Marfaux British Cemetery.

Stonehouse, James, e. Stockton, Durham, r. New Town, Stockton-on-Tees, 235672, Acting Company Sergeant Major, DOW, 10/11/17, aged 39, buried at Etaples Military Cemetery.

Stott, William, b. Kirby Hill, Yorks, e. Newcastle-on-Tyne, 20845, Private, KIA, 28/03/18, Formerly 24030, Royal Horse, & Royal Field Artillery, aged 26, buried at Bienvillers Military Cemetery, obituary *Harrogate Advertiser* 27/4/18.

Swallow, Charlie, b. Bradford, Yorks, e. Bradford, 22381, Private, aged 26, KIA, 23/05/18, buried at Bienvillers Military Cemetery, obituary in *Bradford Weekly Telegraph* 14/6/18

Swift, Allan Whitty, b. Burley, Leeds, e. Leeds, 15/868, Private, KIA, 20/07/18, buried at Marfaux British Cemetery.

Swinscoe, James, b. Womersley, Yorks, e. Dewsbury Yorks, 21/410, Private, KIA, 20/07/18, commemorated on the Soissons Memorial.

Sykes, Joe, b. Slaithwaite, Yorks, e. Halifax, Yorks, 63852, Private, KIA, 29/07/18, commemorated on the Soissons Memorial, obituary in *Bradford Weekly Telegraph* 7/6/18

Sykes, Ralph, b. Bradford, Yorks, e. Bradford, 41744, Private, DOW, 01/04/18, aged 24, buried at Doullens Communal Cemetery Extension No.1.

Taylor, Harold, b. Seacroft, Yorks, e. York, 42366, Private, KIA 20/07/18, commemmorated on the Soissons Memorial.

Taylor, John, b. North Reston, Lincs, e. Lincoln, 201944, Lance Corporal, KIA, 20/07/18, buried at Marfaux British Cemetery.

Taylor, Thomas, b. Barony, Lanark, e. Glasgow, 51853, Private, KIA, 20/07/18, Formerly 24297, Royal Scots., buried at Marfaux British Cemetery.

Teasdale, Joseph, e. Newcastle-on-Tyne, 54619, Private, KIA, 31/07/18, aged 23, buried at Rethel French National Cemetery.

Thacker, James, b. Clayton, Yorks, e. Bradford, Yorks, 201689, Lance Corporal, KIA, 20/07/18, aged 23, buried at Marfaux British Cemetery, obituary in *Bradford Weekly Telegraph* 23/8/18

Thompson, Frank Horace, b. Noramby, Lincs, e. Lincoln, 202011, Acting Lance Corporal, KIA, 26/03/18, buried at Bienvillers Military Cemetery.

Thompson, Samuel, b. Leeds, e. Leeds, 202141, Private, DOW, 27/05/17, aged 27, buried at Ervillers Military Cemetery.

Thornton, Herbert, b. Leeds, e. Leeds, 49368, Private, KIA, 20/07/18, aged 32, buried at Marfaux British Cemetery.

Thorpe, Albert, b. Chesterfield, Derbyshire, e. Chesterfield, 53745, Private, KIA, 20/07/18, aged 18, buried at Marfaux British Cemetery.

Tucker, Douglas, b. Bristol, e. Leeds, 4579, Private, KIA, 06/02/17, aged 17, buried at Courcelles-Au-Bois Communal Cemetery Extension.

Tunnicliffe, Percy, b. Burton-on-Trent, e. Burton-on-Trent, 53773, Private, KIA, 20/07/18, aged 19, buried at Marfaux British Cemetery.

Turner, Edgar, e. York, r. York, 201176, Lance Corporal, KIA, 01/03/17, aged 21, commemorated on the Thiepval Memorial.

Turpin, Harry, b. York, e. York, 3978, Lance Corporal, KIA, 15/02/17, aged 22, commemorated on the Thiepval Memorial, obituary *Yorkshire Evening Post* 2/3/17.

Tyler, Gilbert Ringham, b. Thilby, Lincs, e. Bourne, Lincs, 42330, Private, KIA, 31/07/18, aged 21, buried at Chambrecy British Cemetery.

Upshaw, Fred William Edward, b. Salters Lode, Denver, Norfolk, e. Norwich, r. Downham Market, 20502, Private, KIA, 20/07/18, formerly 2469, East Anglian Ambulance, buried at Marfaux British Cemetery.

Vernon, Allen, b. Leeds, e. Leeds, 48908, Private, KIA, 20/07/18, buried at Marfaux British Cemetery.

Wade, Willie, b. Bradford, Yorks, e. Bradford, 41994, Private, KIA, 21/05/18, aged 34, buried at Bienvillers Military Cemetery, obituary in *Bradford Weekly Telegraph* 31/5/18

Waite, Robert, e. Knaresborough, Yorks, 200956, Private, KIA, 10/09/17, buried at Favreuil British Cemetery.

Wakeling, Albert Edward, b. Croydon, Surrey, e. Kingston-on-Thames, 20933, Private, KIA, 21/05/18, Formerly 235940, Royal Field Artillery,

Waldby, Robert Alfred, b. St. Lukes, Harrogate, Yorks, e. Harrogate, 201531, Private, KIA, 20/07/18, buried at Marfaux British Cemetery, obituary *Harrogate Advertiser* 10/8/18.

Walker, Rupert, e. Harrogate, Yorks, r. Ripon, Yorks, 200894, Private, KIA, 30/03/18, aged 27, buried at Couin New British cemetery.

Walkington, Alma, e. York, r. Kirk Hammerton, Yorks, 201516, Private, KIA, 16/02/17, buried at Ten Tree Alley Cemetery, obituary *Harrogate Herald* 21/3/17.

Ware, George, b. York, e. York, 201812, Private, KIA, 15/05/17, aged 21, buried at Croisilles Railway Cemetery, obituary *Yorkshire Herald* 31/ 5/17.

Warn, Abraham, b. Laughton, Lincs, e. Market Deeping, Lincs, r. Market Deeping, 202055, Private, KIA, 17/02/17, aged 37, commemorated on the Thiepval Memorial.

Watkins, George William, b. Birmingham, e. Wolverhampton, 53758, Private, Died, 17/09/18, buried at St Sever Cemetery Extension Rouen.

Watson, Ebenezer, b. Gateshead, Durham, e. Felling-on-Tyne, 54546, Private, KIA, 31/07/18, buried at Chambrecy British Cemetery

Welby, John, b. York, e. York, 202036, Private, DOW, 21/11/17, aged 21, buried at Rocquigny-Equancourt Road British Cemetery, Manancourt

Welton, Tom, b. Brigg, Lincs, e. York, 203590, Private, KIA, 20/07/18, commemorated on the Soissons Memorial.

Whatley, John William, b. York, e. York, 201669, Private, KIA, 08/04/17, aged 33, commemorated on the Memorial to the Missing at Arras.

Whetstone, Walter, b. Wortley, Leeds, e. Leeds, 63858, Private, KIA, 30/07/18, aged 18, buried at Chambrecy British Cemetery.

Whincup, Thomas, e. Knaresborough, Yorks, r. Knaresborough, 201289, Private, KIA, 29/07/18, aged 21, buried at Chambrecy British Cemetery.

Whiston, Frederick, b. Hanley, Staffs, e. Lichfield, 242122, Private, DOW, Home, 08/11/18, aged 24, buried at Wetley Rocks (St. John) Churchyard.

Whitaker, Sydney, b. Grassington, Yorks, e. Skipton, Yorks, 201989, Private, KIA, 03/05/17, commemorated on the Memorial to the Missing at Arras.

White, Bernard, b. Monk Bretton, Yorks, e. Barnsley, Yorks, 270215, Private, DOW, 21/11/17, aged 19, buried at Grevillers British Cemetery.

Whiting, William, b. Bradford, Yorks, e. Bradford, 240119, Private, KIA, 22/07/18, aged 24, buried at Terlincthun British Cemetery, Wimille, obituary in *Bradford Weekly Telegraph* 6/9/18

Wilcock, Reggie, b. York, e. York, 200225, Private, KIA, 03/05/17, aged 19, buried at London Cemetery, Neuville-Vitasse.

Wilding, Charles Smith, b. Whitby, Yorks, e. Hull, Yorks, 13954, Lance Corporal, KIA, 25/07/18, aged 25, commemorated on the Soissons Memorial.

Wildman, Henry Dennis, e. Selby, 2640, Private, DOW, 05/02/17, aged 25, buried at Mesnil Communal Cemetery Extension.

Wilkins, James, e. Harrogate, Yorks, r. Cheltenham, 3114, Private, KIA, 18/02/17, commemorated on the Thiepval Memorial.

Wilkinson, Arthur, b. Bradford, Yorks, e. Bradford, r. Manningham, Yorks, 16/201, Private, KIA, 22/11/17, commemorated on the Cambrai Memorial, Louverval

Wilkinson, William, b. Quarrington, Lincs, e. Boston, Lincs, r. Boston, 4535, Private, KIA, 06/02/17, aged 25, buried at Courcelles-Au-Bois Communal Cemetery Extension

Williamson, Arthur, b. Bradford, Yorks, e. Bradford, 241625, Private, KIA, 29/07/18, commemorated on the Soissons Memorial.

Wilson, Alfred, b. Walthamstow, Essex, e. Walthamstow, 20507, Lance Corporal, DOW, 20/11/17, formerly 1964, East Anglian Field Ambulance, buried at Metz-En-Couture Communal Cemetery British Extension

Wilson, Frank, b. Leeds, e. York, 202615, Private, KIA, 20/07/18, commemorated on the Soissons Memorial.

Wilson, Gilbert, e. Huddersfield, 50217, Private, KIA, 22/11/17, aged 30, commemorated on the Cambrai Memorial, Louverval.

Winkley, Edward, b. Salford, Lancs, e. Salford, 20512, Private, KIA, 20/11/17, formerly T/291700, A.S.C, commemorated on the Cambrai Memorial, Louverval

Winterburn, John William, e. Harrogate, Yorks, r. Harrogate, 201029, Private, KIA, 20/02/17, aged 26, buried at Ancre British Cemetery, Beaumont-Hamel obituary *Harrogate Herald* 7/3/17.

Wise, William Charles, b. York, e. York, 4199, Private, DOW, 18/02/17, aged 28, buried at Varennes Military Cemetery.

Woolsoncroft, Thomas, e. Mansfield, r. Sutton-in-Ashfield, Notts, 47104, Private, DOW, 21/11/17, aged 21, buried at Rocquigny-Equancourt Road British Cemetery, Manancourt, obituary *Nottingham Free Press* 1/11/18

Worrall, Arthur Francis, b. Leicester, e. Leicester, 57806, Private, DOW, 21/03/18, buried at Roclincourt Military Cemetery

Wortley, William, e. York, r. York, 201373, Private, KIA, 03/05/17, commemorated on the Memorial to the Missing at Arras

Wrightson, Percival, e. Harrogate, Yorks, r. Harrogate, 200999, Sergeant, DOW, 05/05/17, aged 30, buried in Boulogne Eastern Cemetery, obituary *Harrogate Herald* May 1917.

Youll, William Bowden, b. Wallsend-on-Tyne, e. Wallsend-on-Tyne, 46108, Private, KIA, 26/03/18, Formerly 31419, K.O.Y.L.I., commemorated on the Memorial to the Missing at Arras

Young, Robert Elliott, b. Barnard Castle, Durham, e. Stockton-on-Tees, 60672, Private, KIA, 20/07/18, buried at Marfaux British Cemetery.

Youngs, Clement, e. Saxmundham, Norfolk, 203771, Private, KIA, 13/09/17, formerly1830, 6th Cyclist Res. Battn., Suffolk Regt., buried at Favreuil British Cemetery

Appendix 2
Officer Roll of Honour
2/5th Battalion West Yorkshire
Regiment 1914 - 1918

Airey, Norman George, 2/Lt, Killed in action, 22/11/17, commemorated on the Cambrai Memorial, Louverval.

Annely, Ernest George, 2/Lt, Killed in action, 03/05/17, aged 29, commemorated on the Memorial to the Missing at Arras.

Dale, Alwyn Percy, OBE, Major, Killed in action, 01/03/17, buried at Queens Cemetery, Bucquoy, obituary in *Yorkshire Gazette* 27/7/18.

De Ville, Charles Arthur, 2/Lt, Killed in action, 20/07/18, buried at Marfaux British Cemetery.

Donkersley, Reynold, 2/Lt, MC, Killed in action, 20/07/18, aged 23, buried at Marfaux British Cemetery.

Gibson, Thomas Ernest, 2/Lt, Killed in action, 28/11/17, aged 23, commemorated on the Cambrai Memorial, Louverval.

Hutchinson, Hanley, Lt, Died of wounds, 01/09/17, aged 26, buried at Grevillers British Cemetery.

Kermode, Edgar Marsden, 2/LT, DSO, MC & BAR DCM, Died of wounds, 27/07/18, aged 22, buried at St Imoges Churchyard, near Marfaux, commemorated on the East Window at St Peter's Church, Shipley and in the Prince of Wales' Own Regiment of Yorkshire museum at York.

Knowles, Frank Henry, Captain, Killed in action, 03/05/17, aged 30, commemorated on the Memorial to the Missing at Arras.

Schindler, William Barron, 2/Lt, Killed in action, 20/07/18, aged 23, buried at Marfaux British Cemetery.

Skirrow, Geoffrey, Acting Captain, Killed in action, 27/08/18, aged 22, buried at Mory Abbey Military Cemetery, commemorated on the family tomb Addingham Churchyard, Yorkshire.

Smith, Norman Herbert, 2/Lt, Killed in action, 20/11/17, aged 20. Buried at Flesquieres Hill Cemetery.

Wilson, Arnold, 2/Lt, Killed in action, 03/05/17, aged 22, commemorated on the Memorial to the Missing at Arras, obituary in *Bradford Weekly Telegraph* 27/4/17.

Officers serving with the 2/5th at the time of their death

Churchman, Charles Harvey, Captain, 6th Battalion Suffolk Regiment, killed in action 03/05/1917, aged 22, commemorated on the Memorial to the Missing at Arras

Cole, William Thomas 2/Lt, 4th Battalion Yorkshire Regiment, killed in action 29/07/1918, aged 23, buried at Chambrecy British Cemetery

Grigson, Kenneth Walton, MC, Captain, 7th Battalion Devonshire Regiment, killed in action 20/07/1918, buried at Marfaux British Cemetery.

Hutchinson, George Russell, 2/Lt, 2/8th Battalion West Yorkshire Regiment, killed in action 26/11/1917, aged 22, commemorated on the Cambrai Memorial, Louverval.

Jennings, William, 2/Lt, 5th Battalion Yorkshire Regiment, killed in action, 31/07/1918, buried at Beaurepaire French National Cemetery, Pontavert.

Officers of 2/5th killed while attached to other units

Hutchinson, William, 2/Lt, Killed in action, 22/11/17, aged 22, attached 2/8th Battalion West Yorkshire Regiment, commemorated on the Cambrai Memorial, Louverval

Officers Captured

Wilcox, Harry, Lt, B Company, wounded and captured 03/05/1917 at Bullecourt, aged 24, held at Karlsruhe camp.

Appendix 3
Honours and Awards
2/5th Battalion West Yorkshire
Regiment 1914 - 1918

Commanding Officers

Bottomley, Richard Arthur Augustus, Lieutenant Colonel, 2/5th Battalion West Yorkshire Regiment, formerly Commanding 2nd Volunteer Battalion West Yorks at Bradford 1906 – 08. Territorial Decoration, Military Member for West Riding Territorial Force County Association, Mentioned in Dispatches on the list of those brought to notice of the Secretary of State for War for distinguished services in connection with the war.

Josslyn, John J., Lieutenant Colonel, attached from 6th Battalion Suffolk Regiment, CMG, DSO, OBE, TD, Croix de Guerre, three times Mentioned in Dispatches, Member of the Order of St Michael and St George, Order of Saint Apostolic and Grand Duke Vladimir (Russian) and the Saint Anne, 2nd Class with Swords (Russian). The DSO was in the *London Gazette* (LG) on 1/1/18, for an act of gallantry not in the presence of the enemy. His OBE was listed on 7/6/18 and amended to the Military division on 15/4/19.

Waddy Richard H. Lieutenant Colonel, attached from 1st Battalion Somerset Light Infantry, DSO Birthday Honours List, LG 3/5/1918 for distinguished service in connection with military operations in France and Flanders. Mentioned in Dispatches LG 23/5/1918. Awarded Croix de Guerre in July 1918 for actions at Marfaux and Mont de Bligny, LG 7/10/19.

Officers

Airey, John Croft, Lieutenant, attached from 10th Royal Scots, MC, LG 7/11/18, for his actions at the engagement at Marfaux.

Anderson, John Miller, Lieutenant, MC, LG 11/1/19 while attached to 5th Battalion Devonshire Regiment as adjutant. Won for a patrol action of which no details are known.

Bailey, R, Second Lieutenant, MC and Bar, awarded after he left the Battalion on 11/7/1918. The MC was listed with a citation on 11/1/19, he was attached to 2/4 Y&L, the Bar was listed on 2/4/19 and on 10/12/19 with a citation.

Bardsley, Ernest Harrison, Lieutenant, MC, LG on 7/11/18 for his actions at Marfaux.

Donkersley, Reynold Second Lieutenant, MC, LG 16/9/18 reported in Brigade orders 11/6/18 for patrol and raiding work.

Foster, Robert Joseph, Second Lieutenant, Mentioned in Dispatches on 27/12/18.

Friend, Charles, Lieutenant, MC and Croix De Guerre. Attached to 185 Infantry Brigade HQ, MC Citation LG on 11/1/19 and Croix de Guerre on 7/10/19. Also Mentioned in Dispatches LG 23/5/18.

Green, Arthur Estough, Captain, MC LG 16/8/17 for his role in the second Battle of Bullecourt, citation printed in Brigade Orders 1/6/17.

Grigson, Kenneth Walton, MC, Captain, 7th Battalion Devonshire Regiment attached, recorded in war diary on 21/6/18, awarded in Birthday Honours list.

Gwynn, Arthur Joseph, Second Lieutenant, MC, LG 7/11/18 for actions in the engagement at Marfaux.

Heaton, Hedley Francis, Captain MC, LG 9/12/19, for conspicuous gallantry at Avesnes-le Sec, from 11 to 16 October, 1918.

Kermode, Edgar Marsden, Second Lieutenant, DSO, MC and Bar, DCM. DCM for bravery on 19/12/15 for rescuing the wounded under shellfire while a private in the 1/6th West Yorks in the Ypres salient. MC for a patrol action on 6/7 September 1917 with Second Lieutenant Simpson, LG 7/3/18, Bar to the MC for his action at the defence of Bucquoy 26/3/18, LG 16/9/18, and DSO for a trench raid at Biez Wood on 25/ 5/18, LG 16/9/18. Mentioned in Dispatches LG 27/12/18.

McLintock, WJ, Second Lieutenant MC, LG on 7/11/18, Croix de Guerre (France) LG 7/1/19.

Riley, Bernard Mann, Lieutenant MC, LG 7/11/18 for actions as Battalion Intelligence Officer at the engagement at Marfaux.

Riley, T, Captain & QM, MC, New Years Honours List, LG 1/1/18.

Sawyer, Edward Charles, Lieutenant, MC, for bravery in bringing up supplies under fire. Citation LG 5/7/1918. Award made on 1/1/18 recorded in the war diary, relating his action at the Battle of Cambrai on 20/11/17.

Simpson, J H, Second Lieutenant, Croix de Guerre (French) reported in Brigade orders 21/6/18 for an action on 25/5/18, related to his role in the Biez Wood raid, LG 17/8/18.

Skirrow, Geoffrey, acting Captain, Croix de Guerre (French) avec Palme, LG 14/7/17 for patrol work before the first Battle of Bullecourt.

Smith, Arthur Wilfred Lucius, Lieutenant, MC, LG on 18/6/17, reported in *Yorkshire Herald* 15/5/1917 for fighting and reconnaissance patrols near

Croisilles in April 1917. Also awarded the Croix de Guerre at an unknown date.

Stuart GF, Lieutenant, DSO, LG 5/7/18 while serving with 2/6th West Yorks. Mentioned in Dispatches 23/5/18.

Tewson, Harold Vincent, Second Lieutenant, MC LG 5/7/18. LG on 4/2/18, citation printed 5/7/18 for bravery in leading his men under fire. Award made on 1/12/18 recorded in war diary and relating to his action at the Battle of Cambrai on 20/11/17.

Veal, Leo Francis, Second Lieutenant, MC, LG 5/7/18, award made on 1/1/18 in war diary relating to securing an exposed flank at the Battle of Cambrai.

Walker, Raymond Butler, Second Lieutenant, Mentioned in Dispatches LG 27/12/18.

Wilson, Arthur George, Second Lieutenant, MC while attached to the RAF, LG 26/7/18.

Awards Won by Non Commissioned Officers and Men of the 2/5th

Abbott J, Sgt, 200783, MM, LG 6/7/17 for Bullecourt.

Allen A E, Pte, 42016, MM, LG 7/2/19.

Allinson W B, Pte, 241936, MM LG 10/12/18 for the action at Marfaux.

Appleby, SP, L/Cpl, 202109, MM, LG 11/12/18.

Aves CA, Pte, 52004, MM, LG 7/2/1919.

Beetham H, Pte, 203773, DCM, LG29/10/18 for bringing in the wounded under fire.

Bell S D, Cpl, 11307, MM, for actions at Cambrai on 20/11/1917, LG12/3/18.

Bevens, G H, L/Cpl, 42028, MM, for actions at Cambrai on 20/11/17, LG 12/3/18.

Bingham T, Pte, 202093, for actions at Cambrai, LG12/3/18.

Boult J R, Pte, 57492, MM, LG 10/12/18.

Bradley J, L/Cpl, 201126, MM and Bar, MM LG 6/7/1917 for Bullecourt, Bar for action at Bucquoy 25/3/18, LG 29/8/18

Brear G W, L/Cpl, 267154, MM LG 11/12/18.

Briggs F (sometimes Buggs), L/Cpl, 42032, MM, LG 13/3/18, for actions at Cambrai where he was wounded.

Bromfield J, Pte, 201906, MM, LG 11/12/18 for the action at Marfaux

Bryant C E, Pte, 203630, MM for Bucquoy 25/3/18, LG 26/9/18

Burdett T H, Cpl, 42435, MM, LG 10/12/18.

Campbell R W, Sgt 238027, DCM, LG 30/10/18 for Marfaux.

Cole A, Cpl, 200985, MM, LG 7/2/19.

Collinson A E, L/Cpl, 202019, MM, for actions at Cambrai on 20/11/17, LG 12/3/18.

Cope R, Pte, 52034, MM for Bucquoy 25/3/18, LG 29/8/18

Coulter W J, CSM, 200713, Mentioned in Dispatches LG 22/5/17

Cross A, Pte, 59207, MM, LG 10/12/18 when serving with 10th Btn West Yorks.

Crowther C, L/Cpl, 265469, MM LG 11/12/18.

Cust J W, L/Cpl, 3717, MM, for fighting Patrol near Croisilles with Lt Smith. LG 26/5/17

Dagg J T, Pte, 40973, MM, LG 7/2/19.

Damme R, L/Cpl, 42044, MM, LG 16/11/17, possibly for a patrol 6/9/17 with Kermode

Davies S, (of Birmingham), CQMS, 42000, Croix de Guerre LG 3/10/19

Day A, Pte, 201980, MM, LG 10/12/18.

Doe C, Pte, 200982, MM, for actions at Cambrai, LG 12/3/18.

Ewbank J, L/Cpl, 201557, original regimental number 3787, MM and Bar. MM LG 26/5/17 for repairing communications under fire, Bar for action at Bucquoy, LG 29/8/18.

Falconer J S, L/Cpl, 20166, MM, LG 10/12/18. DCM with 8th WYR LG 2/12/19

Foster W V, Pte, 200858, MM, for actions at Cambrai, LG12/3/18.

Grasby J W, Pte, 201361, MM, for actions at Cambrai, LG 12/3/18.

Greaves G E, CQMS, 200047, MM, LG 10/12/18.

Haigh W Pte 48379, MM for Bucquoy 25/3/18, LG 29/8/18

Holliday R, L/Cpl, 201935, MM, LG 6/7/17 for Bullecourt.

Hudson T, Cpl, 200463, MM, LG 7/2/19.

Huggins J W Sgt, 201012, MM, LG 12/3/18 for Cambrai.

Irving J, Sgt, 201115, MM for Bullecourt. LG 29/8/18

Johnson J, Pte, 59588, MM, LG 7/2/19.

Keatley JC, L/Cpl, 268521, MM, LG 6/7/17 for Bullecourt.

Kelly J H, Pte (LCpl), 201997 MM LG 14/5/19, 8 WYR. Pte Kelly has a 5th WYR number so may have transferred to 8th West Yorks on disbandment.

Lamb C W, L/Cpl, 200904, MM for Bucquoy 25/3/18. LG 29/8/18

Lumley G, Pte, 201544 MM LG 11/2/19, 8 WYR

Lyons, H. Sgt, 201566 MM LG 7/10/18

Marston T, L/Cpl, 4265, MM for a covering the retreat of a patrol at Ten Tree Alley on 17/2/1917. LG 26/4/17

McGregor J, Pte, 20476, MM, for actions at Cambrai, where he was wounded, LG 12/3/18.

Moody J A, Cpl, 42438, MM, for actions at Cambrai where he was wounded, LG 12/3/18.

Molyneaux C, A/Cpl 200778 Meritorious Service Medal LG 17/6/18

Page H, Sgt, 200046 Meritorious Service Medal LG 28/9/17 (for gallantry)

Page P, Pte, 41785, MM, LG 7/2/19.

Pearson HA Sgt, 201129, MM, for actions at Cambrai where he was wounded, LG 12/3/18.

Pickard L, CSM, 240010 Meritorious Service Medal LG 17/6/18.

Pickthall W, Pte, 2746, MM, LG 11/5/17, for the rescue of 2/Lt H A Girling in Ten Tree Alley February 1917.

Plant H G, Pte, 57191, MM, LG 10/12/18.

Platt B T, Pte, 20484, MM, LG 7/2/19. Bar to MM LG 11/2/19 55731 Pte BT Platt 4 Y & L formerly 20484 WYR.

Plumb F, L/Cpl, 3700, MM, for the rescue of 2/Lt Girling under fire at Ten Tree Alley 17/2/1917, LG 24/4/17.

Pope A, CQMS, 20026, MM, LG 10/12/18.

Priestley H, L/Sgt, 252897, MM and Bar. MM LG 26/4/17, Bar LG 12/3/18 for Cambrai.

Rathke W E, CSM, 201195, DCM, LG 18/7/17, for his actions with 'B' Company at the second Battle of Bullecourt.

Raw J R, Cpl, 42120, MM, LG 10/12/18.

Raynor W, Pte, 53706, MM, LG 10/12/18.

Richmond W E, RQMS, 200372, MM, LG 10/12/18.

Roberts F, CQMS 241134, Croix de Guerre LG 3/10/19

Ross D G, Pte, 57460, MM LG 11/12/18.

Rushworth G, Pte, 38216, MM for Bucquoy 25/3/1918, LG 26/9/18.

Sheard B, Pte, 201163, MM, LG 10/12/18.

Shepherd H, L/Cpl, 305451, MM, for 6/7 September 1917 fighting patrol with Kermode and Simpson. LG 19/11/17, corrected 6/8/18

Sigsworth W, Sgt, 200950, MM, LG 10/12/18.

Smith H, Pte, 20928, MM, LG 21/1/19 when serving as 49797 4th Btn West Riding Regiment.

Smith J, Pte, 201202, DCM, MM for actions at Cambrai on 20/11/17, LG12/3/18. DCM Citation 30/10/18.

Smith J E, Sgt, 201174, 2/5 WYR, Medaille Militaire LG 11/3/19.

Stones J, L/Cpl, 203581, Décoration Militaire (Belgian), LG 21/9/17.

Symonds W, Sgt, 4252, MM, for Bullecourt. LG 29/8/18.

Taylor W, L/Cpl, 5264, MM for the rescue of 2/Lt Girling under fire at Ten Tree Alley 17/2/1917, LG 24/4/17.

Waite R, L/Cpl, 200162, MM, LG 9/7/17. Name corrected to WAKE LG 28/9/17.

White J H, Cpl, 200436, MM, LG 26/8/18.

Wilson A, Sgt 266804 Meritorious Service Medal LG 17/6/18.

Wright A H, Sgt, 201138, MM, LG 7/2/19.

Appendix 4
Officers Known to Have Served 2/5th Battalion West Yorkshire Regiment 1914 – 1918

Surname	Initial	Rank	Dates of Service
Ablitt	B E	2/Lt	Sept 1914 to Sept 1915, transferred to 1/5th, wounded on 1st July 1916.
Airey	N G	2/Lt	Aug 1917 until killed in November 1917.
Airey	J C	Lt	Attached 10th Royal Scots served at least Jan 1917 to August 1918.
Allen	NCBH	2/Lt	Enlisted Oct 1914, commissioned April 1914, joined 1/5th in France July 1915.
Almond	C S	2/Lt	Feb 1917 to August 1918, wounded at Bullecourt 3/5/1917, employed by Ministry of Labour from early 1918.
Anderson	J M	Capt	July 1915 to August 1918, later adjutant of 1/5th Devons.
Annely	E G	2/Lt	April 1917 until killed in May 1917.
Armistead	J H	Lt	October 1914 until transfer to 1/5th in October 1915.
Armitage	S	2/Lt	May 1915 to April 1916 after which Machine Gun Corps.
Ash	F S	2/Lt	November 1917 to March 1918.
Avis	F	2/Lt	November 1917 to June 1918, acting adjutant early 1918.
Bailey	R	2/Lt	February 1918, posted to Base July 1918.
Banks	H	2/Lt	Reported at Pourcy July 1918.

Surname	Initial	Rank	Dates of Service
Bardsley	E H	Lt	Transferred from 2/7th June 1917, to August 1918. Wounded at Marfaux 20/7/18
Barrett	N K	2/Lt	Reported at Pourcy 22 July 1918.
Barker	H T		Attached 7th Battalion Devonshire Regiment, sometime Intelligence officer served from at least January 1917. Transfer date unknown.
Behrens	J H	2/Lt	Posted from 2/6th in January 1918.
Bickersteth	C W	2/Lt	December 1914 to his transfer to the Reserve battalion in August 1917 was unfit from his accidental wounding 20/4/1917.
Birbeck	L S	2/Lt	Enlisted into 2/5th August 1914, commissioned in 1/5th November 1915, returned to 2/5th July 1917 and served until transfer to RFC in September 1917.
Bottomley	R A A	Lt Col	From founding of Battalion in October 1914 to May 1916.
Bower	H M	Capt	March 1915 to August 1916, attached to No2 Infantry Records Office, York, too old for overseas service.
Bulmer	C	Capt	October 1914 until transfer to Reserve Battalion in early 1918, did not return to 2/5th after wounding on 3/5/1917.
Catterall	T	2/Lt	September 1916 to August 1918.
Chadwick	G S	Lt	March 1915 to August 1917.
Churchman	C H	Capt	attached 6th Suffolk Regiment, date unknown, killed at Bullecourt 3/5/1917.
Clough	F V	2/Lt	Intermittent service in 1/5th, 2/5th and 3/5th, as well as attachment to 9th Battalion.
Clough	W		Intermittent service in 1/5th, 2/5th and 3/5th. Present in 2/5th in July and August 1918.
Clubb	A D	2/Lt	December 1915 to March 1916, transferred to 1/5th.
Clubb	P	2/Lt	March 1915 to June 1918. Platoon Commander in B Company at Bullecourt, later OC 'B' Company.

Surname	*Initial*	*Rank*	*Dates of Service*
Cole	W T	2/Lt	Originally a sergeant in 2/5th, commissioned in May 1918 into 4th Yorkshire Regiment, posted to 2/5th in July 1918 and killed at Bligny.
Cork	S	2/Lt	Posted in late July 1918.
Corke	C A	2/Lt	November 1917 to June 1918.
Couch	A W	2/Lt	Lt 9th Battalion Hampshire attached to 62nd Division from July 1916 to January 1917.
Cowan	A G	2/Lt	Served Sept 1917 to June 1918.
Cross	E P	Capt & adj	October 1914 until deemed medically unfit in December 1915, Military Representative on the Northumberland Tribunal.
Cross	H B	2/Lt	
Dale	A P	Major	October 1914 until killed on 1 March 1917.
Davidson	R M	2/Lt	A Company Commander on 22/11/17, wounded in Cambrai operations – no other details.
De Lacey	P	2/Lt	Dates of service unknown, wounded three times, including May 1918 and at Marfaux 20/7/1918.
De Ville	C A	2/Lt	March 1918 until killed at Marfaux 20/7/1918.
Dickes	A	2/Lt	Dates of service unknown, wounded at Marfaux 20/7/1918.
Dodsworth	B	2/Lt	Originally commissioned November 1907, served from December 1914 to March 1915, found permanently unfit with heart disease.
Donkersley	R	2/Lt	Served from January 1918, wounded in May 1918, served until killed near Marfaux in July 1918.
Fairbank	A S	Lt	Reported to 2/5th in June 1917.
Fisher	J H	2/Lt	Posted from 2/6th in January 1918, name engraved on the Bucquoy Jug listing all officers who fought with 2/5th at Bucquoy March 1918, posted to Base July 1918.
Foster	G B	2/Lt	Served January 1917 to August 1918, wounded at Bullecourt 3/5/17 and again at Cambrai 27/11/17.

Surname	Initial	Rank	Dates of Service
Foster	R J	2/Lt	Dates of service unknown.
Fox	G N S	2/Lt	Served very briefly in early 1918, killed while attached to 2nd West Yorks 27/3/1918.
Friend	C	2/Lt	April 1915 to September 1916, then until 28/2/19 attached to HQ 185 Brigade as Intelligence Officer.
Gaunt	A	Capt	June 1917 until attached elsewhere in August 1917, role unknown.
Gibson	T E	2/Lt	Reported in France June 1917 until killed 28 November 1917.
Girling	H A	2/Lt	Attached from 10th Royal Scots, wounded 17/2/17.
Gould	C	2/Lt	Dates uncertain, served at Bucquoy and until August 1918.
Gray	W D	2/Lt	May 1915 to August 1918.
Green	A E	Lt	October 1914 to August 1918, wounded at Bullecourt 3/5/17, transferred to Royal Engineers, served with army of occupation.
Green	R	Major	March 1915 to August 1918, was found medically unfit in May 1918 at age 46.
Greenwood	J J G	Capt	Dates uncertain, wounded May 1918.
Grigson	K W	Capt	attached from 7th Battalion Devonshire from January 1917 (possibly earlier) until killed at Marfaux in July 1918.
Gwynn	A J	2/Lt	Posted from 2/6th in January 1918, decorated for his role at Marfaux.
Hall	J	2/Lt	Posted from 2/6th June 1918, served until an unknown date.
Harris	G S	2/Lt	served intermittently from April 1915 until posted to the Reserve Battalion in November 1917.
Heaton	H F	Capt	March 1915 at least to August 1918, adjutant from June 1916, attached East Kent Yeomanry as adjutant February to May 1918.
Hering	M O L	2/Lt	March 1915 to December 1915, posted to 1/5th, badly gassed and posted to 1st East Yorks at Lucknow.
Holditch	W J	2/Lt	August 1917 to May 1918.

Surname	Initial	Rank	Dates of Service
Holland	A	2/Lt	Exact dates unknown, served from at least February 1917.
Hubie	J E	2/Lt	June 1917 to June 1918 when posted to 1/5th West Yorks.
Hutchinson	H	Lt	March 1915 until killed in September 1917.
Hutchinson	W	2/Lt	Attached to 2/8th killed 22/11/1917.
Hutchinson	G R	2/Lt	Attached from Leeds Rifles, killed 27/11/1917
Jacques	R	2/Lt	February 1918 to May 1918.
Jennings	W	2/Lt	Posted from Yorkshire Regiment and killed July 1918 at Bligny.
Josselyn	J	Lt Col	6th Suffolks CO from June 1916 to August 1917, invalided for shell shock and wounds 27/8/17. Commanded Brigade in Russia 1918.
Kenworthy	F B	2/Lt	From June 1918.
Kermode	E M	2/Lt	August 1917 until killed 27/07/1918.
Kitson	A	2/Lt	August 1917 to July 1918.
Knowles	F H	Capt	March 1915 until killed 03/05/1917.
Lee	A B	2/Lt	June 1915 to September 1915, posted to 1/5th.
Leslie	C G	2/Lt	June to August 1918.
Lucas	A H	Capt	Posted from 2/6th in January 1918
Lupton	H	2/Lt	August 1915 to December 1917, wounded 9/5/17, sent back to UK with shell shock December 1917.
Macartney	W S	Lt	May 1917 to August 1918.
Marston	W H	Lt	July 1916 until returns to England with right hand amputated April 1917.
McConnell	J W	Major	March 1915 to December 1915.
McLintock	W J	2/Lt	Served at Bucquoy and Marfaux.
Moffat	J	2/Lt	January 1917 to June 1917. Attached from 7th Devons.
Morant	G A McK	Capt	Attached from Leeds Pals, date and role unknown, killed 16/4/1918.
Newton	G H	2/Lt	March 1915 to February 1916, posted to 1/5th.

Surname	Initial	Rank	Dates of Service
Nicholson	E	2/Lt	Reported in France 30 June 1918, posted to Base July 1918.
Pearson	W A	Capt	March 1915 to December 1915, Posted to Command Depot in Ireland 9 Feb 1916 medically unfit for general service.
Pearson	H E	2/Lt	March 1915 to mid 1916.
Peter	F H	Major	Attached from 1 RWF April 1917, end of attachment unknown date.
Phillips	F G	Capt	Details Unknown.
Phillips	C K	Lt	March 1915 to December 1915.
Pinkerton	A	2/Lt	Bucquoy Jug, transfers to RE in June 1918.
Platnauer	H M	Capt	March 1915 to December 1915, transfers to 3/5th.
Potts	W E	2/Lt	May 1918.
Preston	F V	2/Lt	Reported in France June 1917, to August 1918.
Preston	H	2/Lt	June 1918 to August 1918.
Pringle	G L K	Capt & MO	March 1915 to August 1918.
Puckridge	G M	Capt	Attached from 7th Devons, dates unknown.
Reed		2/Lt	Reported in France July 1918.
Reynolds	A E	Lt	Reported in France June 1917, served until early 1918.
Riley	B M	Lt	Dates of service uncertain. Posted from 2/6th in January 1918, also served with 1/6th, wounded at Marfaux 22/7/1918.
Riley	T	Captain & QM	March 1915 to August 1918.
Robinson	W		Reported in France June 1917 to early 1918.
Samuel	H B	2/Lt	May 1916 to September 1917, request transfer to Jewish unit.
Sawney	L T	2/Lt	Transfer from 2/7th 21/6/1918, wounded at Marfaux.
Sawyer	E C	Lt	June 1915 to August 1918.
Schindler	W B	2/Lt	June 1916 until killed 20/7/1918.
Scoby	H H	Lt	June 1915 to August 1915.
Scott	H C	Capt	April 1915.

Surname	*Initial*	*Rank*	*Dates of Service*
Scott	H S	2/Lt	October 1916 to November 1917, attached RFC.
Sharpe	L	2/Lt	July 1916 to August 1918, originally attached from 13th Worcestershire Regt, acting Adjutant early 1918.
Simpson	J H	2/Lt	July 1917 to August 1918, wounded at Marfaux 20/7/1918.
Sinnott	T D	2/Lt	March 1915 to August 1918, mostly employed as Divisional Grenade officer from April 1916.
Skirrow	G	Capt	March 1915 until August 1918. Killed while attached 2/4th KOYLI 27/08/1918.
Smith	A W L	Lt	March 1915, wounded at Bullecourt 3/5/17, service post May 1917 uncertain.
Smith	N H	2/Lt	March 1916, reported in France June 1917, killed on 20/11/1917.
Smith	S	Lt	Posted from 2/7th 21 June 1918.
Stoddard	J W	2/Lt	March 1915 to August 1918, Asst Comdt 62nd Divisional School from February 1917.
Stuart	G F	2/Lt	Posted from 2/6th in January 1918 but may have already been serving with 2/5th in January 1917, to February 1918.
Stuart	K	Capt	Dates uncertain, Company Commander in 1918.
Swann	C R	2/Lt	June 1918 to August 1918.
Tasker	H	Lt	Reported in France June 1917, to August 1918.
Tennant	J S	2/Lt	March 1915 to April 1916.
Tewson	H V	2/Lt	November 1917 to August 1918.
Thacker	H H	Lt	March 1915 to December 1915.
Thackery	E A	2/Lt	June 1918, posted to Base July 1918.
Thompson	J L	Capt	March 1915 to August 1918, wounded 28/1/18.
Titchener	A W	2/Lt	September 1917 to February 1918.
Veal	L F	Lt	Reported in France June 1917 to August 1918.
Vero	W	2/Lt	Posted from 2/6th in January 1918, wounded 22/4/18.

Surname	*Initial*	*Rank*	*Dates of Service*
Waddy	R H	Lt Col	1st Battalion Somerset Light Infantry, Commanding Officer September 1917 to August 1918.
Wade	J A	2/Lt	July 1917 until August 1918.
Walker	L F	2/Lt	November 1917 to August 1918, wounded in Cambrai operation.
Walker	R B	2/Lt	June to August 1918.
Watson	A J	2/Lt	August 1917 to early 1918, wounded in 20/11/17 near Havrincourt.
Watson	J F	Capt	March 1915 to February 1917, found medically unfit in May 1916, posted 25th Battalion DLI.
Waugh	E R	Lt	Reported in France June 1918, served until an unknown date, wounded at Marfaux 20/7/1918.
Wesley-Smith	J L	Lt	Listed as Lt J L Smith in Army List. March 1917 to December 1917, disabled at Bullecourt May 1917.
Weston	F G	2/Lt	From at least January 1918, attached from 8th WYR.
White	R F	Capt	June 1917 to August 1918, wounded at Marfaux 20/7/1918.
White	F	2/Lt	July 1917 to August 1918.
Whittle	W K	Lt	June 1917 to August 1918.
Wilcock	H E	2/Lt	October 1917 to July 1918, accidentally injured July 1918.
Wilcox	H	2/Lt	May 1917 to August 1918, wounded and captured at Bullecourt.
Willey	W M	2/Lt	Listed on Bucquoy Jug – no other details discovered.
Wilson	A G	2/Lt	July 1917 to September 1917, posted to RFC.
Wilson	A	2/Lt	Date of posting unknown, killed at Bullecourt 03/05/1917.
Wright	H R	2/Lt	July 1917 to August 1918.
Wrightson	E	2/Lt	August 1917 to August 1918.
Wrigley	M J	2/Lt	Exact dates unknown around June 1918.

Index